KT-244-577

Modern Knitting
Illustrated

Easy-to-follow instructions for
indoor and outdoor garments to
suit all members of the family

by

JANE KOSTER
and MARGARET MURRAY

ODHAMS PRESS LIMITED · LONG ACRE · LONDON · W.C.2

A family act ! John and Joan agree with Mother that their sleeveless pullovers are ideal for the outdoor life. Instructions for making both Mother's and the children's jerkins are given in this book.

Contents

*Black and white in knitting and crochet—fashion's leading alliance:
This smart little jumper will distinguish itself anywhere, but is at its
best worn with a black tailored suit. Instructions are for 34 in. bust.*

Women's Garments

Afternoon Jumper

A KNITTED JUMPER WITH A
CROCHETED FLOWER INSET

MATERIALS

5 2-oz. spools black thread No. 20.
2 balls white crochet cotton No. 40.
2 No. 10 and 2 No. 12 knitting needles.
A No. 6 crochet hook.
3 small white buttons.

MEASUREMENTS

Length, 18 ins.
Bust size, 34 ins.
Sleeve seam, 4½ ins.

TENSION

With No. 12 needles about 11 sts. to
1 in.; with No. 10 needles about 10 sts.
to 1 in.; both measured over patt. in
double thread.

N.B.—Work with black thread used
double throughout.

The Front and Back Alike.—With No.
12 needles and double black thread cast
on 154 sts.

Work in patt.:—

1st row.—* K. 1, w.fd., sl. 1 p.w., w.bk.;
rep. from * to end.

2nd row.—* P. 1, w.bk., sl. 1 p.w.,
w.fd.; rep. from * to end.

These 2 rows form patt. Continue in
patt. until work measures 3 ins., ending
row on wrong side, i.e., 2nd patt. row.

Change to No. 10 needles and continue
in patt., inc. 1 st. both ends of every 12th
row until there are 174 sts. Continue
straight until work measures 12 ins.,
ending row on wrong side.

Shape Armholes thus: Continue in patt.,
cast off 6 sts. beg. of next 2 rows, dec. 1
st. both ends of every row until 142 sts.
remain.

Work 4 rows straight in patt.

Cast off.

Work a second piece in same way.

The Sleeves.—With No. 12 needles and
double black thread cast on 116 sts.

Work in patt. for 1 in., inc. 1 st. both
ends of next row, then continue in patt.
until work measures 1½ ins.

Change to No. 10 needles and continue
in patt., inc. 1 st. both ends of 7th row
and every following 12th row until 124
sts.

Continue straight until work measures
4½ ins., ending row on the wrong
side.

Shape Top thus: Continue in patt., dec.
1 st. both ends of next row and every
following 3rd row until 98 sts. remain,
then dec. both ends of every alternate row
until 82 sts. remain.

Cast off 3 sts. beg. of every row until
22 sts. remain.

Cast off.

The Yoke.—With No. 12 needles and
double black thread cast on 94 sts.

The jumper is knitted throughout with double thread in order to give it a neat, firm texture; the crocheted rosettes are inset into the jumper to form the smart and unusual yoke. The sleeves have a tiny crocheted border.

Work 16 rows in patt.

Next row.—Patt. 11, cast off 72 patt. to end.

Continue in patt. on last set of 11 sts. for 4½ ins., finishing straight outside edge.

Next row.—Patt. 11, cast on 37 sts. Work in patt. on 48 sts. for 2¼ ins. Cast off.

Rejoin thread to other 11 sts. at inside edge and work to match first side.

THE ROSETTE INSET

The Crochet Rosettes.—With crochet hook and single white thread make 6 ch. and join into a ring with a sl.st.

1st round.—5 ch., 1 tr. into ring, * 2 ch., 1 tr. into ring; rep. from * 6 times,

2 ch., 1 sl.st. into 3rd of 5 ch. at beg. of round.

2nd round.—Work 1 d.c., 1 tr., 1 long tr., 1 tr., 1 d.c. into each of the 8 sp.

3rd round.—Work 4 ch., 1 s.c. into each tr. of 1st round, keeping the loops at the back of petals of 2nd round.

4th round.—Work 1 d.c., 2 tr., 3 long tr., 2 tr., 1 d.c. into each of the 8 loops of 4 ch.

Fasten off.

Make 67 of these rosettes, 21 for neck border, 46 for yoke.

Sew pairs of petals together, as shown in illustration.

Arrange 13 for back and front of yoke, with 10 for each shoulder; join at right angles the whole forming an oblong.

Work outer border as follows:—

Join white cotton to a petal, * work 5 ch., 1 d.c. into next petal of same flower, 10 ch. 1 d.c. into first petal of next flower; rep. from * all round, working 10 ch. at each corner.

Next round.—3 ch. (representing 1 tr.), * 2 ch., miss 2 ch., 1 tr. into next ch.; rep. from * all round, making 5 ch., 1 tr. into same ch. as last tr. at each corner.

Join at end of round with 2 ch., 1 sl.st. into first 3 ch.

Next round.—1 d.c. into each tr. and each ch. to end.

Next round.—With single black thread work 1 d.c. into each d.c. with 3 d.c. into each corner.

Now work inside border in the same way, but work 1 long tr. into join between petals at each corner to keep work square, and in next round work 2 tr. at right angles at each corner without ch. between.

When working d.c. rounds omit 2 or 3 at corners to keep work flat.

Sew rosettes together for neck border, arranging 7 for front of neck, 4 at right angles for each shoulder and 3 for each side of back of neck.

Work round these in same way as for yoke, but leaving opening at centre back and working down each short side edge of back opening in same border.

The Sleeve Borders.—With single white thread make a ch. about 10 ins. long to fit round lower edge of sleeve.

1st row.—1 tr. into 5th ch. from hook, * 2 ch., miss 2 ch., 1 tr. into next ch.; rep. from * to end.

2nd row.—Work 1 d.c. into each tr. and each ch. of previous row, then work 1 d.c. into each ch. of foundation edge.

Using single black thread, work a row of d.c. into each d.c. on each side of insertion.

Work a second strip in same way.

Make-up.—Press knitted fabric lightly on wrong side with hot iron over damp cloth.

Join side seams.

Sew crochet yoke border neatly in position to back and fronts.

Now sew the knitted yoke neatly to inside edge of crochet yoke, with opening to centre back; then sew the neck border into position.

Work a row of black d.c. down each back opening edge, making small chain loops for buttons on right side.

Sew on buttons to match loops.

Sew sleeve borders round lower edges of sleeves.

Join sleeve seams and sew into armholes, matching seams with side seams.

Press all seams carefully on wrong side.

Detail of the crochet rosettes, also shown as a necklet on page 78.

Three smart girls, who know the value of comfort, choose to wear knitted jumpers at informal afternoon tea parties; the high-necked, cable-fronted jumper is enchanting knitted in any pastel shade.

Brunettes will be flattered in the striped, multi-coloured jumper, and the more vivid the colours chosen for the stripes, the smarter it will be. Blondes, of course, will choose the charming black and white model.

Cable-panelled Jumper

FOR THE HOSTESS

MATERIALS

6 oz. of 3-ply wool.
1 pair No. 10 and No. 12 needles and a short spare needle pointed at each end.
5 buttons.
A press fastener.

MEASUREMENTS

Length, 19 ins.
Bust size, 34 ins.
Sleeve seam, 5 ins.

TENSION

$7\frac{1}{2}$ sts. to 1 in. measured over stocking stitch.

The Front.—With No. 12 needles cast on 98 sts and k. 10 rows.

Continue in st.st. and patterned panels thus:—

1st row.—K. 12, * k. 1, m. 1, k. 2 tog., k. 1, m. 1, k. 2 tog., p. 2, k. twice into each of next 2 sts., p. 2, k. 1, m. 1, k. 2 tog., k. 1, m. 1, k. 2 tog., k. 10; rep. from * twice, k. 2 (104 sts.).

2nd row.—P. 12, * k. 1, m. 1, k. 2 tog., k. 1, m. 1, k. 2 tog., k. 2, p. 4, k. 2, p. 1, m. 1, k. 2 tog., k. 1, m. 1, k. 2 tog., p. 10; rep. from * twice, p. 2.

3rd row.—K. 12, * k. 1, m. 1, k. 2 tog., k. 1, m. 1, k. 2 tog., p. 2, sl. next 2 sts. on to a spare needle and leave at front of work, k. next 2 sts., then k. 2 sts. from spare needle, p. 2, k. 1, m. 1, k. 2 tog., k. 1, m. 1, k. 2 tog., k. 10; rep. from * twice, k. 2.

4th row.—As 2nd row.

5th row.—K. 12, * k. 1, m. 1, k. 2 tog., k. 1, m. 1, k. 2 tog., p. 2, k. 4, p. 2, k. 1, m. 1, k. 2 tog., k. 1, m. 1, k. 2 tog., k. 10; rep. from * twice, k. 2.

These 4 rows, i.e., rows 2 to 5 inclusive, form the patt.

Continue in patt. until work measures $3\frac{1}{2}$ ins., ending with a row on wrong side.

Change to No. 10 needles and continue in st.st. and patt. panels, inc. 1 st. at both ends of next row and every 4th row following until 136 sts. are on the needle, working the extra sts. at each side in st.st. fabric. Continue without shaping until work measures $12\frac{1}{2}$ ins., ending with a row on wrong side.

Shape Armholes thus: Keeping continuity of st.st. and patterned panels, cast off 8 sts. at beg. of next 2 rows, then dec. 1 st. at both ends of every row until 104 sts. remain. Continue without shaping until work measures $17\frac{1}{2}$ ins., ending with a row on wrong side.

Shape for Neck and Shoulder thus:—

Next row.—Work across 42 sts., cast off next 20 sts., work to end of row.

Continue in st.st. and patterned panel on remaining 42 sts., dec. 1 st. at neck edge on the next 10 rows.

Now continue on 32 sts. until work measures 19 ins., ending at armhole edge.

Cast off 8 sts. on next 4 rows, beg. at armhole edge.

Rejoin wool to second set of sts. at neck edge and work to match first side.

The Back.—Proceed as given for front until work measures $12\frac{1}{2}$ ins., ending with a row on wrong side.

Shape for Armholes and Divide for Back Opening thus: Keeping continuity of st.st. and patterned panels, cast off 8 sts. at beg. of next 2 rows, then dec. 1 st. at both ends of every row until 104 sts.

If you have never knitted cable stitch, you will be surprised how easy and fascinating it is; this jumper has three cable panels back and front.

remain, thus ending with row on wrong side of work. Now work 1 row across all sts.

Next row.—Work across 50 sts., turn, cast on 4 sts. for underwrap. Leave remaining 54 sts. on a spare needle.

Continue in st.st. and patt. with the 4 underwrap sts. in g.st. (each row k.), until work measures 19 ins., ending at opening edge.

Shape Neck and Shoulder thus:—

1st row.—Cast off 16 sts., work to end of row.

2nd row.—Cast off 8 sts., work to last 2 sts., work 2 tog.

3rd row.—Work 2 tog., work to end of row.

Rep. last 2 rows twice.

Cast off remaining sts.

Now place 5 pins in the underwrap, the first one about ¼ in. down from neck edge, the others at about 1-in. intervals below it to provide a guide for the buttonholes.

Rejoin wool at opening edge to the 54 sts. for other side of back and work in st.st. and patt. with the 4 sts. at opening edge in g.st. for the overwrap (replacing the cable patt.) exactly as given for the first side, making buttonholes at the points indicated in the underwrap as follows:—

1st row of Buttonhole.—Beg. at opening edge, k. 2. w.fd., k. 2 tog., work to end of row.

2nd row.—Work in patt. to last 4 sts.. k. 4.

The Sleeves.—With No. 12 needles cast on 82 sts. and k. 10 rows.

Continue in st.st. and patt. as follows:

1st row.—K. 32, (k. 1, m. 1, k. 2 tog.) twice, p. 2, k. twice into each of next 2 sts., p. 2, (k. 1, m. 1, k. 2 tog.) twice, k. 32.

2nd row.—P. 32, (k. 1, m. 1, k. 2 tog.) twice, k. 2, p. 4, k. 2, (k. 1, m. 1, k. 2 tog.) twice, p. 32.

3rd row.—K. 32, (k. 1, m. 1, k. 2 tog.) twice, p. 2, cross next 4 sts., p. 2, (k. 1, m. 1, k. 2 tog.) twice, k. 32.

4th row.—As 2nd row.

5th row.—K. 32, (k. 1, m. 1, k. 2 tog.) twice, p. 2, k. 4, p. 2, (k. 1, m. 1, k. 2 tog.) twice, k. 32.

Rep. last 4 rows, i.e., rows 2 to 5 inclusive, until work measures 2 ins., inc. 1 st. at both ends of every 4th row, working these extra sts. in the st.st.

Change to No. 10 needles and continue in st.st. and patt., inc. on every 4th row until 100 sts. are on needle, working the extra sts. in st.st. as before.

Continue without shaping until work

Detail of the cable with pretty lace stitch panels on either side of it.

measures 5 ins. ending with row on wrong side.

Shape Top thus: Work 8 rows in st.st. and patt., dec. 1 st. at both ends of each row.

Next row.—Work to end of row.

Next 3 rows.—Dec. 1 st. at both ends of each row.

Rep. these last 4 rows 8 times (30 sts.).

Now cast off 6 sts. at beg. of next 4 rows. Cast off remaining sts.

The Neck Border.—With No. 12 needles cast on 12 sts. and work in patt. thus:—

1st row.—K.

2nd row.—K.

3rd row.—K. 2, p. 2, k. 4, p. 2, k. 2.

4th row.—K. 4, p. 4, k. 4.

5th row.—K. 2, p. 2, cross next 4 sts., p. 2, k. 2.

6th row.—As 2nd row.

7th row.—K. 2, p. 2, k. 4, p. 2, turn.

8th row.—K. 2, p. 4, k. 4.

9th row.—As 5th row.

10th row.—As 6th row.

Rep. the last 8 rows, i.e., rows 3 to 10 inclusive, until shortest edge of work measures approximately 14½ ins., ending with a 10th patt. row.

Next 2 rows.—K. to end.

Cast off.

Make-up.—Press work lightly on wrong side using a hot iron over a damp cloth.

Back stitch shoulder seams. Join side and sleeve seams and sew sleeves into armholes, matching seams to side seams and with centre of pattern panel of sleeve to shoulder seam.

Pin the centre of the longest edge of the neck band to centre front of neck edge and stitch neatly round neck edge, ending at underwrap and overwrap edges, overlapping the band over neck edge for about ⅛ in. Stitch underwrap at lower edge.

Sew buttons on to match buttonholes. Press all seams.

Fasten neck border with a press fastener.

Multi-coloured Blouse

FOR ALMOST ANY OCCASION

MATERIALS

4 oz. of 3-ply wool in maroon.
1 oz. 3-ply wool in green.
1 oz. 3-ply wool in yellow.
1 pair each of No. 10 and No. 12 needles.
3 small buttons.

MEASUREMENTS

Length, 19 ins.
Bust size, 34 ins.
Sleeve seam, 5 ins.

TENSION

7 sts. to 1 in. measured over st.st. and g.st. stripes.

The Back and Front of Blouse are Alike: Begin at side edge and work in stripes of st.st. and g.st. in maroon, green and yellow. Carry colours not in use along side of work to avoid ends.

With No. 10 needles and maroon wool cast on 29 sts. and k. 1 row.

Cast on 6 sts., p. to end.
Change to yellow wool.

3rd row.—K. to end.

4th row.—Cast on 6 sts., k. to end.
Change to maroon wool.

5th row.—K. to end.

6th row.—Cast on 6 sts., p. to end.
Change to green wool.

7th and 8th rows.—Rep. 3rd and 4th rows once.
Change to maroon wool.

9th row.—K. twice into 1st st., k. to end.

10th row.—Cast on 6 sts., p. to end.
Change to yellow wool.

11th row.—As 9th row

12th row.—As 4th row.
Change to maroon wool.

13th row.—As 9th row.

14th row.—Cast on 28 sts., p. to end.
Change to green wool.

15th row.—As 9th row.

16th row.—K. to end.
Change to maroon wool.

17th row.—As 9th row.

18th row.—P. to end.
Change to yellow wool.

19th row.—As 9th row.

20th row.—K. to end inc. 1 st. at end of row.
Change to maroon wool.

21st row.—As 9th row.

22nd row.—P. to end, inc. 1 st. at end of row.
Change to green wool.

23rd and 24th rows.—Rep. 19th and 20th rows once.

This completes side and armhole shapings (104 sts.).

Now continue in st.st. and g.st. stripes until work measures about 2 ins. from the 28 cast-on sts., i.e., 14th row, ending with 2 rows in g.st.

Shape for Waist thus:—

* Change to maroon wool.

Next row.—K. to last 26 sts., turn.

Next row.—P. to end. Change to yellow or green wool.

Work 2 rows in g.st. to end of row.

Rep. last 4 rows twice *.

Continue in st.st. and g.st. stripes for 2 ins., ending with 2 rows in g.st.

Rep. from * to * once.

Continue in st.st. and g.st. stripes for 3 ins., ending with 2 rows in g.st.

** Rep. from * to * once.

Continue in st.st. and g.st. stripes for 2 ins., ending with 2 rows in g.st. **.

Rep. from ** to ** twice, ending second rep. with 2 rows in st.st. and working for only 1 in. instead of 2 ins.

Shape for Second Armhole and Side Edge thus:—

1st and 2nd rows.—Work 2 rows in g.st., dec. 1 st. at beg. of 1st row and end of 2nd row.

3rd and 4th rows.—Work 2 rows in st.st. dec. 1 st. at beg. of 1st row and end of 2nd row.

5th and 6th rows.—Rep. 1st and 2nd rows once.

7th row.—K. to end, dec. 1 st. at beg. of row.

8th row.—P. to end

9th row.—As 7th row.

10th row.—K. to end.

11th row.—As 7th row.

12th row.—Cast off 28 sts., p. to end.

13th row.—As 7th row.

14th row.—Cast off 6 sts., k. to end.

15th row.—As 7th row.

16th row.—Cast off 6 sts., p to end.

17th row.—K. to end.

18th row.—Cast off 6 sts., k. to end.

19th row.—K. to end.

20th row.—Cast off 6 sts., p. to end.

21st and 22nd rows.—Rep. 17th and 18th rows once.

23rd and 24th rows.—Rep. 19th and 20th rows once.

Cast off in maroon wool.

Work a second piece in same way.

Detail of the stripe stitch

The Back Yoke.—With No. 10 needles and maroon wool cast on 99 sts. and work in moss st. thus:—

1st row.—* K. 1, p. 1; rep. from * to last st., k. 1; rep. this row for 4½ ins.

Shape Shoulder thus: Cast off 7 sts. at beg. of next 4 rows, then cast off 8 sts. at beg. of next 4 rows.

Cast off remaining 39 sts.

The Right Front of Yoke.—With No. 10 needles cast on 53 sts. in maroon wool. Work in moss st. for ¾ in.

Next row.—Moss st. 2, cast off 3 sts. for a buttonhole, moss st. to end.

Next row.—Moss st. to last 2 sts., cast on 3 sts., moss st. to end.

* Continue in moss st. for 1 in.; then make another buttonhole in next 2 rows.

Rep. from * once.

Continue in moss st. until work measures 3 ins., ending at buttonholed front edge.

Shape Neck thus: Cast off 11 sts. at beg. of next row, then dec. 1 st. at this same edge on every row until 30 sts. remain.

Continue without shaping until work measures 4½ ins., ending at straight edge.

Shape Shoulder thus:—

Next row.—Cast off 7 sts., moss st. to end.

Next row.—Moss st. to end.

Rep. last 2 rows once.

Next row.—Cast off 8 sts., moss st. to end.

Next row.—Moss st. to end.

Cast off remaining 8 sts.

The Left Front of Yoke.—With No. 10 needles cast on 53 sts. in maroon wool and work in moss st. for 3 ins.

Shape Neck and Shoulder as given for right front of yoke.

The Sleeves.—With No. 12 needles and maroon wool cast on 75 sts. and work 1 in. in moss st.

Continue in moss st., inc. 1 st. at both ends of next row and every following 4th row until work measures 2 ins.

The yoke and sleeves of this jumper are in moss stitch, and the rest in garter stitch ridges ; the original was maroon, green and yellow.

Change to No. 10 needles and continue in moss st., inc. at both ends of every 4th row until 91 sts. are on needle.

Continue without shaping until work measures 5 ins.

Shape Top thus: Dec. 1 st. at both ends of next 2 rows, then work 1 row straight.

Rep. these 3 rows until 29 sts. remain. Cast off.

The Collar.—With No. 10 needles and maroon wool cast on 17 sts. and work in moss st. for 8 rows.

9th row.—Moss st. 13, turn.

10th row.—Moss st. to end.

Rep. these 10 rows until work measures $13\frac{1}{2}$ ins. on the shorter edge.

Then work 8 rows in moss st.

Cast off in moss st.

Make-up.—Press all pieces of work carefully on wrong side with a hot iron over a damp cloth.

Join shoulder seams of yoke .

Place right front edge over left front edge, overlapping first 5 or 6 sts. so that the two fronts are same size as back of yoke.

Stitch front edges together at lower edge.

Join shaped side seams of bodice with a narrow backstitch seam.

Place lower edge of back and front of yoke over top edge of bodice and stitch neatly and firmly into position.

Join sleeve seams and backstitch sleeves into armholes, matching seams with side seams and arranging any extra fullness at top of sleeve.

Pin centre of shortest edge of collar to centre back of neck and stitch collar round neck edge to within $\frac{1}{2}$ in. of each front edge.

Sew on buttons to correspond with buttonholes.

Press seams.

These three smart girls, having achieved success in the drawing room, turn their attention to sports wear. First choice is a sleeveless pullover to wear over shirt blouses; it gives warmth yet allows freedom of movement.

Second choice is a classic jumper which can be worn successfully on both formal and informal occasions. A cotton shirt blouse completes the trio's selection. To be effective it should be in a brilliant shade of bouclé yarn.

Classic Jersey

UNBEATABLE FOR SPORTSWEAR

MATERIALS

5 oz. of 2-ply wool.
1 pair each of No. 12 and No. 14 needles.
6 buttons.

MEASUREMENTS

Length from shoulder, 18½ ins.
Bust. 34 ins.
Sleeve seam, 5 ins.

TENSION

With No. 12 needles 9 sts. to 1 in.

The Front.—Using No. 14 needles cast on 127 sts. and work in moss st. (every row alike) as follows:—

K. 1, * p. 1, k. 1; rep. from * to end of row.

Rep. this row for ¾ in. Now, with right side of work facing and continuing on No. 14 needles, change to patt.:—

1st row.—K. 1, * p. 1, k. 1; rep. from * to end of row.

Detail of the stitch used for the classic jersey shown on page 19.

2nd row.—P. 1, * (p. 1, k. 1) twice, p. 2; rep. from * to end of row.

Rep. these 2 rows until work measures 3½ ins.

Change to No. 12 needles and inc. 1 st. at both ends of next and every following 8th row until 151 sts. are on needle.

Continue without shaping until work measures 12 ins. from commencement.

Shape Armholes thus: Cast off 6 sts. at beg. of next 2 rows, then dec. 1 st. at each end of every row until 115 sts. remain.

Work straight until armhole measures 5 ins.

Change to No. 14 needles and shape neck:—

Work in patt. over 49 sts. and leave on a spare needle, cast off the centre 17 sts. and work on the remaining 49 sts.; dec. 1 st. at neck edge every row until 36 sts. remain.

Work without shaping until front measures 18½ ins., ending at armhole edge.

Shape Shoulder thus: Cast off 9 sts., work to end of row.

Next row.—Work to end of row. Rep. these 2 rows twice. Cast off 9 sts.

Return to the 49 sts. left on spare needle, rejoin wool and work to correspond with first side.

The Back.—Work exactly as given for front until armholes are reached, then with right side of work facing, shape armholes and divide for opening thus:—

Cast off 6 sts. at beg of row, work in patt. over 64 sts., moss st. 11. Leave the remaining 70 sts. on spare needle.

Next row.—Moss st. 11, work in patt. until 2 sts. remain, k. 2 tog.

Continue thus, dec. 1 st. at armhole edge on every row until 12 dec. have been made and 63 sts. remain on needle. At the same time, when armhole measures $\frac{3}{4}$ in., make a buttonhole on moss-st. band thus:—

With wrong side of work facing, moss st. 4. Cast off 3 sts., moss st. 4, patt. to end. In the following row cast on 3 sts. over the 3 cast off in previous row.

When armhole shaping is completed work straight until armhole measures 5 ins., making buttonholes at intervals of 1¼ ins. all the way up.

The round-necked classic jumper has its place in every wardrobe. This model was knitted in stone colour, in 2-ply wool.

Change to No. 14 needles and continue in the same way until work measures 18½ ins.

Shape Neck and Shoulder: With wrong side of work facing, cast off 21 sts., work to end of row.

Next row.—From armhole edge, cast off 9 sts., work until 2 sts. remain, k. 2 tog.

Next row.—K. 2 tog., work in patt. to end of row. Rep. the last 2 rows twice more. Cast off the remaining 9 sts.

Rejoin wool to the sts. left on spare needle and cast on 11 sts. for underwrap. Work to correspond with first side, but omitting buttonholes and reversing all shapings.

The Sleeves.—Using No. 14 needles cast on 97 sts. and work in moss st. as for front for ¾ in. Change to No. 12 needles and patt. and inc. 1 st. at both ends of next and every following 6th row until there are 121 sts. on needle.

Work without inc. until sleeve measures 5 ins.

Shape Top thus: Cast off 6 sts. at the beg. of each of the next 2 rows, then dec. 1 st. at both ends of every alternate row until 49 sts. remain.

Then dec. at both ends of every row until there are 37 sts. left. Cast off.

The Neck Band.—Using No. 14 needles cast on 9 sts. and work 6 rows in moss st.

Next row.—Make a buttonhole, moss st. 3, cast off 3 sts., moss st. to end. In the following row cast on 3 sts. over those cast off in the previous row. Continue in moss st. until neck band measures 13 ins. Cast off.

Make-up.—Press the work very lightly on the wrong side, using a warm iron and a damp cloth.

Join side, shoulder and sleeve seams. Stitch sleeves into armholes, placing seams to side seams and arranging the extra fullness at the top of sleeve. Stitch neck band to edge of neck. Sew the underwrap neatly into position at back. Neaten buttonholes.

Press all seams. Sew on buttons to correspond with buttonholes.

Cotton Shirt

TO PARTNER SLACKS

MATERIALS
10 oz. cotton or rayon bouclé.
1 pair each of No. 10 and No. 12 needles.
3 buttons.

MEASUREMENTS
Length, 19 ins.
Bust, 34 ins.
Sleeve seam, 5 ins.

TENSION
With No. 10 needles 5½ sts. to 1 in.

The Back.—With No. 12 needles cast on 72 sts. and work in k. 1, p. 1 rib for 3 ins., inc. 1 st. at end of last row of ribbing.

Change to No. 10 needles and work in moss st. (every row alike) thus:—

K. 1, * p. 1, k. 1; rep. from * to end of row.

Inc. 1 st. at each end of 3rd and every following 6th row until there are 93 sts. on needle.

Detail of moss stitch used for shirt knitted in cotton bouclé.

Continue without shaping until the work measures 12 ins., ending with a row on wrong side of work.

Shape Armholes thus: Cast off 5 sts. at beg. of the next 2 rows, then dec. 1 st. at both ends of every alternate row until 69 sts. remain.

Continue without shaping until the work measures 17 ins.

Change to No. 12 needles and continue in moss st. for 1½ ins. more, ending with row on wrong side of work.

Shape Shoulder thus: Cast off 6 sts. at the beg. of each of the next 4 rows, then cast off 5 sts. at the beg. of the next 4 rows.

Cast off remaining 25 sts.

The Front.—Work exactly as given for back until armhole shaping is finished and 69 sts. remain, finishing with a row on wrong side of work.

Now Divide for Front Opening thus: Moss st. 31 sts.; sl. these sts. on to a spare needle and work on the remaining 38 sts. for 1¼ ins., finishing with a row on wrong side of work.

Next row.—Make a buttonhole as follows:—

Moss st. 3, cast off 3, moss st. to end.

In the following row cast on 3 sts. over those cast off in the previous row.

Work for a further 2½ ins., making 2 more buttonholes at intervals of 1¼ ins. Work ¼ in. after third buttonhole. Work should now measure 17 ins.

Now change to No. 12 needles and shape neck thus:—

Cast off 10 sts., work to end. Now dec. 1 st. at neck edge every row until 22 sts. remain.

Work without shaping until armhole measures the same as back, ending at armhole edge.

Shape Shoulders thus: Cast off 6 sts. at the beg. of next row, turn and work back.

Rep. these 2 rows once.

Next row.—Cast off 5 sts., work to end; turn and work back. Cast off 5 sts.

Return to the 31 sts. left on spare needle and cast on 7 sts. for underwrap, work to correspond with right side, omitting buttonholes and reversing all shapings.

The Sleeves.—With No. 12 needles cast on 61 sts. and work in moss st. as for back for 1 in.

Change to No. 10 needles and inc. at both ends of next and every following 4th row until there are 73 sts. on needle. Work without shaping until sleeve measures 4½ ins., then shape top thus:—

Cast off 3 sts. at the beg. of the next 2 rows, then dec. 1 st. at each end of every row until 55 sts. remain. Now dec. 1 st. at each end of every alternate row until there are 21 sts. left. Cast off.

The Collar.—With No. 12 needles cast on 12 sts. * Work 10 rows in moss st.

Next row.—Moss st. 9, turn. Work back to end; rep. from * until short edge measures about 12 ins. Work 10 rows. Cast off.

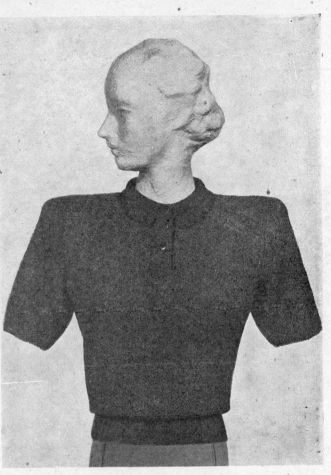

A shirt to wear with slacks is best knitted in cotton; choose a bright, clear colour—this was pillar-box red—and a simple stitch. The Peter Pan collar gives it a neat neckline.

Make-up.—Press the work lightly on the wrong side, using a hot iron over a damp cloth.

Join the side, shoulder and sleeve seams Stitch sleeves into armholes, placing seams to side seams and easing fullness at top of shoulder.

Sew underwrap into position at lower edge of front opening.

Sew collar to neck to within 4 sts. of edges of fronts.

Neaten buttonholes. Press all seams. Sew on buttons to match buttonholes.

Pullover

TO WEAR IN SPRING AND AUTUMN

MATERIALS

5 oz. 3-ply wool.
1 pair No. 10 and 1 pair No. 12 needles.

MEASUREMENTS

Length, 20 ins.
Bust, 34 ins.

TENSION

7½ sts. to 1 in.

The Front.—With No. 10 needles cast on 113 sts. and work in k. 1, p. 1 rib for ¾ in.

Continue in patt. as follows:—

1st row.—K. 1, * k. 1, p. 5, k. 1, p. 1; rep. from * to end.

2nd row.—K. 1, * (p. 1, k. 2) twice, p. 1, k. 1; rep. from * to end.

3rd row.—K. 1, * p. 3, (k. 1, w.fd., k. 1) all into next st., p. 4; rep. from * to end.

Detail of stitch used for sleeveless pullover.

4th row.—* K. 4, p. 1, k. into back of next st. (this will be referred to as k.b.l.) p. 1, k. 3; rep. from * to last st., k. 1.

5th row.—K. 1, * p. 2, k. 2 tog., m. 1, p. 1, m. 1. sl. 1, k. 1, p.s.s.o. p. 3; rep. from * to end.

6th row.—* K. 3, p. 1, k.b.l., k. 1, k.b.l., p. 1, k. 2; rep. from * to last st., k. 1.

7th row.—K. 1, * p. 1, k. 2 tog., m. 1, p. 3, m. 1, sl. 1, k. 1, p.s.s.o., p. 2; rep. from * to end.

8th row.—* K. 2, p. 1, k.b.l., k. 3, k.b.l., p. 1, k. 1; rep. from * to last st., k. 1.

9th row.—K. 1, * k. 2 tog., p. 5, sl. 1, k. 1, p.s.s.o., p. 1; rep. from * to end.

10th row.—K. 1, * p. 1, k. 5, p. 1, k. 1; rep. from * to end.

11th row.—K. 1, * k. 1, p. 5, k. 1, p. 1; rep. from * to end.

12th row.—As 10th row.

These 12 rows form the patt.; rep. them once more.

Change to No. 12 needles and rep. the patt. twice.

Change to No. 10 needles and continue in patt., inc. 1 st. at both ends of next and every following 4th row 8 times, working the extra sts. into patt. as soon as there are sufficient increasings worked (129 sts.).

Continue in patt. without further inc. until work measures 13 ins., ending with a 10th patt. row.

Shape for Armholes and Divide for Neck Opening thus: Cast off 8 sts. at beg. of the next 2 rows.

Next row.—Work in patt. over 56 sts., turn and work back, dec. 1 st. at end of row. Now continue in patt., dec. 1 st. at both ends of every alternate row until 8 dec. have been worked at each edge.

Now dec. at neck edge only until 33 sts. remain.

Continue in patt. until work measures 20 ins., ending at armhole edge.

Shape Shoulder thus:—

Next row.—Cast off 11 sts., work in patt. to end.

Next row.—Work in patt. to end.

Rep. last 2 rows once.

Cast off remaining sts.

Rejoin wool to second set of sts. at neck edge, work 2 sts. tog., patt. to end of row. Now work second side to correspond with first.

The Back.—Work exactly as for front until armholes are reached.

Shape for Armholes thus: Cast off 8 sts. at beg. of next 2 rows. Now dec. 1 st. at both ends of every alternate row until 8 sts. have been decreased at each armhole edge.

Continue in patt. without further dec. until work measures 20 ins., ending with row on wrong side.

Shape Shoulders thus: Cast off 11 sts. at beg. of next 6 rows.

Cast off remaining sts.

The Neck Border.

—With No. 12 needles cast on 6 sts. and work in k. 1, p. 1 rib for 19 ins. Cast off in rib.

The Armhole Borders.—With No. 12 needles cast on 6 sts. and work in k. 1, p. 1 rib for 17 ins. Cast off in rib.

Make-up.—Backstitch shoulder seams.

Stitch armhole borders evenly round armholes.

Join side seams.

Stitch neck border round neck edge, joining cast-on and cast-off edges at centre front.

Press the garment lightly on wrong side, using a hot iron over a damp cloth.

A sleeveless pullover worn over a shirt blouse, with slacks, makes a useful outfit for gardening.

Charming Bedjacket

WITH LONG OR SHORT SLEEVES

MATERIALS

6 oz. 3-ply wool in a pastel shade (8 oz. for long sleeves), and a small ball of white for the crochet edging.
1 pair each No. 12, No. 10 and No. 9 needles.
A medium-size crochet hook.
7 buttons.

MEASUREMENTS

Length, 19 ins.
To fit a 34-in. to 36-in. bust loosely.
Sleeve seam, 4½ ins. or 18 ins.

TENSION

1 patt. measures about 1 in. on the No. 9 needles.

The Back.—Using No. 12 needles cast on 105 sts. and work in g.st. for ¾ in.
Change to No. 10 needles and proceed in patt. as follows:—

1st row.—* K. 4, m. 1, k. 2 tog.; rep. from * to last 3 sts. k. 3.

2nd row.—* P. 3, k. 1, m. 1, k. 2 tog.; rep. from * to last 3 sts., p. 3.

Rep. these 2 rows twice more.

7th row.—* K. 1, m. 1, k. 2 tog., k. 3; rep. from * to last 3 sts., k. 1, m. 1, k. 2 tog.

8th row.—* K. 1, m. 1, k. 2 tog., p. 3; rep. from * to last 3 sts., k. 1, m. 1, k. 2 tog.

Rep. these 2 rows twice more.

These 12 rows form patt. Rep. them until work measures 3½ ins. from beg.

Change to No. 9 needles and beg. side shaping by inc. 1 st. at both ends of next and every following 4th row until there are 129 sts. on the needle, working extra sts. into patt. as soon as possible.

Continue without shaping until work measures 13 ins. from beg.

Shape Armholes thus: Cast off 6 sts. at beg. of next 2 rows.

Then dec. 1 st. at both ends of every row until there are 105 sts. on the needle.

Continue without shaping until the 12th row of a patt. has been worked, then commence ribbed yoke thus:—

Next row.—* P. 2, k. 4; rep. from * to last 3 sts., p. 1, p. 2 tog.

The Ribbed Yoke. 1st row.—* K. 2, p. 4; rep. from * to last 2 sts., k. 2.

2nd row.—* P. 2, k. 4; rep. from * to last 2 sts., p. 2.

Rep. these 2 rows of ribbing until work measures 19 ins. from beg.

Shape Neck and Shoulders thus: Cast off 7 sts. at beg. of the next 8 rows. Then cast off remaining sts.

The Left Front.—Using No. 12 needles cast on 51 sts. and work in g.st. for ¾ in. Change to No. 10 needles and proceed

Detail of pattern for the bedjacket.

The older woman will delight in this bedjacket designed for her on simple lines, with long sleeves. A short-sleeved version of the bedjacket is given too, and both models fit 34-36 bust sizes.

in patt. as used for back until work measures $3\frac{1}{2}$ ins. from beg., ending with a row on wrong side of work.

Change to No. 9 needles and continue in patt., inc. 1 st. at the beg. of next row, and at beg. of every following 4th row until there are 63 sts. on the needle. Continue without shaping until work measures 13 ins. from beg., ending with a row on wrong side of work.

Shape Armholes thus: Cast off 6 sts. at beg. of next row. Then dec. 1 st. at this edge on every row until there are 51 sts.

Continue without shaping until the 12th patt. row has been worked; then commence the ribbed yoke thus:—

Next row.—* P. 2, k. 4; rep: from * to last 3 sts., p. 1, p. 2 tog.

The Ribbed Yoke. 1st row.—* K. 2, p. 4; rep. from * to last 2 sts., k. 2.

2nd row.—* P. 2, k. 4; rep. from * to last 2 sts., p. 2.

Rep. these 2 rows until work measures 16 ins. from beg.

Change to No. 10 needles and continue in rib until work measures $17\frac{1}{2}$ ins. from beg., ending with a row on wrong side.

Change to No. 12 needles and dec. for top of yoke as follows:—

Next row.—* P. 2 tog., k. 4; rep. from * to last 2 sts., p. 2 tog.

Next row.—P. 2 tog., p. 3, * k. 1, p. 4; rep. from * to last 6 sts., k. 1, p. 3, p. 2 tog.

Continue in rib as follows:—

1st row.—* K. 4, p. 1; rep. from * to last 4 sts., k. 4.

2nd row.—* P. 4, k. 1; rep. from * to last 4 sts., p. 4.

Rep. these 2 rows until work measures 19 ins. from beg., ending with a row on wrong side of work.

Shape Shoulders thus:—

Next row.—Cast off 13, rib to end.

Next row.—Rib to end.

Rep. these 2 rows once more.

Cast off remaining sts.

The Right Front.—Work exactly as given for left front until work measures $3\frac{1}{2}$ ins. from beg. Now change to No. 9 needles and begin side shaping, inc. 1 st. at end of next and every following 4th row, instead of at beg., and shaping armholes when work measures 13 ins. from beg., but ending with a row on right side of work. Work yoke as given for left front, but shape shoulders when work measures 19 ins. from beg., ending with a row on right side.

The Sleeves.—Using No. 12 needles cast on 75 sts. and work in g.st. for $\frac{3}{4}$ in.

Change to No. 10 needles and proceed in patt. as for back, inc. 1 st. at both ends of the 7th and every following 4th row until there are 87 sts. on needle and changing to No. 9 needles when the sleeve measures $2\frac{1}{2}$ ins. from beg. Continue without shaping until work measures $4\frac{1}{2}$ ins. from beg.

Shape Top thus: Dec. 1 st. at both ends of the next and every alternate row until there are 55 sts. on needle. Then dec. 1 st. at both ends of every row until 29 sts. remain. Cast off.

The Right Front Band and Collar.—Using No. 12 needles cast on 9 sts. and work in g.st. for $\frac{1}{2}$ in.

Make a buttonhole in next 2 rows as follows:—

Next row.—K. 3, cast off 3, k. 3.

Next row.—K. 3, cast on 3, k. 3.

Continue in g.st. making buttonholes at intervals of 2 ins. until 7 buttonholes in all have been worked. Work a further $\frac{1}{2}$ in. in g.st. The band should now measure 14 ins. from the beg.

Begin the Collar Shaping thus: With the right side of work facing, k. 7, inc. in next st., k. 1.

Continue in g.st., inc. 1 st. at this edge on every 8th row until there are 16 sts. on needle.

Continue without further shaping until the work measures $21\frac{1}{2}$ ins. from the beg.

Cast off.

The Left Front Band and Collar.— Work exactly as given for right front, omitting the buttonholes.

Make-up.—Press all the knitting on the wrong side, except the yoke ribbing, using a warm iron over a damp cloth.

Join the side, sleeve and shoulder seams. Stitch the sleeves into armholes, easing in any fullness towards the top. Join the collar at centre back and placing this seam to centre back of neck, stitch the shaped edges of collar in position, continuing down g.st. border.

The Crochet Edges.—With right side of work facing and using a medium-size crochet hook and white wool, work all round fronts, collar, lower edge and lower edge of sleeves, as follows:—

* 1 d.c., miss about ½ in. of edge, 6 tr. into next st.; rep. from * all round.

Press all seams. Sew on buttons.

The bedjacket can be made with long or short sleeves, and left plain or trimmed with crochet edgings.

Instructions for Long Sleeves

With No. 9 needles cast on 87 sts. Continue in 12 row patt. until work measures 16 ins., ending row on wrong side.

Shape Top as for short sleeve.

The Cuff.—With No. 12 needles cast on 60 sts. Work 2 ins. in g.st. Cast off.

Run a thread along cast-on edge of sleeve and sew to top of cuff, easing in fullness. Cuffs may be left open and fastened with press studs. Join sleeve seam. Sew sleeves into armholes.

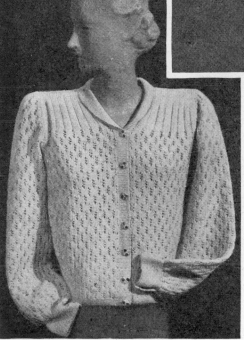

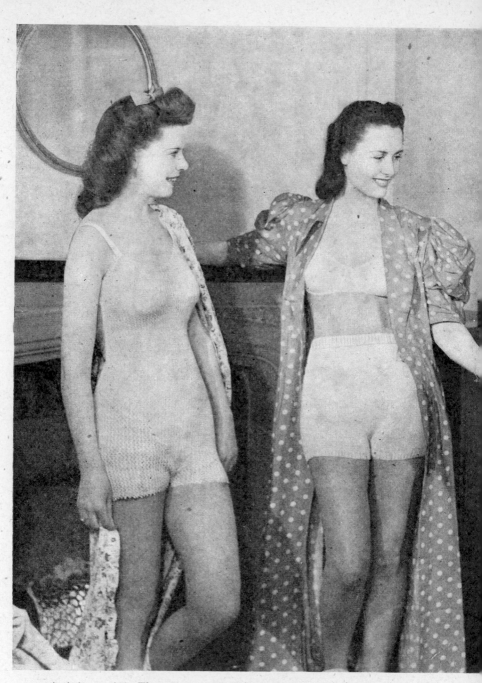

And yet again: Three smart girls begin the day well with wool next the skin. Camiknickers are the choice of one, and she has made them in open-work stitch, in pale pink wool, combining prettiness with warmth.

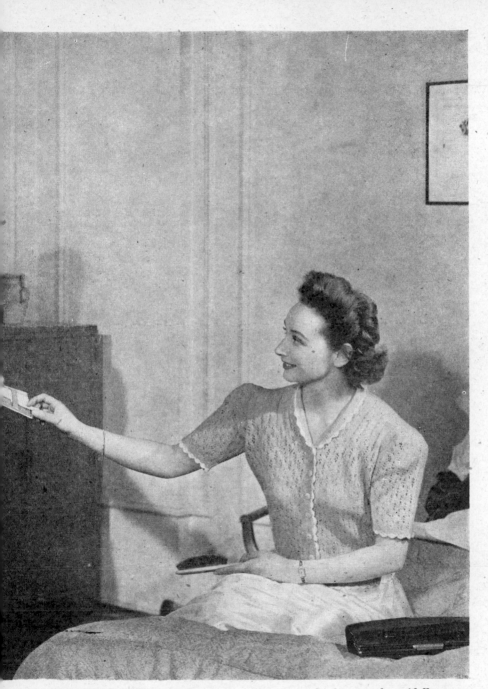

Very brief panties are the choice of the second; they are beautifully knitted to fit snugly, and show no wrinkles. The third still wears her bedjacket, the short-sleeved version with its dainty crocheted edges.

Camiknickers

KNITTED IN TWO PIECES

MATERIALS

3 oz. 2-ply wool.
2 No. 8, 2 No. 10 and 2 No. 12 knitting needles.
A medium crochet hook.
About ¾ yd. ribbon for shoulder straps.
3 small buttons.

MEASUREMENTS

Length at side seam, 22 ins.
Bust size, 32 ins. to 34 ins.

TENSION

With No. 8 needles, 6 sts. to 1 in. over patt.

The Front and Back are Alike.—With No. 8 needles cast on 51 sts. Work in patt. :—

1st row.—K. 1, * k. 2 tog., m. 1; rep. from * to last 2 sts., k. 2.

2nd row.—P. 2, * sl. m. st. of previous row, p. 1; rep. from * to last st., p. 1.

3rd row.—K. 2, * m. 1, sl. 1, k. 1, p.s.s.o.; rep. from * to last st., k. 1.

4th row.—As 2nd row.

These 4 rows form patt. Continue in patt. until work measures 3½ ins., finishing 3rd patt. row. Leave sts. on spare needle.

Work a second piece in same way, then join as follows:—

Next row.—P. 2, * sl. m. st. of previous row, p. 1; rep. from * to last st., now p. this last st. tog. with 1st st. from 51 sts. on spare needle, p. 1, ** sl. m. st. of previous row, p. 1; rep. from ** to last st., p. 1 (101 sts.).

Continue in patt. across all sts. until work is 8 ins.

Change to No. 10 needles, continue in patt. until work is 13½ ins.

The camiknickers are knitted in two pieces and the gusset. The waist is on finer needles, to fit snugly.

Change to No. 12 needles, continue in patt. until work is 16½ ins. Change to No. 10 needles, continue in patt. until work is 22 ins., finishing 4th patt. row. Keeping continuity of patt.

Shape Top thus:—

Next row.—Patt. 49, k. 2 tog., turn. Leave remaining 50 sts. on spare needle.

Continue in patt. on 50 sts., dec. 1 st. both ends of every row until 4 sts. remain. Work 4 tog., fasten off.

Rejoin wool and work on other 50 sts. to match. Work a second piece in same way.

The Gussets.—With No. 10 needles cast on 45 sts. Work in st.st. for 2½ ins.

Continue in st.st., dec. 1 st. both ends of every row until 21 sts., then dec. both ends of every alternate row until 3 sts. remain. K. 3 tog. and fasten off.

With No. 10 needles cast on 45 sts. Work 4 rows in st.st.

5th row.—K. 2, * cast off 3 sts., k. 16 counting st. already on needle; rep. from * once, cast off 3 sts., k. to end.

6th row.—P. 2, * cast on 3, p. 16; rep. from * once, cast on 3, p. 2.

Continue in st.st. until work is 2½ ins., then shape as for first gusset.

Detail of stitch, showing the waist knitted on finer needles.

Make up. Press work lightly with a hot iron over a damp cloth.

Sew gussets into position with points to centre leg opening. Join side seams.

Sew on ribbon for shoulder straps and buttons to plain gusset matching with buttonholes in other side. Work a row of picot edge all round legs and top edges. Press seams.

Tailored Panties

SNUG AND SLIM FITTING

MATERIALS

3 oz. 3-ply wool.
2 No. 10 and 2 No. 12 knitting needles.
A fine crochet hook.
1 yd. bias binding or some fine round elastic.
2 or 3 small buttons or press fasteners.

MEASUREMENTS

Length at side edge, 15 ins.
Waist, 24 ins. to 27 ins.

TENSION

7½ sts. to 1 in.

The Front. The Right Leg.—With No. 12 needles cast on 68 sts. and work 1 in. in k. 1, p. 1 rib. Leave these sts. on a spare needle.

The Left Leg.—Work as for right leg, then join legs and work for gusset as follows:—

Change to No. 10 needles.

The panties are tailored to fit smoothly over the hips, and in at the waist. The stitch is stocking stitch.

1st row.—K. 68 sts. of left leg. Cast on 26 sts. for gusset, k. 68 sts. of right leg (162 sts.).

2nd row.—P.

3rd row.—K. 68, k. 2 tog., k. to last 70 sts., k. 2 tog. k. 68.

4th row.—P.

Rep. the last 2 rows until the gusset sts. are reduced to 4.

25th row.—K. 68, (k. 2 tog.) twice, k. 68.

26th row.—P.

27th row.—K. 67, (k. 2 tog.) twice, k. 67.

28th row.—P.

29th row.—K

30th row.—P.

31st row.—K. 65, k. 2 tog., k. 2, k. 2 tog., k. 65.

Work 3 rows st.st.

Next row.—K., dec. on either side of the 2 centre sts. as in 31st row.

Rep. last 4 rows 3 times, and after that work 5 plain rows instead of 3 between dec. rows until 104 sts. remain.

Continue in st.st. without further shaping until work measures 13½ ins. from cast-on leg edge. Change to No. 12 needles and continue in k. 1, p. 1 rib until work measures 15 ins. Cast off in rib.

The Back. — Work exactly as for front until work measures 13½ ins., ending with a row on wrong side.

Shape Back thus:—

Next 2 rows.—Work to last 11 sts., turn.

Next 2 rows.—Work to last 21 sts., turn.

Next 2 rows.—Work to last 31 sts., turn.

Next 2 rows.—Work to last 41 sts. turn.

Next 2 rows.—Work right across.

Change to No. 12 needles and work 1½ ins. in k. 1, p. 1 rib.

Cast off loosely in rib.

Make-up.—Press work lightly on wrong side with hot iron and damp cloth, avoiding the ribbing.

Join leg and gusset seams. Join side seams leaving an opening at the top of left side seam.

Face the waist and opening with bias binding and fasten opening with press fasteners, or neaten the edges of the opening with a row of d.c., make 2 or 3 small button loops and sew on buttons to correspond. The waist may have fine elastic threaded through the top edge of the ribbing instead of the bias binding.

Opera-top Vest

IN THREE SIZES

MATERIALS

4 oz. 2-ply wool (for any of the 3 sizes).
1 pair No. 10 and 1 No. 5 needle.
Ribbon for shoulder straps.

MEASUREMENTS

Length: Size 1, 26 ins.; size 2, 27 ins.; size 3, 28 ins.

Bust: Size 1, 32 ins. to 34 ins.; size 2, 36 ins. to 38 ins.; size 3, 40 ins. to 42 ins.

TENSION

6½ sts. to 1 in. over st.st.

The vest is worked throughout with 1 No. 10 and 1 No. 5 needle, with the exception of the ribbing at waist and the patterned border at top edge.

The numbers of sts. in brackets refer to the two larger sizes.

The Front.—Using the No. 5 needle cast on 104 sts. (117) (130). Now work in g.st. (each row k.) for 4 rows, using 1 No. 10 and 1 No. 5 needle.

Continue in patt. as follows:—

1st row.—K.

2nd row.—P.

3rd row.—* P. 2 tog., p. 2 tog., k. 1, (m. 1, k. 1) 4 times, p. 2 tog., p. 2 tog.; rep. from * to end of row.

4th row.—P.

These 4 rows form one pattern. Rep. them twice more, then work 4 rows in g.st.

Continue in st.st. until work measures 11½ ins. ending with row on wrong side. Now start shapings for waist.

Next row.—K. 26 (31) (34), sl. 1, k. 1, p.s.s.o., k. 9, k. 2 tog., k. 26 (29) (36), sl. 1, k. 1, p.s.s.o., k. 9, k. 2 tog., k. 26 (31) (34).

Work 7 rows without dec.

The vest has feather-pattern border at the top and lower edges; it can be knitted in three sizes.

Be lovely, be warm! Here is a vest that has the charm of simplicity.
It will keep you warm without looking or feeling bulky. The original
was knitted in pale blue and looked pretty enough to add to a trousseau.

Next row.—K. 26 (31) (34), sl. 1, k. 1 p.s.s.o., k. 7, k. 2 tog., k. 26 (29) (36), sl. 1, k. 1, p.s.s.o., k. 7, k. 2 tog., k. 26 (31) (34).

Work 7 rows without dec.

Next row.—K. 26 (31) (34), sl. 1, k. 1, p.s.s.o., k. 5, k. 2 tog., k. 26 (29) (36), sl. 1, k. 1, p.s.s.o., k. 5, k. 2 tog., k. 26 (31) (34).

Work 7 rows without dec.

Next row.—K. 26 (31) (34), sl. 1, k. 1 p.s.s.o., k. 3, k. 2 tog., k. 26 (29) (36) sl. 1, k. 1, p.s.s.o., k. 3, k. 2 tog., k. 26 (31) (34). Work 7 rows without dec.

Next row.—K. 26 (31) (34), sl. 1, k. 1, p.s.s.o., k. 1, k. 2 tog., k. 26 (29) (36), sl. 1, k. 1 p.s.s.o., k. 1, k. 2 tog., k. 26 (31) (34).

Work 7 rows without dec.

Next row.—K. 26 (31) (34), sl. 1, k. 2 tog., p.s.s.o., k. 26 (29) (36), sl. 1, k. 2 tog., p.s.s.o., k. 26 (31) (34). Work should now measure about 16½ ins. from lower edge. If not, continue without shaping until it does.

Change to No. 10 needles and work in k. 1, p. 1 rib on the 80 (93) (106) sts. for 3 ins., ending with row on wrong side.

Change to 1 No. 10 and 1 No. 5 needle and inc. for bust as follows:—

Next row.—K. 26 (31) (34), inc. 2 in next st. by knitting into back, front and back again, k. 26 (29) (36), inc. 2 in next st., k. 26 (31) (34).

Work 3 rows in st.st.

Next row.—K. 26 (31) (34), inc. 1 st. in next st., by knitting into back and front of next st., k. 1, inc. in next st., k. 26 (29) (36), inc. in next st., k. 1, inc. in next st., k. 26 (31) (34).

Rep. the last 4 rows 4 times more; working 2 extra sts. between each pair of increases each time, until there are 104 (117) (130) sts. on needle.

Continue in st.st. without further inc. until work measures 24½ ins. (25½) (26½), ending with row on wrong side.

Change to 2 No. 10 needles and work 4 rows in g.st.

Then rep. the 4 rows of lace patt. 3 times.

Work 4 rows in g.st. Cast off.

The Back.—Continue exactly as given for front until the waist ribbing has been worked, ending with row on wrong side (80) (93) (106) sts.

Continue in st.st. without shaping until work measures 24½ ins. (25½) (26½), ending with row on wrong side.

Change to 2 No. 10 needles and work 4 rows in g.st., dec. 1 st. each end of 1st row.

Now work 12 rows in lace patt. and 4 rows in g.st. to match front.

Cast off loosely.

Make-up.—Press the work lightly on the wrong side using a warm iron and damp cloth.

Sew up side seams.

Attach ribbon shoulder straps.

Press seams.

Detail of the feather-pattern which trims the vest.

Shirt-waisted Dress

SMART TO WEAR IN TOWN OR COUNTRY

MATERIALS

16 oz. 3-ply wool.
2 No. 12 and 2 No. 14 knitting needles
5 buttons.
A leather belt
A fine crochet hook.

MEASUREMENTS

Length, 39½ ins.
Bust size, 34 ins.
Sleeve seam, 5 ins.

TENSION

With No. 12 needles 8½ sts. to 1 in.
measured over st.st.

The Front.—With No. 12 needles cast on 225 sts. Work in patt.:—

1st row.—K. 4, * k. twice into next st., k. 7; rep. from * to last 5 sts., k. twice into next st., k. 4.

2nd row.—P. 4, * p. 2 tog., p. 7; rep. from * to last 6 sts., p. 2 tog., p. 4.

Rep. these 2 rows until work measures 6 ins., ending 2nd patt. row.

Next row.—K. 4, * k. twice into next st., k. 2 tog., k. 5; rep. from * to last 5 sts., k. twice into next st., k. 4.

Next row.—P. 4, * p. 2 tog., p. 6; rep. from * to last 6 sts., p. 2 tog., p. 4.

Continue in fancy rib with only 6 sts. instead of 7 between until work measures 12 ins., ending 2nd patt. row.

Next row.—K. 4, * k. twice into next st., k. 2 tog., k. 4; rep. from * to last 5 sts., k. twice into next st., k. 4.

Next row.—P. 4, * p. 2 tog., p. 5; rep. from * to last 6 sts., p. 2 tog., p. 4.

Continue in fancy rib with only 5 sts.
instead of 6 between until work measures 18 ins., ending 2nd patt. row.

Next row.—K. 4, * k. twice into next st., k. 2 tog., k. 3; rep. from * to last 5 sts., k. twice into next st., k. 4.

Next row.—P. 4, * p. 2 tog., p. 4; rep. from * to end.

Continue in fancy rib with only 4 sts. instead of 5 between until work measures 24 ins., ending 2nd patt. row.

Change to No. 14 needles. Dec. for waist:—

Next row.—K. 5, * k. 1, k. 2 tog., k. 2; rep. from * to last 4 sts., k. 4 (117 sts.).

Next row.—K. 1, * p. 1, k. 1; rep. from * to end.

Rep. this row for 1½ ins., ending row on wrong side.

Change to No. 12 needles and work for bodice:—

Next row.—K. 4, (k. twice into next st., k. 1) 18 times, moss st. 37, (k. 1, k. twice into next st.) 18 times, k. 4.

Next row.—P. 4, (p. 2 tog., p. 4) 9 times, moss st. 25, turn.

Leave remaining sts. on a spare needle.

Continue in moss st. and patt. on these 74 sts., inc. 1 st. at side edge on next row and the following 8th row until work measures 1½ ins. from top of waist band, ending front edge.

Next row.—Make a buttonhole thus: Moss st. 4, cast off 4 for buttonhole, moss st. to end of panel, patt. to end.

Next row.—Patt. to moss st. panel, moss st. to last 4 sts., cast on 4, moss st. 4.

Continue in patt. and moss st. making further buttonholes at intervals of 2 ins. from beg. of previous buttonhole, still

You'll never get tired of this knitted tailored dress. The fancy rib is worked on fine needles to make a firm fabric, essential for a large knitted garment, which will wear splendidly and keep its smart shape.

inc. at side edge on every 8th row until 6 increasings have been worked in all (80 sts. at end of a 2nd patt. row).

Continue straight with regular buttonholes until work measures 7½ ins. from top of waist band, ending side edge.

Shape Armhole thus: Cast off 8 sts. beg. of next row, dec. 1 st. at this same edge on next 10 rows. (*N.B.*—When dec. on a 2nd patt. row regard double patt. sts. as 1 st.)

Continue straight on 62 sts. until 5 buttonholes have been made in moss st. panel, then continue without further buttonholes until work measures 11 ins. from top of waist band, ending front edge.

Begin Yoke thus: Continue in moss st. across all sts. until work measures 14 ins. from top of waist band, ending armhole edge.

Shape Shoulder thus:—

Next row.—Cast off 10 sts., moss st. to end.

Next row.—Moss st. to end.

Rep. last 2 rows twice.

Next row.—Cast off 9 sts., moss st. to end.

Cast off remaining sts.

Rejoin wool to sts. for left side of front at opening edge, work thus:—

Cast on 13 sts. for underwrap, moss st. these 13 sts. and next 12 sts., * p. 4, p. 2 tog.; rep. from * to last 4 sts., p. 4.

Continue in moss st. and patt. on 74 sts., inc. 1 st. at side edge on next row and every following 8th row until 6 increasings have been worked. Continue straight until work measures 7½ ins. from top of waist band, ending side edge.

Shape Armholes and complete front to match right front omitting buttonholes.

The Back.—Work as for front until moss st. waist band is completed.

Change to No. 12 needles and work for bodice:—

Next row (right side facing).—(K. 1, k. twice into next st.) 8 times, (k. 4, k. twice into next st., k. 1, k. twice into next st.,

k. 1, k. twice into next st.) 10 times, (k. 1, k. twice into next st.) 5 times, k. 1.

Next row.—P. 4, * p. 2 tog., p. 4; rep. from * to end (134 sts.).

Continue in patt., inc. 1 st. both ends of next row and every following 8th row until 146 sts. on needle at end of a 2nd patt. row. Continue straight in patt. until work measures 7½ ins. from top of waist band.

Shape Armholes thus: Continuing in patt., cast off 8 sts. beg. of next 2 rows (regarding double patt. sts. as 1 st.), then dec. 1 st. both ends of every row until 110 sts. remain, at end of a 2nd patt. row.

Continue straight until work measures 11 ins. from top of waist band.

Begin Yoke thus: Continue in moss st. across all sts. for 3 ins.

Shape Neck and Shoulders thus: Cast off 10 sts. beg. of next 6 rows, cast off 9 sts. beg. of next 2 rows.

Cast off remaining sts.

The Sleeves.—With No. 12 needles cast on 85 sts. Work 1 in. in moss st.

Continue in moss st., inc. 1 st. both ends of next row and every following 4th row until 103 sts. on needle. Continue straight until work measures 5 ins

Shape Top thus: Dec. 1 st. both ends of every alternate row until 63 sts. remain, then dec. both ends of every row until 33 sts.

Cast off 11 sts. beg. of next 2 rows. Cast off 11 sts.

The Collar.—With No. 12 needles cast on 73 sts. Work in moss st. for 1¼ ins.

Continue in moss st., cast off 12 sts. beg. of next 2 rows, 4 sts. beg. of next 8 rows.

Cast off remaining sts.

Make-up.—Press work lightly on wrong side, using a hot iron over damp cloth.

Backstitch shoulder seams.

Join side seams.

Join sleeve seams, backstitch sleeves into armholes matching seams.

Pin centre of cast-off edge of collar to centre back of neck and sew collar round neck edge, ending about 1 in. from front edges.

Turn collar and front edges back as far as top buttonhole to form revers.

Sew lower edge of left front underwrap along back of right front.

Sew on buttons to match with buttonholes. The buttons may be "made" ones, in the same wool as the frock.

Press seams.

Now work 2 rows of d.c. all round lower edge, sleeve edges, collar and front edges, taking care not to draw in edges.

Fasten a leather belt round waist.

The dress has yoke, collar and revers in moss stitch, and the bodice and skirt in fancy rib; detail of the stitch is shown on the left. Fine needles are used to give a closely knitted fabric which hangs well.

Cardigan Suit

TO WEAR IN SPRING AND AUTUMN

MATERIALS

22 oz. 3-ply crêpe wool.
2 No. 7, 2 No. 12 and 2 No. 10 knitting needles and a short spare needle pointed each end.
1 yd. petersham.
Press fasteners.
8 buttons.
A small piece of bias binding.
2 shoulder pads.

MEASUREMENTS

The Jacket: Length, 23 ins.
Bust, 34 ins.
Sleeve seam, 18 ins.
The Skirt: Length, 25 ins.
Waist, 26–28 ins.

TENSION

Using No. 7 needles, 8 sts. to 1 in. measured over patt.

THE SKIRT

The Front and Back are Alike.—With No. 7 needles cast on 177 sts. Work in patt.:—

1st row.—P. 1, * w.bk., sl. 1 p.w., w.fd., p. 1; rep. from * to end.

2nd row.—Sl. 1 p.w., * w.bk., k. 1, w.fd., sl. 1 p.w.; rep. from * to end.

These 2 rows form patt. Continue in patt. until work measures 4 ins., ending 2nd patt. row.

Keeping continuity of patt. throughout, dec. 1 st. both ends of next row and every following 14th row until work measures 19½ ins., ending on wrong side.

Now begin waist darts. When there are an uneven number of sts. after these decreasings, keep continuity of patt. by

slipping 2 sts. at dec. points on p. rows and knitting 2 sts. at dec. points on k. rows. Continue to dec. on every 14th row at both ends of row throughout.

Next row.—Patt. 37, p. 2 tog., patt. 3, p. 2 tog., patt. to last 44 sts., p. 2 tog., patt. 3, p. 2 tog., patt. 37. Work 13 rows in patt., allowing for dec. sts.

Next row.—Patt. 35, p. 2 tog., patt. 3, p. 2 tog., patt. to last 42 sts., p. 2 tog., patt. 3, p. 2 tog., patt. 35.

Work 13 rows in patt.

Next row.—Patt. 33, p. 2 tog., patt. 3, p. 2 tog., patt. to last 40 sts., p. 2 tog., patt. 3, p. 2 tog., patt. 33. Work 13 rows in patt., allowing for dec. sts.

Next row.—Patt. 31, p. 2 tog., patt. 3, p. 2 tog., patt. to last 38 sts., p. 2 tog., patt. 3, p. 2 tog., patt. 31.

Continue in patt. across all sts., still dec. regularly at side edges until work measures 23½ ins., finish row on wrong side.

Change to No. 12 needles and continue in patt. until work measures 25 ins., finish row on wrong side.

Cast off loosely as follows: K. 1, * k. 2 tog., pass previous st. over; rep. from * to last st., k. 1, pass previous st. over.

Work second piece in same way.

The Underwrap.—With No. 12 needles cast on 5 sts. and work 5½ ins. in patt. Cast off.

Make-up.—Press work lightly with a hot iron over a damp cloth on wrong side.

Join side seams with very narrow back-stitch seams, leaving left side seam open for about 5½ ins. at waist.

Sew side edge of underwrap along back edge of side opening, then face the top

*Beauty and the Beast, both dressed for autumn, Billy in his coat
of tan, his mistress in a navy suit; the suit is knitted in crêpe wool,
and in a plain stitch with cable bands on the tailored cardigan jacket.*

edge with the strip of bias binding. Sew petersham in position round waist, fasten this with hooks and eyes and fasten opening with press fasteners. Press seams.

THE JACKET

The Back.—With No. 7 needles cast on 146 sts. Work in patt.:—

1st row.—* P 1, w.bk., sl. 1 p.w. w.fd.; rep. from * to end.

2nd row.—* K. 1, w.fd., sl. 1 p.w., w.bk.; rep. from * to end.

These 2 rows form patt. which is used throughout. Continue in patt. until work measures 5 ins. ending 2nd row.

Change to No. 10 needles and continue in patt. until work measures 7 ins., ending 2nd row

Change to No. 7 needles and continue in patt., inc. 1 st. both ends of next row and every following 10th row until 170 sts., working extra sts. into patt. Continue straight until work measures 16 ins.

Shape Armholes thus: Cast off 6 sts. beg. of next 2 rows, dec. 1 st. both ends of every row until 126 sts. remain.

Continue straight until work measures 23 ins., finishing 2nd row.

Shape Shoulders thus: Cast off 8 sts. beg. of next 10 rows. Cast off.

Detail of the stitch and cable band on the jacket.

The Right Front.—With No. 7 needles cast on 70 sts. Work 5 ins. in patt. as given for back, ending 2nd row.

Change to No. 10 needles, continue in patt. until work measures 7 ins., ending 2nd row.

Change to No. 7 needles. Continue in patt., inc. 1 st. at end of next row and every following 10th row until 82 sts., working extra sts. into patt. Continue straight until work measures 16 ins., ending shaped side edge.

Shape Armhole thus: Cast off 6 sts. beg. of next row, dec. 1 st. at same edge on every row until 60 sts. remain. Continue straight until work measures 18½ ins., ending straight front edge.

Shape Front Edge thus: Dec. 1 st. beg. of next row and every alternate row until 40 sts. remain. Continue straight until work measures 23¼ ins., ending armhole edge.

Shape Shoulder thus:—

Next row.—Cast off 8 sts., work to end.

Next row.—Patt. to end.

Rep. last 2 rows 3 times.

Cast off 8 sts.

The Left Front.—Continue as right front until work measures 7 ins., ending 2nd row.

Change to No. 7 needles. Continue in patt., inc. 1 st. beg. of next row and every following 10th row until 82 sts., working extra sts. into patt. Continue straight until work measures 16 ins., ending shaped side edge.

Shape Armhole, Front Edge and Shoulder as for right front.

The Sleeves.—With No. 7 needles cast on 80 sts. Work in patt. as given for back for 10 rows, then inc. 1 st. both ends of next row and every following 12th row until 112 sts. Continue straight until work measures 17 ins., ending 2nd row.

Shape Top thus: Dec. 1 st. beg. of every row until 48 sts. remain.

K. 3 tog. at beg. of each row until 12 sts. remain. Cast off 12 sts.

The Front Border.— With No. 10 needles cast on 12 sts., k. 2 rows.

** 3rd row.—K. to end.

4th row.—K. 2, p. 8, k. 2.

5th row.—K. 2, twist next 8 sts. thus: sl. next 4 sts. on to a spare needle, leave at back of work, k. next 4 sts., k. 4 sts. from spare needle, k. 2.

6th row.—K. 2, p. 8, k. 2.

7th row.—Make a buttonhole: k. 4, cast off 4, k. to end.

8th row.—K. 2, p. 2, cast on 4, p. 2, k. 2.

9th row. — As 3rd row.

10th row. — As 4th row.

11th row. — As 5th row.

12th row.—As 6th row.

13th row.—As 3rd row.

14th row.—As 4th row.

Rep. last 6 rows, i.e., rows 9 to 14 inclusive, twice more ******.

Now rep. from ****** to ****** 6 times, then rep. rows 3 to 8 inclusive once more (8 buttonholes).

Continue in cable patt. with g.st. border without buttonholes until band is correct length to fit all round front and back of neck edges when slightly stretched, allowing for top buttonhole to come just below commencement of right front shaping.

K. 2 rows, then cast off.

The Cuffs.—With No. 10 needles cast on 12 sts., k. 2 rows.

3rd row.—K. to end.

4th row.—K. 2, p. 8, k. 2.

5th row.—K. 2, twist next 8 sts., k. 2.

The suit is designed to fit a 32- or 34-in. bust measurement, and was knitted in navy blue in the original. The plain skirt is shown folded in half.

6th row.—As 4th row.

7th and 8th rows.—As 3rd and 4th rows. Rep. last 6 rows until band measures 9 ins. Cast off.

Work a second strip in same way.

Make-up.—Press work lightly with a hot iron over a damp cloth.

Join side and shoulder seams with very narrow backstitch.

Sew cuffs very neatly to lower edge of sleeves, then join sleeve seams with narrow backstitch. Backstitch sleeves into armholes, matching seams, and keeping extra fullness to top of sleeve.

Pin front border into position round front and back of neck edges with top buttonhole just below commencement of right front shaping and sew on neatly. Sew on buttons to match buttonholes.

Press seams. Sew in shoulder pads.

Twin Set

FOR THE OLDER WOMAN

MATERIALS

16 oz. real Shetland 2-ply wool or ordinary 3-ply fingering.

(To make garments separately you require 7 oz. for jumper, 9 oz. for cardigan.)

2 No. 10 and 2 No. 12 knitting needles.

A fine crochet hook.

6 small buttons for jersey.

7 buttons for cardigan.

1 press fastener.

MEASUREMENTS

The Jersey: Length, 19 ins.

Bust, 38 ins.

Sleeve, 5 ins.

The Cardigan: Length, 21 ins.

Bust, 39 ins.

Sleeve, 17 ins.

TENSION

$7\frac{1}{2}$ sts. to 1 in. over st.st.

THE JERSEY

The Back.—With No. 10 needles cast

Detail of stitch showing plain knitting and pattern panel.

on 115 sts.

Change to No. 12 needles, work in k. 1, p. 1 rib for 3 ins.

Change to No. 10 needles.

Continue in st.st., inc. 1 st. both ends of 5th row and every following 6th row until 137 sts. are on needle. Continue straight until work measures $11\frac{1}{2}$ ins., ending p. row.

Shape Armholes thus: Cast off 8 sts. beg. of next 2 rows, dec. 1 st. both ends of every row until 109 sts. remain. Continue without shaping until work measures $14\frac{1}{2}$ ins., finishing p. row.

Begin Yoke thus:—

1st row.—P. 2, * w.bk., pass needle p.w. through 1st and 2nd sts. on left-hand needle, k. into front of 3rd st. and sl. this st. off, pass needle p.w. again through 1st st. and (p. 1, k. 1) into back of 2nd st. slipping this st. off, now (p. 1, k. 1) into back of 1st st. and sl. off in usual way, p. 3; rep. from * to end, ending p. 2, instead of p. 3.

2nd row.—K. 2, * p. 5, k. 3; rep. from * to last 7 sts., p. 5, k. 2.

3rd row.—P. 1, * k. 2 tog., k. 3,sl.1, k. 1, p.s.s.o., p. 1; rep. from * to end.

4th row.—K. 2, * p. 3, k. 3; rep. from * to last 5 sts., p. 3, k. 2.

These 4 rows form patt. of yoke.

Continue in patt. for $4\frac{1}{2}$ ins., ending with a 4th patt. row.

Shape Shoulders and Neck thus:—

Next row.—Cast off 9 sts., patt. across next 32 sts., including st. already on needle after casting off, k. 2 tog., turn.

Work on these sts. only in patt. for one shoulder (leaving remaining 66 sts. for neck and other shoulder):—

Simple lines are most becoming to the woman with the fuller figure, as you can see from this elegant twin set, which was knitted in a delicate shade of grey-green shetland wool. The jumper beneath has short sleeves.

Next row.—K. 2 tog., patt. to end.

Next row.—Cast off 9 sts., patt. to last 2 sts., p. 2 tog.

Next row.—K. 2 tog., patt. to end.

Rep. last 2 rows once. Cast off remaining sts.

Rejoin wool at needle point. Cast off centre 23 sts., work in patt. to last 11 sts.. k. 3, p. 3, k. 3, p. 2.

Next row.—Cast off 9 sts., patt. to last 2 sts., k. 2 tog.

Next row.—P. 2 tog., patt. to end. Rep. last 2 rows twice. Cast off remaining sts.

The Front.—With No. 10 needles cast on 132 sts. Change to No. 12 needles, work in k. 1, p. 1 rib for 3 ins.

Change to No. 10 needles. Continue in st.st., inc. 1 st. both ends of 5th row and every following 6th row until 154 sts. are on needle. Continue straight until work measures 11½ ins., finishing p. row.

Shape Armholes and Begin Front

Opening: Cast off 8 sts. beg. of next 2 rows. dec. 1 st. both ends of next 3 rows.

Next row.—P. 2 tog., p. 64, turn. Leave remaining 66 sts. on spare needle.

Continue in st.st. on these 65 sts., dec. 1 st. at armhole edge on every row until 61 sts. remain. Continue straight until work measures 14½ ins., finishing with a k. row.

Begin Yoke thus:—

Next row.—(P. 4, p. 2 tog., p. 4) 6 times, p. 1 (55 sts.).

Continue in patt. as given for back yoke until work measures 3 ins. from beg. of yoke, finish front opening edge with a 4th patt. row.

Shape Neck and Shoulder thus: Continue in patt., cast off 9 sts. beg. of next row, dec. 1 st. at neck edge on every row until 37 sts. remain, counting at end of a 4th patt. row.

Continue straight in patt. until work

The cardigan has a panel of fancy rib down the front and along the lower edge; the pocket is knitted in one with the panel.

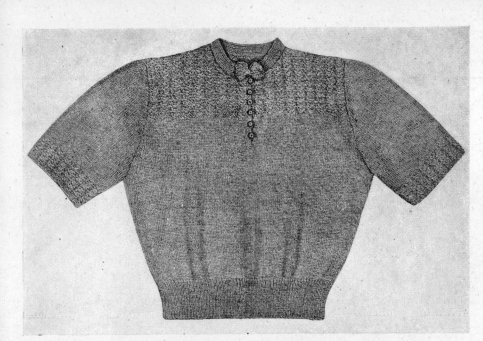

The jumper is knitted plain, with a yoke of the pattern stitch. The narrow neck edging and simple bow give a soft finish.

measures 4½ ins. from beg. of yoke, finishing armhole edge.

Next row.—Cast off 9 sts., patt. to last 2 sts., k. 2 tog.

Next row.—P. 2 tog., patt. to end.

Rep. last 2 rows twice.

Cast off remaining sts.

Sl. other 66 sts. on to No. 10 needle with point to opening edge, rejoin wool and cast on 4 sts. for underwrap.

Continue in st.st. with these 4 underwrap sts. in moss st. (k. 1, p. 1) alternately, dec. 1 st. at armhole edge on every row until 65 sts. remain. Continue straight until work measures 14½ ins., finishing front opening edge with a k. row.

Begin Yoke thus:—

Next row.—Moss st. 4, p. 1, (p. 4, p. 2 tog., p. 4) 6 times.

Continue in patt. as given for back yoke with underwrap sts. in moss st. until work measures 3 ins. from beg. of yoke, finishing armhole edge with a 4th patt. row.

Shape Neck and Shoulder thus:—

Next row.—Patt. to last 15 sts., k. 3, p. 3, k. 3, p. 2, moss st. 4.

Next row.—Cast off 13 sts., patt. to end.

Continue in patt., dec. 1 st. at neck edge on every row until 37 sts. remain. Continue straight until work measures 4½ ins. from beg. of yoke, finishing armhole edge.

Shape Shoulder as for first shoulder.

The Sleeves.—With No. 10 needles cast on 79 sts. Work in patt. as for back yoke, beg. with a 4th patt. row until work measures 2 ins., finishing with a 4th patt. row.

Continue in st.st., inc. 1 st. both ends of next row and every 4th row until 93 sts., then continue straight until work measures 5 ins., finishing with a p. row.

Shape Top thus: Cast off 5 sts. beg. of next 2 rows, dec. 1 st. beg. of every row

*The jumper of the twin set has short sleeves edged with the pattern.
The woman with a fuller figure will want to avoid a heavy look in her
woollens, and so should knit them in fine wool and on thin needles.*

until 47 sts. remain. Then dec. 1 st. at beg. and end of every row until 27 sts. remain.

Cast off 5 sts. beg. of next 4 rows.

Cast off remaining sts.

Neck Band.—With No. 12 needles cast on 7 sts. Work 14 ins. in moss st. Cast off.

The Tie.—With No. 12 needles cast on 7 sts. Work 6 ins. in moss st. Cast off.

Make-up.—Press work lightly on wrong side with hot iron over damp cloth.

Join side and sleeve seams.

Backstitch shoulder seams.

Backstitch sleeves into armholes, matching seams.

Sew lower edge of underwrap along back of right front edge.

Pin centre of one side of neck band to centre back of neck; sew band round neck edge, ending at right front edge and beg. of moss st. underwrap on left front.

Tie the shorter strip into a knot and attach to right front edge of neck band, fasten to other side with a press fastener.

Work a row of fine d.c. down right front edge of opening and make 6 small button loops at regular intervals.

Sew on buttons to match.

Press seams.

THE CARDIGAN

The Back.—With No. 10 needles cast on 121 sts. Work in patt.:—

1st row (wrong side facing).—K. 2, * p. 3, k. 3; rep. from * to last 5 sts., p. 3, k. 2.

2nd row.—P. 2, * w.bk., pass needle p.w. through 1st and 2nd sts. on left-hand needle and k. into front of 3rd st., sl. this st. off needle, pass needle p.w. again through 1st st. and (p. 1, k. 1) into back of 2nd st., slipping this st. off, now (p. 1, k. 1) into back of 1st st. and sl. off in usual way, p. 3; rep. from * to end, ending p. 2 instead of p. 3.

3rd row.—K. 2, * p. 5, k. 3; rep. from * to last 7 sts., p. 5, k. 2.

4th row.—P. 1, * k. 2 tog., k. 3, sl.1, k. 1, p.s.s.o., p. 1; rep. from * to end.

Rep. last 4 rows once more, then 1st row again.

Continue in st.st. until work measures 4 ins., finishing p. row.

Now inc. 1 st. both ends of next row and every following 6th row until 145 sts. on needle. Continue straight until work measures 13 ins., finishing p. row.

Shape Armholes thus: Cast off 8 sts. beg. of next 2 rows, dec. 1 st. both ends of every row until 109 sts. remain. Continue without shaping until work measures 21 ins., finishing p. row.

Shape Neck and Shoulders thus: Cast off 12 sts. beg. of next 2 rows, 13 sts. beg. of next 4 rows.

Cast off remaining sts.

The Right Front.—With No. 10 needles cast on 43 sts. Work 9 rows in patt. as given for back, then continue in st.st. until work measures 4 ins., finishing p. row. Leave sts. on spare needle.

The Front Border and Pocket.—With No. 10 needles cast on 59 sts. Work in patt. with k. 1, p. 1 rib front border thus:—

1st row.—K. 2, * p. 3, k. 3; rep. from * to last 15 sts., p. 3, k. 2, (k. 1, p. 1) 5 times.

Work 4 more rows in patt. on 49 sts. with 10 border sts. in rib, thus finishing front edge. Now make a buttonhole:—

Next row.—Rib 3, cast off 4 for buttonhole, rib to end of border, work in patt. to end.

Next row.—Patt. to last 6 sts., rib 3, cast on 4, rib 3.

Continue in patt. and rib until work measures 2½ ins., finishing front edge.

Make a second buttonhole in next 2 rows, then continue in patt. and rib until work measures 4 ins., finishing row on right side with a 4th patt. row.

Next row.—Cast off 30 sts. for pocket, patt. to last 10 sts., rib 10.

Next row.—Rib 10, patt. 19, then on to same needle k. 43 sts. from spare needle.

Continue in st.st. with patt. and ribbed front borders making regular buttonholes in ribbed border at intervals of 2 ins. from each previous buttonhole, at the same time inc. 1 st. at side edge on next k. row and every following 6th row until there are 84 sts. on needle.

Continue straight until 7 buttonholes have been worked in ribbed border.

Work 4 rows after last buttonhole, thus finishing front edge, then shape front edge thus:—

Next row.—Rib 10, patt. 19, sl. 1, k. 1, p.s.s.o., k. to end. Dec. in this way on every 4th row at neck edge while shaping armhole thus: Cast off 8 sts. beg. of next row, dec. 1 st. at same edge on next 8 rows, then dec. 1 st. at same edge on every alternate row 6 times (22 sts. dec. armhole edge).

Continue with armhole edge straight, dec. on every 4th row at front edge until 44 sts. remain, then continue without shaping until work measures $21\frac{1}{4}$ ins., finishing armhole edge.

Shape Shoulder thus:—

Next row.—Cast off 8 sts., work to end.

Next row.—Work to end.

Rep. last 2 rows twice.

Next row.—Cast off all sts. to ribbed border, rib to end.

Continue in rib on 10 sts. for $2\frac{1}{4}$ ins. for back of neck border. Cast off in rib.

The Left Front, the Front Border and Pocket.—With No. 10 needles cast on 59 sts. Work in patt. with k. 1, p. 1 rib front border thus:—

1st row.—(K. 1, p. 1) 5 times, k 2 * p. 3, k. 3 ; rep. from * to last 5 sts., p. 3, k. 2.

Continue in patt. on 49 sts. with 10 sts. in rib until work measures 4 ins., finishing at front border edge with a 4th patt. row.

Next row.—Rib 10, patt. 19, cast off 30 sts. for pocket. Break off wool, leave sts. on a spare needle.

With No. 10 needles cast on 43 sts. Work 9 rows in patt. as given for back, then continue in st.st. until work measures 4 ins., finishing p. row.

Next row.—K. to end, then work in

patt. and rib across first set of 29 sts.

Continue in st.st. with patt. and ribbed front borders, inc. 1 st. at side edge on next k. row and every following 6th row until there are 84 sts. on needle.

Continue without shaping until work measures same as right front to beg. of front shaping, finishing side edge.

Shape Front Edge thus:—

Next row.—K. to 2 sts. before patt. border, k. 2 tog., patt. to last 10 sts., rib 10.

Dec. in this way on every 4th row at the same time shaping armhole exactly as given for right front. Now complete front shapings and shoulder and back of neck border as given for right front.

The Sleeves.—With No. 12 needles cast on 61 sts. Work 9 rows in patt. as given for back.

Continue in st.st. until work measures $2\frac{1}{2}$ ins., finishing p. row, then inc. 1 st. both ends of next row and every following 6th row until work measures 3 ins.

Change to No. 10 needles and continue to inc. on every 6th row until there are 107 sts. on needle.

Continue without shaping until work measures 17 ins., finishing p. row.

Shape Top thus:—Cast off 5 sts. beg. of next 2 rows, dec. 1 st. beg. of every row until 37 sts. remain.

Cast off 5 sts. beg. of next 6 rows. Cast off remaining sts.

Make-up.—Press work lightly on wrong side with hot iron over damp cloth.

Join side and sleeve seams. Backstitch shoulder seams. Backstitch sleeves into armholes, matching seams.

Sew side edges of pockets to main part and sew lower edge of pocket into position, then sew inside edge of main part along inside edge of ribbed front border to complete pocket.

Join back of neck border seam and sew this border along back of neck edge with join to centre.

Sew on buttons. Press seams.

Three-way Cape

TO WEAR INDOORS, OUTDOORS OR AS A BEDCAPE

CAPE WITH PLAITED NECKLINE

MATERIALS

10 oz. of 3-ply wool.
1 pair of No. 10 and No. 14 needles.

MEASUREMENTS

Length down centre back, 19 ins.
Width all round lower edge, 57 ins.

TENSION

11 sts. to 1 in. unstretched.

The cape is made in two halves and seamed up the back. All dec. are worked on wrong side.

The Right Half of Cape.—Using No. 10 needles cast on 314 sts. and work in k. 1, p. 1 rib for 3 ins. With wrong side of work facing, continue thus:—

1st row.—Rib 83 sts., p. 2 tog. (there are now 2 p. sts. which must be kept as p. 2 in rib until next dec.). Continue in rib until 84 sts. remain, p. 2 tog. (again making p. 2 in rib), continue to end of row.

2nd row.—Rib 82 sts., k. 2, rib until 85 sts. remain, k. 2, rib to end.

3rd row.—Rib 83 sts., p. 2, rib until 84 sts. remain, p. 2, rib to end.

4th row.—As 2nd row.

5th row.—Rib 83 sts., p. 2 tog., rib until 84 sts. rem., p. 2 tog., rib to end.

6th, 7th and 8th rows.—Rib across.

Continue in this way, dec. on every 4th row, taking care to make all decreasings after the 83rd st. and before the 82nd st. from end of needle, until 31 dec. rows have been worked. There should now be 87 sts.

between decreasings and 252 sts. on needle.

Now Start Shaping for Yoke.—With right side of work facing, cast off 83 sts., rib 87 sts., including st. already on right-hand needle; cast off remaining sts.

Next row.—Change to No. 14 needles, rejoin wool and with wrong side of work facing, continue in rib, dec. 1 st. at end of first row. Work on these 86 sts. until yoke measures 4 ins., ending with row on right side

Next row.—Rib 44 sts. and leave on a spare needle, cast off next 10 sts., rib to end.

Next row.—Rib until 2 sts. rem., k. 2 tog.

Each cape is based on the same design, but with different neckline finishes.

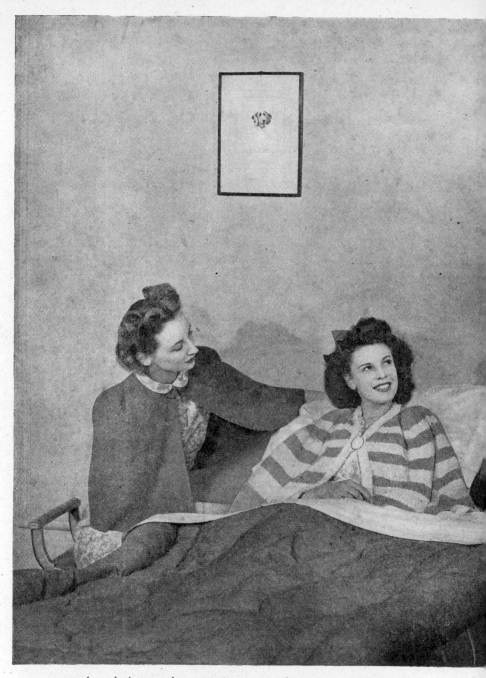

A variation on the same theme; our three smart girls have taken the same design and presented it in three ways: one has given it a plaited neckline and made of it a house cape.

Another has knitted it in stripes, with a fluffy border, and made herself a bedcape; the third has added a little collar and made a cape to wear out of doors, over her lightweight suit.

Next row.—Cast off 2 sts., rib to end.

Rep. the last 2 rows until all sts. are worked off.

Return to the 44 sts. left on spare needle and work in rib for back of yoke, without dec. until 1 in. longer than pointed piece of front yoke. Cast off in rib.

The Left Half of Cape.—Work exactly as for right half until yoke is reached, then continue using No. 14 needles on the first 32 sts. for front yoke, reversing all shapings by ending with row on wrong side of work instead of right side when work measures 4 ins. Work on the last 44 sts. for back of yoke without shaping.

The Shoulder Pad Covers.—Make two.

Using No. 10 needles cast on 24 sts. and work in st.st. for 4 ins. Cast off.

Fold in half diagonally and sew tog. Stuff with cotton wool.

Make-up.—Press all work very lightly on wrong side, with hot iron over damp cloth. Seam the 44 sts. of back yoke tog.

Backstitch the centre back seam of cape close to edge.

Stitch yoke to cape, leaving 1 in. of cape extending beyond yoke at front edges to form front of neck.

Make a thick plait of the wool about 20 ins. long and sew round neck edge, forming ends into a coil at front edges.

Finish with a hook and eye sewn underneath the coils.

To fix the shoulder pads, make a crochet chain about 3 ins. long and stitch ends to outer ends of yoke seams, sew the wider edge of pad to this chain.

Press all seams.

CAPE WITH COLLAR

This is made in exactly the same way as the first cape, but with a collar instead of the plaited neckline.

To Make the Collar.—Using No. 14 needles pick up and k. about 96 sts. round the neck edge. Work 10 rows in k. 1, p. 1 rib, then change to No. 10 needles and continue in rib until the collar is about 2¼ ins. deep. Cast off. Fasten the neck with a button and loop.

BED CAPE

This is made in 2-ply wool instead of 3-ply, using Nos. 8 and 12 needles instead of Nos. 10 and 14. It can be made all in one colour like the 3-ply cape in which case 6 oz. of 2-ply wool will be needed, or like the model shown it can be made in stripes to use up odd quantities of wool. The model took 4 oz. of pale blue, 2 oz. of pink and 1 oz. of white.

The colour stripes are outlined in white worked in holes as follows: End with a row of colour ribbing on the wrong side (a dec. row).

Change to white wool and k. 1 row, then on the next row work "p. 2, m. 1, p. 2 tog." all along the row.

Change to the other colour and k. a plain row, then continue in the rib, working a dec. row to begin (thus making the white stripe replace the 3 rows of rib between the decreasings).

The original was worked in the following stripes: 4 ins. of blue, row of holes in white; 2 ins. of pink, row of holes in white; 1½ ins. of blue, row of holes in white; 1½ ins. of pink, row of holes in white; 1½ ins. of blue, row of holes in white; 1 in. of pink, row of holes in white; 1½ ins. of blue, row of holes in white; ½ in. of pink, row of holes in white, then plain blue throughout.

For the border strip, which is sewn all round the two fronts and the neck, work as follows: Using white wool and No. 12 needles cast on 6 sts. K. 1 row.

1st row.—K. 1, insert the needle into the next st. and pass the wool round the needle and the first finger of the left hand 3 times, then once more round the needle; k. through all threads at once (this is called a loop st.); k. 1, loop st. into next st., k. 1, loop st. into last st.

2nd row.—K. all sts.

Rep. these 2 rows for length required.

Peasant Cardigan

FOR THE FIRST DAYS OF SUMMER

MATERIALS

9 oz. 3-ply wool in white.
1 oz. 3-ply wool in blue.
1 oz. 3-ply wool in pink.
2 No. 6 knitting needles.
A medium size crochet hook.

MEASUREMENTS

Length, $18\frac{1}{2}$ ins.
Bust size, 34 ins.
Sleeve seam, 17 ins.

TENSION

One patt. of 18 sts. measures approximately $3\frac{1}{4}$ ins.

N.B.—Work with double wool throughout. Use separate lengths of wool for each vertical group of knobs in contrasting colours, allowing about $1\frac{1}{2}$ yd. for each group.

Always twist colours carefully when changing from white to contrast and vice versa. Keep white wool always at back of knobs by keeping it always to wrong side of work when working with contrasting colour and carrying it fairly loosely across back of knob.

Additional Abbreviations

W. = white; b. = blue; pk. = pink; work 5 into next st. = work (k. 1, p. 1. k. 1, p. 1, k. 1) all into next st.

The Sleeves.—With double w. wool cast on 40 sts. Work in patt thus:—
1st row.—* K. 2, p. 2; rep. from * to end.
2nd row.—As 1st row.
3rd row.—* P. 2, k. 2; rep. from * to end.
4th row.—As 3rd row. These rows form patt.

Continue in patt. until work measures $3\frac{1}{2}$ ins., then inc. 1 st. both ends of next and every following 8th row until 64 sts. on needle, working extra sts. in patt. Continue straight until work measures 17 ins.

The original cardigan was knitted in white with pink and blue " bobbles." On the right is the detail of the stitch.

Shape Top thus: Dec. 1 st. both ends of next 6 rows, then dec. 1 st. beg. of every row until 12 sts. remain. Cast off 4 sts. beg. of next 2 rows. Cast off 4 sts.

The Back.—With double w. wool cast on 90 sts.

1st row.—* (K. 1, p. 1) 4 times, k. 1. p. 9; rep. from * to end.

2nd row.—* K. 9, (p. 1, k. 1) 4 times, p. 1; rep. from * to end.

Rep. these 2 rows 3 times.

9th row.—* P. 9, (k. 1, p. 1) 4 times, k. 1; rep. from * to end.

10th row.—* (P. 1, k. 1) 4 times, p. 1. k. 9; rep. from * to end.

11th row.—* P. 4 w., work 5 into next st. b., p. 4, rib 9, p. 4 w., work 5 into next st. pk., p. 4, rib 9 w.; rep. from * twice, ending 2nd rep. at end of first 9 sts. in rib.

12th row.—* Rib 9, k. 4 w., p. 5 b., k. 4, rib 9, k. 4 w., p. 5 pk., k. 4 w.; rep. from * once, rib 9, k. 4 w., p. 5 b., k. 4 w.

13th row.—* P. 4 w., sl. 1, k. 1, p.s.s.o., k. 1, k. 2 tog. b., p. 4, rib 9, p. 4 w., sl. 1, k. 1, p.s.s.o., k. 1, k. 2 tog. pk., p. 4, rib 9 w.; rep. from * twice, ending 2nd rep. at end of first 9 sts. in rib.

14th row.—* Rib 9, k. 4 w., p. 3 b., k. 4, rib 9, k. 4 w., p. 3 pk., k. 4 w.; rep. from * once, rib 9, k. 4 w., p. 3 b., k. 4 w.

15th row.—With w. * p. 4, sl. 1, k. 2 tog., p.s.s.o., p. 4, rib 9; rep. from * to end.

16th row.—As 10th row.

17th to 32nd rows.—Rep. rows 9 to 16 inclusive twice.

33rd row.—With w. * (k. 1, p. 1) 4 times, k. 1, p. 9; rep. from * to end, ending last rep. with p. 2 instead of p. 2 tog., m. 1.

34th row.—With w. * k. 9, (p. 1, k. 1) 4 times, p. 1; rep. from * to end.

35th row.—* Rib 9, p. 4 w., work 5 into next st. b., p. 4, rib 9, p. 4 w., work 5 into next st. pk., p. 4 w.; rep. from *

twice, ending 2nd rep. at end of first p. panel.

36th row.—* K. 4 w., p. 5 b., k. 4, rib 9, k. 4 w., p. 5 pk., k. 4, rib 9 w.; rep. from * once, k. 4 w., p. 5 b., k. 4, rib 9 w.

37th row.—* Rib 9, p. 4 w., sl. 1, k. 1, p.s.s.o., k. 1, k. 2 tog. b., p. 4, rib 9, p. 4 w., sl. 1, k. 1, p.s.s.o., k. 1, k. 2 tog. pk., p. 4 w.; rep. from * twice, ending 2nd rep. at end of first p. panel.

38th row.—* K. 4 w., p. 3 b., k. 4, rib 9, k. 4 w., p. 3 pk., k. 4, rib 9 w.; rep. from * once, k. 4 w., p. 3 b., k. 4, rib 9 w.

39th row.—With w. * rib 9, p. 4, sl. 1, k. 2 tog., p.s.s.o., p. 4; rep. from * to end.

40th row.—As 34th row.

41st row.—With w. * rib 9, p. 9; rep. from * to end.

42nd row.—As 34th row.

43rd to 50th rows.—Rep. rows 35 to 42 inclusive once.

51st to 56th rows.—Rep. rows 35 to 40 inclusive once. The last 48 rows, i.e. rows 9 to 56 inclusive, form the patt.

Rep. patt. rows 9 to 32 inclusive once.

Shape Armholes thus: Keeping continuity of patt. beg. at 33rd row, cast off 5 sts. beg. of next 2 rows, then dec. 1 st. each end of next 4 rows (72 sts.).

Continue without shaping to end of a 56th patt. row, then rep. patt. rows 9 to 32 inclusive once more, allowing for dec. sts. at each side.

Shape Shoulders thus: Work as 41st and 42nd rows.

Cast off 8 sts. beg. of next 4 rows, 7 sts. beg. of next 2 rows. Cast off remaining sts.

The Right Front.—With double w. wool cast on 45 sts.

1st row.—* P. 9, (k. 1, p. 1) 4 times, k. 1; rep. from * once, p. 9.

2nd row.—* K. 9, rib 9; rep. from * once, k. 9.

Rep. these 2 rows 3 times.

9th row.—* Rib 9, p. 9; rep. from * once, rib 9.

10th row.—* Rib 9 k. 9; rep. from * once, rib 9.

Pink, white and blue was the colour scheme for this cardigan. It is
gayest worn over a summer dress, or white sports clothes. Designed
for the petite figure, it is very smart for the girl in her late teens.

A little lace jumper should be in every young girl's wardrobe. This model, in pastel shade, is fresh and youthful, and simple enough for the veriest beginner to make. Instructions are given on page 60.

11th row.—Rib 9, p. 4 w., work 5 into next st. b., p. 4, rib 9, p. 4 w., work 5 into next st pk., p. 4, rib 9 w.

12th row.—Rib 9, k. 4 w., p. 5 pk., k. 4, rib 9, k. 4 w., p. 5 b., k. 4, rib 9 w.

13th row.—Rib 9, p. 4 w., sl. 1, k. 1, p.s.s.o., k. 1, k. 2 tog. b., p. 4, rib 9, p. 4 w., sl. 1, k. 1, p.s.s.o., k. 1, k. 2 tog. pk., p. 4, rib 9 w.

14th row.—Rib 9, k. 4 w., p. 3 pk., k. 4, rib 9, k. 4 w., p. 3 b., k. 4, rib 9 w.

15th row.—With w. * rib 9, p. 4, sl. 1, k. 2 tog., p.s.s.o., p. 4; rep. from * once. rib 9.

16th row.—As 10th row.

17th to 32nd rows.—Rep. rows 9 to 16 inclusive twice.

33rd row.—With w. (p. 9, rib 9), twice, p. 9.

34th row.—With w. (k. 9, rib 9) twice. k. 9.

35th row.—P. 4 w., work 5 into next st. pk., p. 4, rib 9, p. 4 w., work 5 into next st. b., p. 4. rib 9, p. 4 w., work 5 into next st. pk., p. 4 w.

36th row.—K. 4 w., p. 5 pk., k. 4, rib 9, k. 4 w., p. 5 b., k. 4, rib 9, k. 4 w., p. 5 pk., k. 4 w.

37th row.—P. 4 w., sl. 1, k. 1, p.s.s.o., k. 1, k. 2 tog. pk., p. 4, rib 9, p. 4 w., sl. 1, k. 1, p.s.s.o., k. 1, k. 2 tog. b., p. 4, rib 9, p. 4 w., sl. 1, k. 1, p.s.s.o., k. 1, k. 2 tog. pk., p. 4 w.

38th row.—K. 4 w., p. 3 pk., k. 4, rib 9, k. 4 w., p. 3 b., k. 4, rib 9, k. 4 w., p. 3 pk., k. 4 w.

39th row.—With w. * p. 4, sl. 1, k. 2 tog., p.s.s.o., p 4, rib 9; rep. from * once, p. 4, sl. 1, k. 2 tog., p.s.s.o., p. 4.

40th row.—As 34th row.

41st row.—With w. (p. 9, k. 9) twice, p. 9.

42nd row.—As 34th row.

43rd to 50th rows.—Rep. rows 35 to 42 inclusive once.

51st to 56th rows.—Rep. rows 35 to 40 inclusive once.

Rep. patt. rows 9 to 33 inclusive once

Shape Armhole thus: Keeping continuity of patt., cast off 5 sts. beg. of next row dec. 1 st. at same edge on next 4 rows (36 sts.).

Continue without shaping to end of a 56th patt. row, then work 6 rows in double moss st. as given for sleeves.

Shape Neck thus: Still working in double moss st., cast off 5 sts. beg. of next row, dec. 1 st. at same edge on next 8 rows (23 sts.).

Continue straight until work measures 18½ ins., ending at armhole edge.

Shape Shoulder thus:—

Next row.—Cast off 8 patt. to end.

Next row.—Patt. to end.

Rep. last 2 rows once.

Cast off remaining sts.

The Left Front.—With double w. cast on 45 sts.

1st row.—* (K. 1, p. 1) 4 times, k. 1, p. 9; rep. from * once, rib 9

2nd row.—* Rib 9, k. 9; rep. from * once, rib 9.

Rep. these 2 rows 3 times.

9th row.—* P. 9, (k. 1, p. 1) 4 times, k. 1; rep. from * once, p. 9.

10th row.—* K. 9, rib 9; rep. from * once, k. 9.

11th row.—* P. 4 w., work 5 into next st. pk., p. 4, rib 9, p. 4 w., work 5 into next st. b., p. 4, rib 9, p. 4 w., work 5 into next st. pk., p. 4 w.

12th row.—K. 4 w., p. 5 pk., k. 4, rib 9, k. 4. w, p. 5 b., k. 4, rib 9, k. 4 w., p. 5 pk., k. 4 w.

13th row.—P. 4 w., sl. 1, k. 1, p.s.s.o., k. 1, k. 2 tog. pk., p. 4, rib 9, p. 4 w., sl. 1, k. 1, p.s.s.o., k. 1, k. 2 tog. b., p. 4, rib 9, p. 4 w., sl. 1, k. 1, p.s.s.o., k. 1, k. 2 tog. pk., p. 4 w.

14th row.—K. 4 w., p. 3 pk., k. 4, rib 9, k. 4 w., p. 3 b., k. 4. rib 9, k. 4 w., p. 3 pk., k. 4 w.

15th row.—With w. * p. 4, sl. 1, k. 2 tog., p.s.s.o., p. 4, rib 9; rep. from * once, p. 4, sl. 1, k. 2 tog., p.s.s.o., p. 4.

16th row.—As 10th row.

17th to 32nd rows.—Rep rows 9 to 16 inclusive once.

33rd row.—With w. * rib 9, p. 9; rep. from * once, rib 9.

34th row.—With w. * rib 9, k. 9; rep. from * once, rib 9.

35th row.—Rib 9, p. 4 w., work 5 into next st. pk., p. 4, rib 9, p. 4 w., work 5 into next st. b., p. 4, rib 9 w.

36th row.—Rib 9, k. 4 w., p. 5 b., k. 4, rib 9, k. 4 w., p. 5 pk., k. 4, rib 9 w.

37th row.—Rib 9, p. 4 w., sl. 1, k. 1, p.s.s.o., k. 1, k. 2 tog. pk., p. 4, rib 9, p. 4 w., sl. 1, k. 1, p.s.s.o., k. 1, k. 2 tog. b., p. 4, rib 9 w.

38th row.—Rib 9, k. 4 w., p. 3 b., k. 4, rib 9, k. 4 w., p. 3 pk., k. 4, rib 9 w.

39th row.—With w. * rib 9, p. 4, sl. 1, k. 2 tog., p.s.s.o., p. 4; rep. from * once, rib 9.

40th row.—As 34th row.

41st row.—*Rib 9, p. 9; rep. from * once, rib 9.

42nd row.—As 34th row.

43rd to 50th rows.—Rep. rows 35 to 42 inclusive once.

51st to 56th rows.—Rep. rows 35 to 40 inclusive once.

Rep. patt. rows 9 to 32 inclusive once.

Shape Armhole as given for right front, then continue as given on 36 sts. to end of a 56th patt. row. Work 5 rows in double moss st. as given for sleeves, then shape neck and complete to match right front.

Make-up.—Press work lightly on wrong side with hot iron over damp cloth.

Join side and shoulder seams with very narrow backstitch, matching patt. in side seams carefully.

Join sleeve seams and backstitch sleeves into armholes.

Press seams.

Work a crochet scallop edging with pk. wool round neck and front edges. Make 7 evenly spaced button loops down right front edge. Make 7 buttons in b. wool and sew on to correspond with loops.

Lacy Jumper

DESIGNED FOR THE YOUNG AND SLIM

MATERIALS

5 oz. of 3-ply wool.
1 pair of No. 10 and No. 12 needles.
A crochet hook.

MEASUREMENTS

Length, 18 ins.
Bust, 34 ins.
Sleeve seams, 5½ ins.

TENSION

Using No. 10 needles and measuring over the lace patt., 7 sts. to measure 1 in.

The Back.—Using No. 12 needles cast on 98 sts. and work in k. 1, p. 1 rib for ¾ in. Change to lace patt. as follows:—

1st row.—K. 2, * m. 1, k. 2 tog. k. 1; rep. from * to end of row.

Rep. this row until work measures 3 ins., ending with row on wrong side.

Continue in k. 1, p. 1 rib for ¾ in

Change to No 10 needles and continue in lace patt. and rib in the same way as before (2¼ ins. lace patt. and ¾ in. k. 1, p. 1 rib), inc. 1 st. at both ends of next and every following 6th row until there are 122 sts. on needle.

Continue without further inc. until

work measures 11½ ins., ending with row on wrong side.

Shape Armholes thus: Cast off 4 sts. at the beg. of each of the next 2 rows, then dec. 1 st. at both ends of every row until 92 sts. remain. Continue in lace patt. and rib as before until work measures 18 ins., ending with row on wrong side.

Shape Shoulders thus: Cast off 8 sts. at the beg. of the next 4 rows, then cast off 7 sts. at the beg. of the following 4 rows.

Leave the rem. 32 sts. on a spare needle.

The Front.—Work exactly as given for back until front measures 15 ins., ending with last row of lace patt. stripe.

Now divide for neck opening thus:—

Work in rib over 46 sts., leave the remaining 46 sts. on a spare needle and continue on the first 46 sts. in rib and lace patt. until work measures 18 ins., ending with row on wrong side.

Shape Shoulders thus: Cast off 8 sts. at beg. of next 2 rows from armhole edge, then 7 sts. at beg. of following 2 rows from this edge. Leave remaining 16 sts. for revers on spare needle.

Rejoin wool at front edge to remaining 46 sts. and work to match first side, reversing shoulder shaping. Leave the remaining 16 sts. for revers on spare needle.

The Neck Border.—Join shoulder seams with a narrow backstitch.

Sl. all sts. left on tops of revers and back of neck on to a No. 10 needle and work in k. 1, p. 1 rib for ¾ in. Cast off.

The Sleeves.—Using No. 12 needles cast on 86 sts. and work in k. 1, p. 1 rib for ¾ in. Continue in lace patt. until work measures 2 ins.

Change to No. 10 needles and continue in lace patt. and rib as for back inc. 1 st. at both ends of next and every following 4th row, until 92 sts. are on needle.

Continue without further inc. until sleeve measures 5½ ins., ending with row on wrong side.

Shape Top thus: Cast off 4 sts. at the beg. of the next 2 rows, then dec. 1 st. at both ends of every row until 72 sts. remain. Dec. 1 st. at both ends of every third row until there are 40 sts. on needle.

Cast off 3 sts. at beg. of each of following 10 rows. Cast off remaining 10 sts.

Make-up.—Press all the work lightly on the wrong side, using a hot iron over a damp cloth.

Join side and sleeve seams with a narrow backstitch. Stitch sleeves into armholes, placing seams to underarm seams and matching the ribbed and lace patt. stripes of sleeve to the corresponding stripes of armhole. Ease fullness at shoulder. Work a picot edging along edges of revers and lightly press them back. Press all seams.

The lacy pattern and the ribbing give the jumper its striped effect. On the right is the stitch detail.

Accent on Simpl...

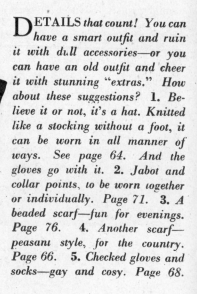

DETAILS *that count! You can have a smart outfit and ruin it with dull accessories—or you can have an old outfit and cheer it with stunning "extras." How about these suggestions?* **1.** *Believe it or not, it's a hat. Knitted like a stocking without a foot, it can be worn in all manner of ways. See page 64. And the gloves go with it.* **2.** *Jabot and collar points, to be worn together or individually. Page 71.* **3.** *A beaded scarf—fun for evenings. Page 76.* **4.** *Another scarf—peasant style, for the country. Page 66.* **5.** *Checked gloves and socks—gay and cosy. Page 68.*

Accessories

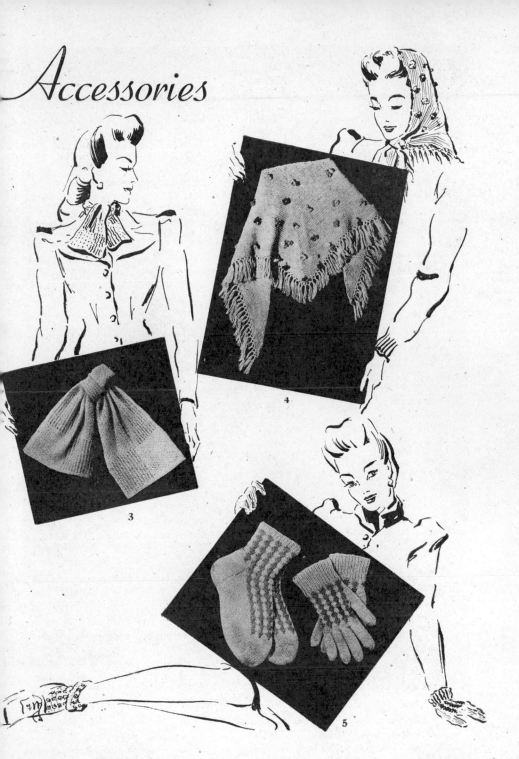

4

3

5

Too good to be true! We'll let you into the secret. This smart hat is simply a circular piece of moss-stitch knitting, like a sock without a foot, and arranged on your head in whichever way suits you best.

Style and Simplicity

A "STOCKING" CAP, AND GLOVES TO MATCH

MATERIALS

5 oz. 3-ply wool.

4 No. 13 needles with points at both ends.

MEASUREMENTS

Cap length, 19 ins.

Gloves to fit average hand.

TENSION

8 sts. to 1 in.

CAP

Cast on 150 sts. (50 on each of 3 needles). Work in moss st. thus:—

1st round.—* K. 1, p. 1; rep. from * to end.

2nd round.—* P. 1, k. 1; rep. from * to end.

Rep. these 2 rounds until work measures 19 ins. Cast off.

THE GLOVES

The Left Hand.—Cast on 60 sts. (20 on each of 3 needles).

Work in moss st. as given for cap for 2½ ins., finish end of round.

Shape Thumb thus:—

1st round.—Moss st. 27, inc. twice in next st. thus: K. into right half of next st. in previous row, then work the st. itself, then work into left half of the same st. in previous row, moss st. 32.

Work 3 rounds without shaping after each inc. round.

5th round.—Moss st. 28, inc. twice in next st., moss st. 33.

9th round.—Moss st. 29, inc. twice in next st., moss st. 34.

13th round.—Moss st. 30. inc. twice in next st., moss st. 35.

17th round.—Moss st. 31. inc. twice in next st., moss st. 36.

21st round.—Moss st. 32, inc. twice in next st., moss st. 37.

25th round.—Moss st. 33, inc. twice in next st., moss st. 38.

26th round.—Moss st. 27, sl. the next 15 thumb sts. on to length of wool, cast on 3 sts., moss st. to end.

27th round.—Moss st. 27, take 3 tog., moss st. to end (60 sts.).

Work 1½ ins. on these sts., finish end of round.

A second suggestion for wearing your hat.

Now begin Fingers thus:—

Fourth Finger.—Moss st. 6, sl. all but last 5 sts. on to length of wool, cast on 5 sts., moss s.. 5. Divide on to 3 needles, work in rounds for 2¼ ins.

Shape Top thus:—

1st round.—K. 1, (take 3 tog., moss st. 3) twice, take 3 tog.

2nd round.—Moss st. to end.

3rd round.—(K. 2 tog.) 5 times. Break off wool. Thread end through remaining sts., draw up and fasten off.

Third Finger.—Moss st. the next 8 sts. off the round, cast on 1 st., moss st. the last 8 sts. of the round, then k. up 3 sts. at base of fourth finger.

Divide sts. on to 3 needles.

Next round.—Moss st. to last 3 sts., take 3 tog. (18 sts.).

Work in moss st. for 2½ ins.

Shape Top thus:—

1st round.—(Moss st. 3, take 3 tog.) 3 times.

2nd round.—Moss st. to end.

3rd round.—* K. 1, k. 2 tog. ; rep. from * to end. Break off wool. Complete as given for fourth finger.

Second Finger.—Moss st. the next 8 sts. of the round. Cast on 1 st., moss st. the last 8 sts. of the round. Pick up and k. 1 st. from base of third finger. Work

2¾ ins. in moss st.

Shape Top and complete as given for third finger.

First Finger.—Sl. the remaining 17 sts. on to 2 needles. Moss st. these, then pick up and k. 1 st. from base of second finger. Work 2½ ins. in moss st. on these sts. Shape top and complete as given for third finger.

The Thumb.—Sl. the 15 thumb sts. on to a needle. Join on wool, then moss st. the sts. on to 2 needles. With the 3rd needle k. up 3 sts. from the opening of the hand. Moss st. for 2¼ ins. Shape and complete as given for third finger.

The Right Hand.—Cast on 60 sts. Work 2½ ins. in moss st., finish end of round.

Shape for Thumb thus:—

1st round.—Moss st. 32, inc. twice into next st., moss st. 27. Work 3 rounds without shaping after each inc. round.

5th round.—Moss st. 33, inc. twice in next st., moss st. 28. Continue thus until 74 sts. are on the needles.

Next round.—Moss st. 32, sl. next 15 sts. on to length of wool, cast on 3 sts., moss st. to end.

Next round.—Moss st. 32, k. 3 tog., moss st. to end.

The remainder of the glove is worked as left hand. Press work.

Triangular Scarf

TRIMMED WITH GAY FLOWER POSIES

MATERIALS

2 oz. 2-ply wool.
1 pair No. 7 needles.
Odd scraps of coloured wool.
A medium-sized crochet hook.

MEASUREMENTS

Sides each 25 ins. ; base, 40 ins.

TENSION

6 sts. to 1 in.

Cast on 305 sts.

1st row.—K. 2 tog., k. to last 2 sts., k. 2 tog.

2nd row.—K. 2 tog., k. 148, k. 3 tog., k. 148, k. 2 tog.

Another peasant touch! The triangular scarf is in plain knitting with bunches of flowers scattered over it. The original scarf was in beige, with gay coloured flowers. Wear it casually tied under the chin.

3rd row.—As 1st row.

4th row.—K. 2 tog., k. 145, k. 3 tog., k. 145, k. 2 tog.

Continue thus, dec. at both ends of every row and knitting 3 tog. in the middle of every alternate row (there will be 3 less sts. in the groups of k. sts. each side of the middle 3 every time) until the row k. 2 tog., k. 1, k. 3 tog., k. 1, k. 2 tog. has been worked. Then work thus:—

Next row.—K. 2 tog., k. 1, k. 2 tog.

Next row.—K. 3 tog.

Draw thread through loop, break off and darn end in neatly on wrong side.

Make a fringe along short sides, using 8-in. lengths of wool so that the finished fringe measures about 3 ins.

Using the coloured wool, make a number of small flowers.

Begin each with 2 or 3 ch. joined into a ring, and work groups of 3 or more trs. with a d.c. between each group, into this ring. For smaller flowers work groups of d.c. with s.c.s between.

Fasten the flowers to the scarf with short loops of green wool so that they hang loosely. Fasten off the ends of green wool firmly behind the flowers.

Gloves and Socks

IN CHEQUERED DESIGN

MATERIALS

4 oz. of double knitting or heavy-weight 4-ply wool in grey.
1 oz. 4-ply wool in red.
2 No. 12 knitting needles.

TENSION

7½ sts. to 1 in.

ADDITIONAL ABBREVIATIONS

Gr. = grey; r. = red.

N.B.—Ordinary 4-ply wool may be substituted for the heavier yarn. In this case No. 11 needles should be used to obtain the correct tension, and it is advisable to work the thumb gusset increasings in every 6th row instead of every 4th, to make the gusset the correct length. 3 oz. of the main colour will be sufficient.

THE GLOVES

The Left-hand Glove.—With No. 12 needles and gr. wool cast on 52 sts. Work 2 ins. in k. 1, p. 1 rib, dec. 1 st. at end of last row.

Next row.—P. to end.

Change to r. wool and patt.:—

1st row.—* K. 3, sl. 3 p.w.; rep. from * to last 3 sts., k. 3.

2nd row.—* P. 3, sl. 3 p.w.; rep. from * to last 3 sts., p. 3.

3rd row.—* K. 4, sl. 1 p.w., k. 1; rep from * to last 3 sts., k. 3.

4th row.—* P. 4, sl. 1 p.w., p. 1; rep. from * to last 3 sts., p. 3.

Change to gr. wool.

5th row.—* Sl. 3 p.w., k. 3; rep. from * to last 3 sts., sl. 3 p.w.

6th row.—* Sl. 3 p.w., p. 3; rep. from * to last 3 sts., sl. 3 p.w.

7th row.—* K. 1, sl. 1 p.w., k. 4; rep. from * to last 3 sts., k. 1, sl. 1 p.w., k. 1.

8th row.—* P. 1, sl. 1 p.w., p. 4; rep. from * to last 3 sts., p. 1, sl. 1 p.w., p. 1.

Change to r. wool. These 8 rows form the patt. for palm and back of hand. Work for thumb gusset in gr. st.st. thus:—

9th row.—Patt. 21, join in gr. wool. (k. twice into next st.) twice, k. 1 gr. join in a fresh ball of r. wool, patt. 27.

10th row.—Patt. 27, p. 5 gr., patt. 21.

11th row.—Patt. 21, k. 5 gr., patt. 27.

12th row.—As 10th row.

13th row.—Patt. 21, k. twice into next st., k. 2, k. twice into next st., k. 1 gr., patt. 27.

14th row.—Patt. 27, p. 7 gr., patt. 21.

15th row.—Patt. 21, k. 7 gr., patt. 27.

16th row.—As 14th row.

17th row.—Patt. 21, k. twice into next st., k. 4, k. twice into next st., k. 1 gr., patt. 27.

Continue in this way, working in patt. with thumb gusset in gr. st.st., inc. 2 sts. in gusset on every 4th row until 61 sts. are on needle.

Work 1 row after last inc. row.

Next row.—Patt. 21, k. 13 gr., turn cast on 1 st. gr.

Next row.—P. 14 gr., turn, cast on 1 st. gr.

Continue in st.st. in gr. on 15 sts. for thumb for 2 ins., finishing p. row.

Shape Top thus:—

Next row.—(K. 1, k. 2 tog.) 5 times.

Next row.—P. 10.

Next row.—(K. 2 tog.) 5 times.

Break off wool, thread end through remaining sts., draw up and fasten off, sew down side edges.

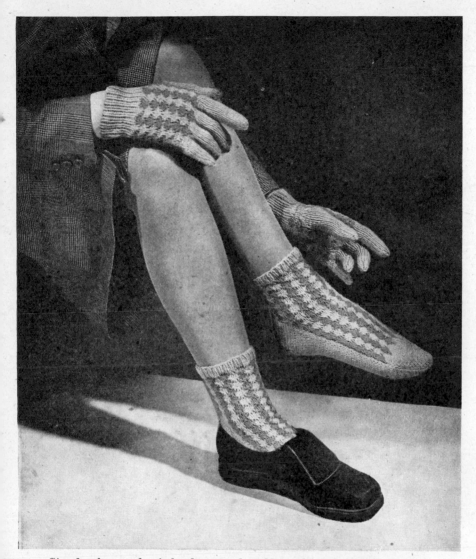

Simple chequered stitch gloves and ankle socks will delight the eye, and comfort cold fingers and toes throughout the autumn and winter. Bright colours are most effective; these were knitted in red and grey.

With right side of work facing, k. up 3 sts. at base of thumb, then continue in patt. to end of row.

Continue in patt. on 51 sts. for 1½ ins., finishing with 4th or 8th patt. row. Break off r. wool. Complete fingers with gr.

Next row.—(K. 3, k. 2 tog.) 10 times.

k. 1 (41 sts.).

Next row.—P. to end.

The First Finger:—

Next row.—K. 26, turn, cast on 1 st.

Next row.—P. 12, turn, cast on 2 sts.

Continue in st.st. for 2½ ins., finishing p. row.

Shape Top thus:—

Next row.—(K. 1, k. 2 tog.) 4 times, k. 2.

Next row.—P. 10.

Next row.—(K. 2 tog.) 5 times.

Break off wool, complete to match thumb.

The Second Finger.—With right side of work facing, rejoin wool and k. up 2 sts. at base of first finger, k. 5 sts., turn, cast on 1 st.

Next row.—P. 13, turn, cast on 1 st.

Continue in st.st. for 3 ins., finishing p. row.

Shape Top and complete as for first finger.

The Third Finger.—With right side of work facing, rejoin wool and k. up 2 sts. at base of second finger, k. 5 sts., turn, cast on 1 st.

Next row.—P. 13, turn, cast on 1 st.

Continue in st.st. for 2½ ins., finishing p. row.

Shape Top and complete as for first finger.

The Fourth Finger.—With right side of

Detail of the chequered stitch.

work facing, rejoin wool and k. up 3 sts. at base of third finger, k. 5 sts.

Continue in st.st. on 13 sts. for 2¼ ins., finishing p. row.

Shape Top thus:—

Next row.—(K. 1, k. 2 tog.) 4 times, k. 1.

Next row.—P. 9.

Next row.—(K. 2 tog.) 4 times, k. 1.

Break off wool and complete to match thumb, sewing down side of hand to wrist edge, matching patt. of hand carefully.

The Right-hand Glove.—Continue exactly as given for left-hand glove until 8 rows in patt. have been worked.

Now reverse the thumb gusset by working 27 sts. in patt. before the gusset and only 21 sts. in patt. after the gusset on k. rows and 21 sts. in patt. before and 27 sts. in patt. after the gusset on p. rows.

Thus 9th row will be: Patt. 27, join in gr. wool, (k. twice into next st,) twice, k. 1 gr., join in a fresh ball of r. wool, patt. 21.

Continue in this way, inc. as before on every 4th row until 61 sts. are on needle.

Work 1 row after last inc. row.

Next row.—Patt. 27, k. 13 gr., turn, cast on 1 st. gr.

Next row.—P. 14 gr., turn, cast on 1 st. gr. Complete thumb, hand and fingers as for right-hand glove.

THE ANKLE SOCKS

With No. 12 needles and gr. wool cast on 58 sts. loosely. Work ¾ in. in k. 1, p. 1 rib, dec. 1 st. at end of last row (57 sts.).

Continue in patt. as given for gloves until work measures 3½ ins., finishing row on wrong side.

Divide for Heel and Instep thus:—

Next row.—Patt. 45, turn.

Next row.—Patt. 33, turn.

Continue in patt. on 33 sts. for 6 ins., finishing row on wrong side.

Break off r. wool. Complete with gr.

Shape Toe thus:—

1st row.—K. 1, sl. 1, k. 1, p.s.s.o., k. to last 3 sts., k. 2 tog., k. 1.

2nd row.—P. to end.

Rep. last 2 rows until 11 sts. remain. Leave sts. on spare needle.

Sl. the two sets of heel sts. on to one needle with side edges to centre forming back seam. With right side of work facing, rejoin gr. wool and work 28 rows in st.st., finishing p. row.

Turn Heel thus:—

1st row.—K. 17, k. 2 tog., turn.

2nd row.—P. 11, p. 2 tog., turn.

3rd row.—K. 11, k. 2 tog., turn.

4th row.—As 2nd row.

Rep. last 2 rows until 12 sts. remain. Now with wrong side of work facing pick up and p. 15 sts. down side of heel flap.

Next row.—K. to end, then k. up 15 sts. down other side of heel flap. P. 1 row, then shape instep:—

Next row.—K. 1, sl. 1, k. 1, p.s.s.o., k. to last 3 sts., k. 2 tog., k. 1.

Next row.—P. to end.

Rep. last 2 rows until 34 sts. remain.

Continue without shaping until work measures same as top part of foot to beg. of toe shapings, finishing p. row and dec. 1 st. at end of last row.

Shape toe as given for top part of foot.

With right side of work outside, graft or cast off two sets of toe sts. tog.

Make-up.—Press work lightly on wrong side with hot iron over damp cloth.

Join foot and leg seams, matching patt. carefully.

Press seams.

New Neckwear

KNITTED IN CROCHET COTTON

MATERIALS

A ball of crochet cotton, No. 50.
2 No. 17 knitting needles.
A fine steel crochet hook.

MEASUREMENTS

Depth of jabot, about 6½ ins.
Width at widest part, 4¼ ins.

TENSION

About 12 sts. to 1 in. over st.st.

ADDITIONAL ABBREVIATIONS

Tw. nt. st. = work twice into next st. (by working k. 1, p. 1 into it).

THE JABOT

Cast on 12 sts. Work 4 rows st.st., ending p. row.

5th row.—K. 2, * m. 1, (always by w.fd.), k. 2; rep. from * to end.

6th row.—(P. 2, tw. nt. st.) twice, p. 5, (tw. nt. st., p. 2) twice.

7th row.—K. 1, (m. 1, sl. 1, k. 1, p.s.s.o., k. 2 tog.) twice (m. 1, k. 1) 3 times. (m. 1, sl. 1, k. 1, p.s.s.o., k. 2 tog.) twice, m. 1, k. 1.

8th row.—P. 4, tw. nt. st., p. 11, tw. nt. st., p. 4.

9th row.—K. 1, k. 2 tog., m. 1, sl. 1, k. 1, p.s.s.o., k. 2 tog., m. 1, sl. 1, k. 1, p.s.s.o., k. 1, m. 1, k. 3, m. 1, k. 1, k. 2 tog., m. 1, sl. 1, k. 1, p.s.s.o., k. 2 tog., m. 1, sl. 1, k. 1, p.s.s.o., k. 1.

10th row.—(P. 2, tw. nt. st.) twice, p. 9, (tw. nt. st., p. 2) twice.

11th row.—K. 1, (m. 1, sl. 1, k. 1, p.s.s.o., k. 2 tog.) twice, m. 1, k. 1, m. 1,

k. 5, m. 1, k. 1, (m. 1, sl. 1, k. 1, p.s.s.o.,
k. 2 tog.) twice, m. 1, k. 1.

12th row.—P. 4, tw. nt. st., p. 2, tw. nt.
st., p. 9, tw. nt. st., p. 2, tw. nt. st., p. 4.

13th row.—K. 1, k. 2 tog., (m. 1, sl. 1,
k. 1, p.s.s.o., k. 2 tog.) twice, m. 1, k. 7,
(m. 1, sl. 1, k. 1, p.s.s.o., k. 2 tog.) twice,
m. 1, sl. 1, k. 1, p.s.s.o., k. 1.

14th row.—(P. 2, tw. nt. st.) twice, p. 13,
(tw. nt. st., p. 2) twice.

15th row.—K. 1, (m. 1, sl. 1, k. 1,
p.s.s.o., k. 2 tog.) twice, m. 1, sl. 1, k. 1,
p.s.s.o., k. 1, k. 2 tog., m. 1, k. 1, m. 1,
sl. 1, k. 1, p.s.s.o., k. 1, k. 2 tog., (m. 1,
sl. 1, k. 1, p.s.s.o., k. 2 tog.) twice, m. 1,
k. 1.

16th row.—P. 4, (tw. nt. st., p. 2) twice,
p. 7, (tw. nt. st., p. 2) twice, p. 2.

17th row.—K. 1, (k. 2 tog., m. 1, sl. 1,
k. 1, p.s.s.o.) twice, k. 1, m. 1, sl. 1, k. 2
tog., p.s.s.o., m. 1, k. 3, m. 1, sl. 1, k. 2
tog., p.s.s.o., m. 1, k. 1, (k. 2 tog., m. 1,
sl. 1, k. 1, p.s.s.o.) twice, k. 1.

18th row.—(P. 2, tw. nt. st.) twice, p.
13, (tw. nt. st., p. 2) twice.

19th row.—K. 1, (m. 1, sl. 1, k. 1,
p.s.s.o., k. 2 tog.) twice, m. 1, sl. 1, k. 1,
p.s.s.o., k. 1, m. 1, k. 5, m. 1, k. 1, k. 2
tog., (m. 1, sl. 1, k. 1, p.s.s.o., k. 2 tog.)
twice, m. 1, k. 1.

20th row.—P. 4, (tw. nt. st., p. 2) twice,
p. 9, (tw. nt. st., p. 2) twice, p. 2.

21st row.—K. 1, (k. 2 tog., m. 1, sl. 1,
k. 1, p.s.s.o.) twice, k. 2 tog., m. 1, k. 1,
m. 1, k. 7, m. 1, k. 1, m. 1, (sl. 1, k. 1,
p.s.s.o., k. 2 tog., m. 1) twice, sl. 1, k. 1,
p.s.s.o., k. 1.

22nd row.—(P. 2, tw. nt. st.) twice, p.
17, (tw. nt. st., p. 2) twice.

23rd row.—K. 1, (m. 1, sl. 1, k. 1,
p.s.s.o., k. 2 tog.) twice, m. 1, sl. 1, k. 1,
p.s.s.o., k. 1, m. 1, k. 9, m. 1, k. 2 tog.,
(m. 1, sl. 1, k. 1, p.s.s.o., k. 2 tog.) twice,
m. 1, k. 1

24th row.—P. 4, (tw. nt. st., p. 2) twice.
p. 13, (tw. nt. st., p. 2) twice, p. 2.

25th row.—K. 1, (k. 2 tog., m. 1, sl. 1,
k. 1, p.s.s.o) twice, k. 2 tog., m. 1, k. 1,

m. 1, k. 11, m. 1, k. 1, m. 1, sl. 1, k. 1,
p.s.s.o., (k. 2 tog., m. 1, sl. 1, k. 1, p.s.s.o.)
twice, k. 1.

26th row.—(P. 2, tw. nt. st.) twice, p.
21, (tw. nt. st., p. 2) twice.

27th row.—K. 1, (m. 1, sl. 1, k, 1,
p.s.s.o., k. 2 tog.) twice, m. 1, sl. 1, k. 1,
p.s.s.o., m. 1, sl. 1, k. 1, p.s.s.o., k. 3, k.
2 tog., m. 1, k. 1, m. 1, sl. 1, k. 1, p.s.s.o.,
k. 3, k. 2 tog., m. 1, (k. 2 tog., m. 1, sl.
1, k. 1, p.s.s.o.) twice, k. 2 tog., m. 1, k.1.

28th row.—P. 4, (tw. nt. st., p. 2) twice,
p. 15, (tw. nt. st., p. 2) twice, p. 2.

29th row.—K. 1, (k. 2 tog., m. 1, sl. 1,
k. 1, p.s.s.o.) twice, k. 2 tog., m. 1, k. 1,
m. 1, sl. 1, k. 1, p.s.s.o., k. 1, k. 2 tog.,
m. 1, k. 3, m. 1, sl. 1, k. 1, p.s.s.o., k. 1,
k. 2 tog., m. 1, k. 1, m. 1, (sl. 1, k. 1,
p.s.s.o., k. 2 tog., m. 1) twice, sl. 1, k. 1,
p.s.s.o., k. 1.

30th row.—(P. 2, tw. nt. st.) twice, p.
21, (tw. nt. st., p. 2) twice.

31st row.—K. 1, (m. 1, sl. 1, k. 1,
p.s.s.o., k. 2 tog.) 3 times, m. 1, sl. 1, k.
2 tog., p.s.s.o., m. 1, k. 5, m. 1, sl. 1, k. 2
tog., p.s.s.o., (m. 1, sl. 1, k. 1, p.s.s.o., k.
2 tog.) 3 times, m. 1, k. 1.

32nd row.—P. 4, (tw. nt. st., p. 2) twice,
p. 13, (tw. nt. st., p. 2) twice, p. 2.

33rd row.—K. 1, (k. 2 tog., m. 1, sl. 1,
k. 1, p.s.s.o.) 3 times, k. 1, m. 1, k. 7,
m. 1, k. 1, (k. 2 tog., m. 1, sl. 1, k. 1,
p.s.s.o.) 3 times, k. 1.

34th row.—(P. 2, tw. nt. st.) 3 times,
p. 13, (tw. nt. st., p. 2) 3 times.

35th row.—K. 1, (m. 1, sl. 1, k. 1,
p.s.s.o., k. 2 tog.) 3 times, m. 1, k. 1, m.
1, k. 9, m. 1, k. 1, m. 1, (sl. 1, k. 1, p.s.s.o.,
k. 2 tog., m. 1) 3 times, k. 1.

36th row.—P. 4, (tw. nt. st., p. 2) twice,
p. 17, (tw. nt. st., p. 2) twice, p. 2.

37th row.—K. 1, (k. 2 tog., m. 1, sl. 1,
k. 1, p.s.s.o.) 3 times, k. 1, m. 1, k. 11,
m. 1, k. 1, (k. 2 tog., m. 1, sl. 1, k. 1,
p.s.s.o.) 3 times, k. 1.

38th row.—(P. 2, tw. nt. st.) 3 times,
p. 17, (tw. nt. st., p. 2) 3 times.

39th row.—K. 1, (m. 1, sl. 1, k. 1,

p.s.s.o., k. 2 tog.)
3 times, m. 1, k. 1,
m. 1, k. 13, m. 1,
k. 1, m. 1, (sl. 1, k.
1, p.s.s.o., k. 2 tog.,
m. 1) 3 times, k. 1.

40th row.—P. 4,
(tw. nt. st., p. 2)
twice, p. 21, (tw.
nt. st., p. 2) twice.
p. 2.

41st row.—K. 1,
(k. 2 tog., m. 1, sl.
1, k. 1, p.s.s.o.) 3
times, k. 1, m. 1,
k. 15, m. 1, k. 1,
(k. 2 tog., m. 1, sl.
1, k. 1, p.s.s.o.) 3
times, k. 1.

42nd row.—(P.
2, tw. nt. st.) 3
times, p. 21, (tw.
nt. st., p. 2) 3
times.

43rd row.—K. 1,
(m. 1. sl. 1, k. 1,
p.s.s.o., k. 2 tog.)
3 times, m. 1, sl. 1,
k. 1, p.s.s.o., k. 5,
k. 2 tog., m. 1, k.
1, m. 1, sl. 1, k. 1,
p.s.s.o., k. 5, k. 2
tog., m. 1, (sl. 1, k.
1, p.s.s.o., k. 2 tog.,
m. 1) 3 times, k. 1.

44th row.—P. 4,
(tw. nt. st., p. 2)

The collar points and jabot are knitted separately; they can be worn together as shown here, or independently.

twice, p. 21, (tw. nt. st., p. 2) twice, p. 2.

45th row. K. 1, (k. 2 tog., m. 1, sl. 1, k. 1, p.s.s.o.) 3 times, m. 1, sl. 1, k. 1, p.s.s.o., k. 3, k. 2 tog., m. 1, k. 3, m. 1, sl. 1, k. 1, p.s.s.o., k. 3, k. 2 tog., m. 1, (k. 2 tog., m. 1, sl. 1, k. 1, p.s.s.o.) 3 times, k. 1.

46th row.—(P. 2, tw. nt. st.) 3 times, p. 19, (tw. nt. st., p. 2) 3 times.

47th row.—K. 1, (m. 1, sl. 1, k. 1, p.s.s.o., k. 2 tog.) 3 times, m. 1, k. 1, m.

1, sl. 1, k. 1, p.s.s.o., k. 1, k. 2 tog., m. 1, k. 5, m. 1, sl. 1, k. 1, p.s.s.o., k. 1, k. 2 tog., m. 1, k. 1, m. 1, (sl. 1, k. 1, p.s.s.o.. k. 2 tog., m. 1) 3 times, k. 1.

48th row.—P. 4, (tw. nt. st., p. 2) 3 times, p. 15, (tw. nt. st., p. 2) 3 times. p. 2.

49th row.—K. 1, (k. 2 tog., m. 1, sl. 1, k. 1, p.s.s.o.) 3 times, k. 2 tog., m. 1, k. 1, m. 1, sl. 1, k. 2 tog., p.s.s.o., m. 1, k. 3, m. 1, k. 1, m. 1, k. 3, m. 1, sl. 1, k. 2

tog., p.s.s.o., m. 1, k. 1, m. 1, (sl. 1, k. 1, p.s.s.o., k. 2 tog., m. 1) 3 times. sl. 1, k. 1, p.s.s.o., k. 1.

50th row.—(P. 2, tw. nt. st.) 4 times. p. 17, (tw. nt. st., p. 2) 4 times.

51st row.—K. 1, (m. 1, sl. 1, k. 1, p.s.s.o., k. 2 tog.) 4 times, k. 2 tog., m. 1, k. 2, k. 2 tog., m. 1, k. 3, m. 1, sl. 1, k. 1, p.s.s.o., k. 2, m. 1, sl. 1, k. 1, p.s.s.o., (sl. 1, k. 1, p.s.s.o., k. 2 tog., m. 1) 4 times, k. 1.

52nd row.—P. 4, (tw. nt. st., p. 2) 3 times, p. 17, (tw. nt. st., p. 2) 3 times, p. 2.

53rd row.—K. 1, (k. 2 tog., m. 1, sl. 1, k. 1, p.s.s.o.) 3 times, (k. 2 tog.) twice, m. 1, k. 4, m. 1, k. 5, m. 1, k. 4, m. 1, (sl. 1, k. 1, p.s.s.o.) twice, (k. 2 tog., m. 1, sl. 1, k. 1, p.s.s.o.) 3 times, k. 1.

54th row.—(P. 2, tw. nt. st.) 3 times, p. 23, (tw. nt. st., p. 2) 3 times.

55th row.—K. 1, (m. 1, sl. 1, k. 1, p.s.s.o., k. 2 tog.) 3 times, k. 2 tog., m. 1, k. 3, m. 1, sl. 1, k. 1, p.s.s.o., k. 3, m. 1, k. 1, m. 1, k. 3, k. 2 tog., m. 1, k. 3, m. 1, sl. 1, k. 1, p.s.s.o., (sl. 1, k. 1, p.s.s.o. k. 2 tog., m. 1) 3 times, k. 1.

56th row.—P. 4, (tw. nt. st., p. 2) twice. p. 25, (tw. nt. st., p. 2) twice. p. 2.

57th row.—K. 1, (k. 2 tog., m. 1, sl. 1, k. 1, p.s.s.o.) twice, (k. 2 tog.) twice, m. 1, k. 2, k. 2 tog., m. 1, k. 1, m. 1, sl. 1, k. 2 tog., p.s.s.o., k. 1, m. 1, k. 3, m. 1, k. 1, k. 3 tog., m. 1, k. 1, m. 1, sl. 1, k. 1, p.s.s.o., k. 2, m. 1, (sl. 1, k. 1, p.s.s.o.) twice, (k. 2 tog., m. 1, sl. 1, k. 1, p.s.s.o.) twice, k. 1.

58th row.—(P. 2, tw. nt. st.) twice, p. 29, (tw. nt. st., p. 2) twice.

59th row.—K. 1, (m. 1, sl. 1, k. 1, p.s.s.o., k. 2 tog.) twice, k. 2 tog., m. 1, k. 3, m. 1, sl. 1, k. 1, p.s.s.o., k. 1, k. 2 tog., m. 1, sl. 1, k. 1, p.s.s.o., k. 3, k. 2 tog., m. 1, sl. 1, k. 1, p.s.s.o., k. 1, k. 2 tog., m. 1, k. 3, m. 1, sl. 1, k. 1, p.s.s.o., (sl. 1, k. 1, p.s.s.o., k. 2 tog., m. 1) twice, k. 1.

60th row.—P. 4, tw. nt. st., p. 29, tw. nt. st., p. 4.

61st row.—K. 1, k. 2 tog., m. 1, sl. 1, k. 1, p.s.s.o., (k. 2 tog.) twice, m. 1, k. 2, k. 2 tog.; m. 1, k. 1, m. 1, sl. 1, k. 2 tog. p.s.s.o., m. 1, k. 1, m. 1, sl. 1, k. 1, p.s.s.o. k. 1, k. 2 tog., m. 1, k. 1, m. 1, sl. 1, k. 2 tog., p.s.s.o., m. 1, k. 1, m. 1, sl. 1, k. 1, p.s.s.o., k. 2, m. 1, (sl. 1, k. 1, p.s.s.o.) twice, k. 2 tog., m. 1, sl. 1, k. 1, p.s.s.o., k. 1.

62nd row.—P. 2, tw. nt. st., p. 10, tw. nt. st., p. 9, tw. nt. st., p. 10, tw. nt. st., p. 2.

63rd row.—K. 1, sl. 1, k. 1, p.s.s.o., (k. 2 tog.) twice, m. 1, sl. 1, k. 1, p.s.s.o., k. 1, m. 1, sl. 1, k. 1, p.s.s.o., k. 1, k. 2 tog., m. 1, sl. 1, k. 1, p.s.s.o., k. 2, m. 1, sl. 1, k. 2 tog., p.s.s.o., m. 1, k. 2, k. 2 tog., m. 1, sl. 1, k. 1, p.s.s.o., k. 1, k. 2 tog., m. 1, k. 1, k. 2 tog., m. 1, (sl. 1, k. 1, p.s.s.o.) twice, k. 2 tog., k. 1.

64th row.—P.

65th row.—Sl. 1, k. 1, p.s.s.o., k. 2, m. 1, k. 3, (m. 1, k. 1, m. 1, sl. 1, k. 2 tog., p.s.s.o.) twice, (m. 1, k. 1) 3 times, m. 1, (sl. 1, k. 2 tog., p.s.s.o., m. 1, k. 1, m. 1) twice, k. 3, m. 1, k. 2, k. 2 tog.

66th row.—P. 10, (tw. nt. st., p. 3) 5 times, p. 7.

67th row.—Sl. 1, k. 1, p.s.s.o., k. 2, m. 1, k. 2, (m. 1, sl. 1, k. 1, p.s.s.o., k. 1, k. 2 tog.) 6 times, m. 1, k. 2, m. 1, k. 2, k. 2 tog.

68th row.—P.

69th row.—Sl. 1, k. 1, p.s.s.o., k. 2, m. 1, k. 3, (m. 1, sl. 1, k. 2 tog., p.s.s.o., m. 1, k. 1) 6 times, k. 2, m. 1, k. 2, k. 2 tog.

70th row.—P. 12, (tw. nt. st., p. 3) 4 times, p. 9.

71st row.—(Sl. 1, k. 1, p.s.s.o., k. 2, m. 1) twice, (sl. 1, k. 1, p.s.s.o., k. 1, k. 2 tog., m. 1) 5 times, k. 2, k. 2 tog., m. 1 k. 2, k. 2 tog.

72nd row.—P.

73rd row.—(Sl. 1, k. 1, p.s.s.o., k. 2, m. 1) twice, (sl. 1, k. 2 tog., p.s.s.o., m. 1, k. 1, m. 1) 4 times, sl. 1, k. 2 tog., p.s.s.o., (m. 1, k. 2, k. 2 tog.) twice.

74th row.—P. 12 (tw. nt. st., p. 3) 3 times, p. 9.

75th row.—(Sl. 1, k. 1, p.s.s.o., k. 2, m. 1) twice, (sl. 1, k. 1, p.s.s.o., k. 1, k. 2 tog., m. 1) 4 times. k. 2, k. 2 tog., m. 1. k. 2, k. 2 tog.

76th row.—P.

77th row.—(Sl. 1, k. 1, p.s.s.o., k. 2, m. 1) twice, (sl. 1, k. 2 tog., p.s.s.o., m. 1, k. 1, m. 1) 3 times, sl. 1, k. 2 tog., p.s.s.o., (m. 1, k. 2, k. 2 tog.) twice.

78th row.—P. 12, (tw. nt. st., p. 3) twice, p. 9.

79th row.—(Sl. 1, k. 1, p.s.s.o., k. 2, m. 1) twice, (sl. 1, k. 1, p.s.s.o., k. 1, k. 2 tog., m. 1) 3 times, k. 2, k. 2 tog., m. 1. k. 2, k. 2 tog.

80th row.—P.

81st row.—(Sl. 1, k. 1, p.s.s.o., k. 2, m. 1) twice, (sl. 1, k. 2 tog., p.s.s.o., m. 1, k. 1, m. 1) twice, sl. 1, k. 2 tog., p.s.s.o., (m. 1, k. 2, k. 2 tog.) twice.

82nd row.—P. 12, tw. nt. st., p. 12.

83rd row.—(Sl. 1, k. 1, p.s.s.o., k. 2, m. 1) twice, (sl. 1, k. 1, p.s.s.o., k. 1, k. 2 tog., m. 1) twice, k. 2, k. 2 tog., m. 1, k. 2, k. 2 tog.

84th and following alternate rows.—P.

85th row.—(Sl. 1, k. 1, p.s.s.o., k. 2, m. 1) twice, sl. 1, k. 2 tog., p.s.s.o., m. 1, k. 1, m. 1, sl. 1, k. 2 tog., p.s.s.o., (m. 1, k. 2, k. 2 tog.) twice.

87th row.—(Sl. 1, k. 1, p.s.s.o., k. 2, m. 1) twice, sl. 1, k. 1, p.s.s.o., k. 1, k. 2 tog., (m. 1, k. 2, k. 2 tog.) twice.

89th row.—(Sl. 1, k. 1, p.s.s.o., k. 2, m. 1) twice, sl. 1, k. 2 tog., p.s.s.o., (m. 1, k. 2, k. 2 tog.) twice.

91st row.—Sl. 1, k. 1, p.s.s.o., k. 2, m. 1, sl. 1, k. 1, p.s.s.o., k. 5, k. 2 tog., m. 1, k. 2, k. 2 tog.

93rd row.—Sl. 1, k. 1, p.s.s.o., k. 2, m. 1, sl. 1, k. 1, p.s.s.o., k. 3, k. 2 tog., m. 1, k. 2, k. 2 tog.

95th row.—Sl. 1, k. 1, p.s.s.o., k. 2, m. 1, sl. 1, k. 1, p.s.s.o., k. 1, k. 2 tog., m. 1, k. 2, k. 2 tog.

97th row.—Sl. 1, k. 1, p.s.s.o., k. 2, m. 1, sl. 1, k. 2 tog., p.s.s.o., m. 1, k. 2, k. 2 tog.

99th row.—Sl. 1, k. 1, p.s.s.o., k. 5, k. 2 tog.

101st row.—Sl. 1, k. 1, p.s.s.o., k. 3, k. 2 tog.

103rd row.—Sl. 1, k. 1, p.s.s.o., k. 1, k. 2 tog.

105th row.—Sl. 1, k. 2 tog., p.s.s.o.
Fasten off.

THE POINTS

The two points are knitted to match the jabot, but they make a very attractive collar, worn alone. They would be smart, too, as cuffs on a dark frock.

Cast on 51 sts. Work 5 rows st.st., ending k. row.

6th row.—(Sl. 1, k. 1, p.s.s.o., k. 2, m. 1) twice, (sl. 1, k. 1, p.s.s.o., k. 1, k. 2 tog., m. 1) 7 times, k. 2, k. 2 tog., m. 1, k. 2, k. 2 tog.

7th row.—P.

8th row.—(Sl. 1, k. 1, p.s.s.o., k. 2, m. 1) twice, (sl. 1, k. 2 tog., p.s.s.o., m. 1, k. 1, m. 1) 6 times, sl. 1, k. 2 tog., p.s.s.o., (m. 1, k. 2, k. 2 tog.) twice.

9th row.—P. 12, (tw. nt. st., p. 3) 5 times, p. 9.

10th row.—(Sl. 1, k. 1, p.s.s.o., k. 2, m. 1) twice, (sl. 1, k. 1, p.s.s.o., k. 1, k. 2 tog., m. 1) 6 times, k. 2, k. 2 tog., m. 1, k. 2, k. 2 tog.

11th row.—P.

12th row.—(Sl. 1, k. 1, p.s.s.o., k. 2, m. 1) twice, (sl. 1, k. 2 tog., p.s.s.o., m. 1, k. 1, m. 1) 5 times, sl. 1, k. 2 tog., p.s.s.o., (m. 1, k. 2, k. 2 tog.) twice.

13th row.—P. 12, (tw. nt. st., p. 3) 4 times, p. 9

Now continue exactly as for the jabot beg. at the 71st row.

Using the crochet hook, work a row of picot edge all round the jabot and along the shaped side edges of the cuffs.

Press work lightly with hot iron over damp cloth.

SPARKLE BY DAY OR BY NIGHT IN

A Beaded Scarf

MATERIALS

2 oz. 3-ply wool.
2,520 small silver beads (sold in 100s).
1 pair No. 10 needles.

MEASUREMENTS

Length, 33 ins.
Width, 9 ins.

TENSION

About 8 sts. to 1 in.

Thread the beads on the wool. When purling st. with beads, pull the wool fairly tightly to prevent beads slipping through to back of work.

Detail of stitch used for the scarf.

Using No. 10 needles cast on 72 sts. and work 4 rows in moss st.

Change to patt. thus:—

1st row.—K. 1, p. 1, k. 1, * k. 1, m. 1, k. 2 tog.; rep. from * 10 times, k. 1, * k. 1, w.fd., sl. 2 beads close to needle, p. 1, k. 2; rep. from second * to last 3 sts., p. 1, k. 1, p. 1.

2nd row.—P. 1, k. 1, p. 34, (k. 1, m. 1, k. 2 tog.) 11 times, k. 1, p. 1, k. 1.

3rd row.—K. 1, p. 1, k. 1, * k. 1, m. 1, k. 2 tog.; rep. from * 10 times, k. 3, * k. 1, w.fd., sl. 2 beads to needle, p. 1, k. 2; rep. from second * to last 5 sts., k. 2, p. 1, k. 1, p. 1.

4th row.—As 2nd row.

Rep. these 4 rows 10 times. Then reverse patt.:—

45th row.—K. 1, p. 1, k. 2, * k. 1, w.td., sl. 2 beads to needle, p. 1, k. 2; rep. from * 7 times, k. 1, m. 1, k. 2 tog. to the last 3 sts., p. 1, k. 1, p. 1.

46th row.—P. 1, k. 1, p. 1, (k. 1, m. 1, k. 2 tog.) 11 times, p. to last 3 sts., k. 1 p. 1, k. 1.

47th row.—K. 1, p. 1, k. 4, * k. 1, w.fd., sl. 2 beads to needle, p. 1, k. 2; rep. from * 6 times, k. 2, (k. 1, m. 1, k. 2 tog.) to last 3 sts., p. 1, k. 1, p. 1.

48th row.—As 2nd row.

Rep. the last 4 rows 10 times.

These 88 rows form one complete patt.

Rep. them until scarf measures 33 ins. or length required.

Finish end of scarf with 4 rows of moss st.

Cast off.

Press scarf very lightly using a warm iron over a damp cloth.

Little silver beads give this scarf its sparkle. They are actually knitted into the fabric, but that doesn't make the knitting difficult or tedious. Try it; the pretty effect is well worth the little extra trouble.

Mₒₑ details ! **1.** *A blouse front knitted in wool and cotton that has a fairy-like effect.* Page 85. **2.** *A rosebud collar.* Page 84. **3.** *A flower necklet for that little black dress.* Page 86. **4.** *Crochet cotton gloves for summer.* Page 80. **5.** *Gaily coloured snood—make one to go with every dress !* Page 88. **6.** *Practical but elegant mesh stockings —for town or country.* Page 90.

4

5

6

Summer Gloves

CROCHETED IN FINE THREAD

MATERIALS

A ball of crochet cotton, No. 60.
A steel crochet hook, No. 6.
About ¼ yd. very narrow (round) elastic.

MEASUREMENTS

To fit an average size hand.

TENSION

Work to produce about 13 spaces to 2 ins. in width.

ABBREVIATIONS

ch.=chain; d.c.=double crochet; tr. =treble; st.=stitch; rep.=repeat; sp.=space or spaces.

The Left-hand Glove.—Begin at bottom of hand and mak 126 ch. Join into a ring with a sl.st. and work in rounds thus:—

1st round.—3 ch., 1 tr. into each of next 3 ch., * 1 ch., miss next ch., 1 tr. into next ch., (2 ch., miss next 2 ch., 1 tr. into next ch.) twice, 1 ch., miss next ch., 1 tr. into each of next 4 ch.; rep. from * 3 times, 1 ch., miss next ch., 1 tr. into next ch., ** 2 ch., miss next 2 ch., 1 tr. into next ch.; rep. from ** 21 times, 3 ch.

2nd round.—1 tr. into next 4 tr. (counting the first 3 ch. as the first tr.), * 2 ch., miss next sp., 1 tr. into next sp., 2 ch., 1 tr. into next sp., 2 ch., 1 tr. into each of next 4 tr.; rep. from * 3 times, 2 ch., miss next sp., 1 tr. into next sp., ** 2 ch., 1 tr. into next sp.; rep. from ** to end, leaving the last sp. of 3 ch. unworked, 2 ch.

3rd round.—1 tr. into each of next 4 tr., 1 ch., 1 tr. into next sp., 2 ch., (1 tr. 2 ch., 1 tr.) all into next sp., 2 ch., 1 tr. into next sp., 1 ch., * 1 tr. into each of next 4 tr., 1 ch., 1 tr. into next sp., (2 ch., 1 tr. into next sp.) twice, 1 ch.; rep. from * 3 times, 1 ch., 1 tr. into next sp., ** 2 ch., 1 tr. into next sp.; rep. from ** to last sp. of 2 ch., (2 ch., 1 tr., 2 ch., 1 tr.) all into next sp., 2 h.

4th round.—1 tr. into each of next 4 tr., 2 ch., miss next sp., 1 tr. into next sp., 2 ch., (1 tr., 2 ch., 1 tr.) all into next sp., 2 ch., 1 tr. into next sp., 2 ch., miss next sp., 1 tr. into each of next 4 tr., work in patt. of tr. and sp. to end of round, working an extra sp. into the increased sp. of last round.

Continue in this way, working in patt. of tr. groups and sp. and inc. 2 sp. in each round for the thumb gusset, working these extra sp. into the increased sp. of previous rounds until 10 rounds have been worked in all; 16 extra sp. in round. 8 on each side of tr. group.

Work 2 rounds in patt. without inc., then beg. thumb:—

Next round.—1 tr. into each of next 4 tr., 1 ch., 1 tr. into next sp., (2 ch., 1 tr. into next sp.) 5 times, 12 ch., 1 tr. into 7th sp., counting back from tr. group for centre of thumb, (2 ch., 1 tr. into next sp.) 5 times, 2 ch.

Next round.—1 tr. into each of next 4 tr., 2 ch., miss next sp., 1 tr. into next sp., (2 ch., 1 tr. into next sp.) 4 times, miss first ch., 1 tr. into next ch., (miss next 2 ch., 1 tr. into next ch.) 3 times, 2 ch., 1 tr. into next sp.

Continue working in rounds of sp. with tr. group until 12 rows have been worked for thumb, counting from 12 foundation ch. at base of thumb and ending at tr. group.

These cool summer gloves are crocheted in cream thread. A small piece of round elastic inserted at the wrist draws the glove in, and keeps it neatly in position; at the same time it gives the crisp frilled effect.

Shape Top thus:—

Next round.—1 d.c. into each of 4 tr., 2 d.c. into each 2 ch. sp. and 1 d.c. into 1 ch. sp. to end.

Next round.—* Miss next d.c., 1 d.c. into each of next 2 d.c.; rep. from * to tr. group.

Next round.—1 d.c. into each st. of previous round.

Next round.—* Miss next d.c., 1 d.c. into next d.c.; rep. from * to end.

Rep. this last round until top is filled in. Fasten off.

Rejoin thread at base of thumb, working 3 ch. into sp. to form a tr., now work in sp. at base of thumb (making 35 sp. between first and last tr. groups for palm of hand) and continue in rounds of sp. and tr. groups until 10 rounds have been worked from base of thumb (22 rounds from beg. of hand). Finish at the 4th tr. group.

Fourth Finger thus:—

Next round.—1 tr. into each of next 4 tr., 1 ch., 1 tr. into next sp., (2 ch., 1 tr. into next sp.) 10 times, 7 ch., 1 tr. into centre sp. between tr. groups.

Continue in rounds of sp. and tr. group, working about 2 sp. into the 7 ch. in next round (making 14 sp. and 4 tr in round), until 12 rounds have been worked from the 7 foundation ch., ending at tr. group.

Shape Top to match with thumb.

Rejoin thread at base of fourth finger beg. at palm of hand and work 2 more rounds in patt., working about 2 sp. into base of fourth finger (making 30 sp. and 4 tr. in round) and finishing at 1st tr. group (24 rounds from beg. of hand).

The First Finger:—

Next round.—1 tr. into each of next 4 tr., 1 ch., 1 tr. into next sp., 2 ch., 1 tr. into next sp., 12 ch., 1 tr. into 10th sp., counting back from tr. group for centre of finger, (2 ch., 1 tr. into next sp.) 8 times, 2 ch.

Continue in rounds of sp. and tr. group, working about 4 sp. into the 12 ch. in next round (making 15 sp. and 4 tr. in round), until 14 rounds have been worked for finger, counting from 12 foundation ch. Finish at tr. group.

Shape Top to match with thumb.

The Second Finger.—Rejoin thread into sp. in palm of hand at base of first finger and make 2 ch.; now work about 4 sp. into base of first finger, 2 sp., a group of 4 tr. and 2 sp. along back of hand, 9 ch., 6 sp. along palm of hand.

Continue in rounds of sp. and tr. group, working about 3 sp. into the 9 ch. in next round (making 17 sp. and 4 tr. in round), until 18 rounds have been worked from 9 foundation ch., ending at tr. group.

Shape Top to match with thumb.

The Third Finger.—Rejoin thread into sp. in palm of hand at base of second finger and make 2 ch., now continue in rounds of sp. and tr. group, working about 3 sp. into base of second finger (making 16 sp. and 4 tr. in round) until 15 rounds have been worked for finger, ending at tr. group.

Shape Top to match with thumb.

The Cuff.—With right side of work facing, work round lower edge of hand as follows: Cut a short length of elastic to fit the wrist when slightly stretched, allowing a bit extra for joining. Place elastic along beg. ch. edge of hand and work a row of d.c. all round this edge, working over the elastic to form a casing thus: Begin at first 4 tr. group and work 1 d.c. into each foundation ch. st., i.e. 126 sts., inc. 4 sts. along palm of hand at regular intervals by working 2 d.c.

into 1 st. 4 times (130 sts. in round). Fasten off elastic securely.

2nd round.—1 ch., * 1 tr. into each of next 4 sts. (these should come directly over 4 tr. groups up back of hand), 1 ch., miss next st., 1 d.c. into next st., (2 ch., miss next 2 sts., 1 d.c. into next st.) twice, 1 ch., miss next st.; rep. from * to end.

3rd round.—* 1 tr. into each of next 4 tr., 2 ch., miss next sp., 1 tr. into next sp., 2 ch., 1 tr. into next sp., 2 ch.; rep. from * to end.

4th round.—* 1 tr. into each of next 4 tr., 1 ch., 1 tr. into next sp., (2 ch., 1 tr. into next sp.) twice, 1 ch.; rep. from * to end.

Rep. last 2 rounds twice, then rep. 3rd round once more.

10th round.—* 3 ch., 1 d.c. into 3rd tr., (3 ch., 1 d.c. into next sp.) 3 times; rep. from * to end.

Fasten off.

The Right-hand Glove.—Begin at bottom of hand and make 126 ch.

Join into a ring with a sl.st. and work in rounds thus:—

1st round.—As 1st round of left-hand glove.

2nd round.—As 2nd round of left-hand glove.

3rd round.—* 1 tr. into each of next 4 tr., 1 ch., 1 tr. into next sp., (2 ch., 1 tr. into next sp.) twice, 1 ch.; rep. from * twice, 1 tr. into each of next 4 tr., 1 ch., 1 tr. into next sp., 2 ch., (1 tr., 2 ch., 1 tr.) all into next sp., 2 ch., 1 tr. into next sp., 1 ch., 1 tr. into each of next 4 tr., 1 ch., 1 tr. into next sp., 2 ch., (1 tr., 2 ch., 1 tr.) all into next sp., ** 2 ch., 1 tr. into next sp.; rep. from ** to end, 1 ch.

4th round.—* 1 tr. into each of next 4 tr., 2 ch., miss next sp., 1 tr. into next sp., 2 ch., 1 tr. into next sp., 2 ch.; rep. from * twice, 1 tr. into each of next 4 tr., 2 ch., miss next sp., 1 tr. into next sp., 2 ch., (1 tr., 2 ch., 1 tr.) all into next sp., 2 ch., 1 tr. into next sp., 2 ch., miss next sp., 1 tr. into each of next 4 tr., 2 ch., miss next sp., 1 tr. into next sp., 2 ch., (1 tr., 2 ch., 1 tr.) all into next sp., ** 2 ch., 1 tr. into next sp.; rep. from ** to end, leaving last sp. of 1 ch. unworked.

Continue in this way to match left-hand glove, working in patt. of sp. and tr. group and inc. 2 sp. in each round for thumb gusset (working these increased sp. into increased sp. of previous round), until 10 rounds have been worked in all. 16 extra sp. in round, 8 on each side of tr. group.

Work 2 rounds without inc., then begin thumb thus:—

Next round.—Work in patt. across back of hand to end of 5th tr. group, 1 ch., 1 tr. into next sp., (2 ch., 1 tr. into next sp.) 5 times, 12 ch., 1 tr. into 7th sp. counting back from tr. group for centre of thumb, (2 ch., 1 tr. into next sp.) 5 times, 2 ch.

Next round.—1 tr. into each of next 4 tr., 2 ch., miss next sp., 1 tr. into next sp., (2 ch., 1 tr. into next sp.) 4 times, miss next ch., 1 tr. into 2nd ch., (miss next 2 ch., 1 tr. into next ch.) 3 times, 2

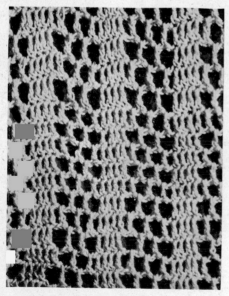

Detail of the crocheted glove stitch.

ch., 1 tr. into next sp.

Continue working in rounds of sp. and tr. group to match left-hand glove.

Rejoin thread at base of thumb and work to match with left-hand glove until fourth finger is reached, ending at 1st tr. group instead of 4th tr. group.

The Fourth Finger:—

Next round.—1 tr. into each of next 4 tr., 1 ch., 1 tr. into next sp., 2 ch., 1 tr. into next sp., 7 ch., 1 tr. into 11th sp., counting back from tr. group.

Continue in rounds of sp. and tr. group, working about 2 sp. into the 7 ch. in next round (14 sp. and 4 tr. in round), finish as for left-hand glove.

Rejoin thread at base of fourth finger, beg. at back of hand, and work 2 rounds to match with left-hand glove, finishing at 4th tr. group.

The First Finger:—

Next round.—1 tr. into each of next 4 tr., 1 ch., 1 tr. into next sp., * 2 ch., 1 tr. into next sp.; rep. from * 7 times, 12 ch., 1 tr. into centre sp. between tr. groups. 2 ch., 1 tr. into next sp., 2 ch.

Continue in rounds of sp. and tr. group, working about 4 sp. into the 12 ch. in next round (making 15 sp. and 4 tr. in round), finish as for left-hand glove.

The Second Finger.—Rejoin thread into space at base of first finger in back of hand and make 2 ch., now work about 4 sp. into side of first finger, 6 sp. along palm of hand, 9 ch., 2 sp., a 4 tr. group, 2 sp. along back of hand.

Continue in rounds of sp. and tr. group, working about 3 sp. into the 9 ch. in next round (making 17 sp. and 4 tr. in round), finish as for left-hand glove.

The Third Finger.—Rejoin thread into sp. at base of second finger in back of hand and work to match left-hand glove.

The Cuff.—Work exactly as given for left-hand glove.

Make-up.—Press work lightly with hot iron over damp cloth.

Fasten in all ends neatly.

A Rosebud Collar

ENCHANTING ON A PLAIN BLACK DRESS

MATERIALS

A ball of crochet cotton, No. 40.
2 No. 18 knitting needles.

MEASUREMENTS

Length at neck edge, 13½ ins.

TENSION

About 14 sts. to 1 in. over st.st.

Cast on 191 sts. and work 6 rows in st.st. beg. with a k. row.

7th row.—K. 5, * k. 2 tog., k. 4; rep. from * to end.

Work 3 rows st.st.

11th row.—K. 5, * k. twice into next st., k. 4; rep. from * to end (191 sts.).

Continue in st.st. on reverse side of work thus:—

12th row.—K.

13th row.—P.

Rep. last 2 rows once.

16th row.—K. 5, * k. 2 tog. w.fd., k. 1, k. 2 tog., w.fd., sl. 1, k. 1, p.s.s.o., k. 1, w.fd., sl. 1, k. 1, p.s.s.o., k. 9; rep. from * to end, ending k. 5, instead of k. 9.

Detail of one section of the rosebud motif.

17th row.—* P. 9, (p. 1, k. 1) into next st., p. 8; rep. from * to last st., p. 1.

18th row.—K. 4, * (k. 2 tog., w.fd.) twice, sl. 1, k. 1, p.s.s.o., k. 2 tog., (w.fd., sl. 1, k. 1, p.s.s.o.) twice, k. 7; rep. from * to end, ending k. 4 instead of k. 7.

19th row.—* P. 7, (p. 1, k. 1) into next st., p. 2, (p. 1, k. 1) into next st., p. 6; rep. from * to last st., p. 1.

20th row.—K. 3, * k. 2 tog., w.fd., k. 1, sl. 1, k. 1, p.s.s.o., k. 2 tog., w.fd., sl. 1, k. 1, p.s.s.o.. k. 2 tog., k. 1, w.fd., sl. 1, k. 1, p.s.s.o., k. 5; rep. from * to end, ending k. 3 instead of k. 5.

21st row.—* P. 8, (p. 1, k. 1) into next st., p. 7; rep. from * to last st., p. 1.

22nd row.—* K. 2, k. 2 tog., w.fd., k. 2, w.fd., k. 1, sl. 1, k. 1, p.s.s.o., k. 2 tog., k. 1, w.fd., k. 2, w.fd., sl. 1, k. 1, p.s.s.o., k. 1; rep. from * to last st., k. 1.

23rd and every alternate row.—P.

24th row.—* K. 1, k. 2 tog., w.fd., k. 3, w.fd., k. 1, w.fd., sl. 2, k. 2 tog., p.s.sts.o., w.fd., k. 1, w.fd., k. 3, w.fd., sl. 1, k. 1. p.s.s.o.; rep. from * to last st., k. 1.

26th row.—K. 2 tog., * w.fd., k. 4, w.fd., k. 3, w.fd., k. 1, w.fd., k. 3, w.fd., k. 4, w.fd., sl. 1, k. 2 tog., p.s.s.o.; rep. from * to end, ending sl. 1, k. 1, p.s.s.o. instead of sl. 1, k. 2 tog., p.s.s.o.

28th row.—* K. 2, w.fd., sl. 1, k. 1, p.s.s.o., k. 2, w.fd., sl. 1, k. 1, p.s.s.o., k. 1, k. 2 tog., w.fd., k. 1, w.fd., sl. 1, k. 1, p.s.s.o., k. 1, k. 2 tog., w.fd., k. 2, k. 2 tog., w.fd., k. 1; rep. from * to last st., k. 1.

30th row.—* K. 1, w.fd., sl. 1, k. 1, p.s.s.o., w.fd., sl. 1, k. 1, p.s.s.o., k. 2, w.fd., sl. 1, k. 2 tog., p.s.s.o., w.fd., k. 3, w.fd., sl. 1, k. 2 tog., p.s.s.o., w.fd., k. 2, k. 2 tog., w.fd., k. 2 tog., w.fd.; rep. from * to last st., k. 1.

32nd row.—* K. 1, k. 2 tog., w.fd., k. 1, w.fd., sl. 1, k. 1, p.s.s.o., k. 3, w.fd., sl. 1, k. 1, p.s.s.o., k. 1, k. 2 tog., w.fd., k. 3, k. 2 tog., w.fd., k. 1, w.fd., sl. 1, k. 1, p.s.s.o.; rep. from * to last st., k. 1.

34th row.—K. 2 tog., * w.fd., k. 3, w.fd., sl. 1, k. 1, p.s.s.o., k. 1, k. 2 tog., w.fd., sl. 1, k. 2 tog., p.s.s.o., w.fd., sl. 1, k. 1, p.s.s.o., k. 1, k. 2 tog., w.fd., k. 3, w.fd., sl. 1, k. 2 tog., p.s.s.o.; rep. from * to end, ending sl. 1, k. 1, p.s.s.o. instead of sl. 1, k. 2 tog., p.s.s.o.

36th row.—K. 1, * w.fd., k. 2 tog. w.fd., k. 1 w.fd., sl. 1, k. 1, p.s.s.o. w.fd., sl. 1, k. 1, p.s.s.o., k. 5, k. 2 tog. w.fd., k. 2 tog , w.fd., k. 1, w.fd., sl. 1 k. 1, p.s.s.o., w.fd , k. 1; rep. from * to end.

38th row.—K. 2, * w.fd., sl. 1, k. 1, p.s.s.o., k. 1, k. 2 tog., w.fd., k. 1, w.fd., sl. 1, k. 1, p.s.s.o., k. 3, k. 2 tog., w.fd., k. 1, w.fd., sl. 1, k. 1, p.s.s.o., k. 1, k. 2 tog., w.fd., k. 3; rep. from * to end ending k. 2 instead of k. 3.

40th row.—K. 1, * w.fd., k. 2, w.fd., sl. 1, k. 2 tog., p.s.s.o., w.fd., k. 2, w.fd., k. 1, w.fd., sl. 1, k. 1, p.s.s.o., k. 1, k. 2 tog., w.fd., k. 1, w.fd., k. 2, w.fd., sl. 1, k. 2 tog., p.s.s.o., w.fd., k. 2, w.fd., k. 1; rep. from * to end.

42nd row.—K. 2, * w.fd., sl. 1, k. 1, p.s.s.o., k. 3, k. 2 tog., w.fd., k. 3, w.fd., sl. 1, k. 2 tog., p.s.s.o., w.fd., k. 3, w.fd., sl. 1, k. 1, p.s.s.o., k. 3, k. 2 tog., w.fd., k. 3; rep. from * to end, ending k. 2 instead of k. 3.

44th row.—K. 1, * w.fd., sl. 1, k. 1, p.s.s.o., w.fd., sl. 1, k. 1, p.s.s.o., k. 1, k. 2 tog., w.fd., k. 2 tog., w.fd., k. 1, w.fd., sl. 1, k. 1, p.s.s.o., k. 1, k. 2 tog., w.fd., k. 1, w.fd., sl. 1, k. 1, p.s.s.o., w.fd., sl. 1, k. 1, p.s.s.o., k. 1, k. 2 tog., w.fd., k. 2 tog., w.fd., k. 1; rep. from * to end.

46th row.—K. 2, * w.fd., sl. 1, k. 1, p.s.s.o., w.fd., sl. 1, k. 2 tog., p.s.s.o., w.fd., k. 2 tog., w.fd., k. 3, w.fd., sl. 1, k. 2 tog., p.s.s.o., w.fd., k. 3, w.fd., sl. 1, k. 1, p.s.s.o., w.fd., sl. 1, k. 2 tog., p.s.s.o., w.fd., k. 2 tog., w.fd., k. 3; rep from * to end, ending k. 2 instead of k. 3.

Cast off very loosely on a p. row.

Press carefully on wrong side with hot iron over damp cloth.

Cotton and Wool

COMBINE TO MAKE THIS BLOUSE FRONT

MATERIALS

1 oz. 2-ply wool.
A ball of crochet cotton No. 40.
2 No. 12 knitting needles.
2 or 3 small buttons for back opening.
½ yd. net or butter muslin.

MEASUREMENTS

Length from shoulder, 18 ins.
Width of front, 13 ins.

TENSION

9 sts. to 1 in. with 2-ply wool.

The Front.—Using crochet cotton cast on 150 sts. * Work ½ in. in k. 1, p. 1 rib.
Change to wool and work ¾ in. in st.st. (1 row k., 1 row p.).
Change to crochet cotton *.
Rep. from * to * until work measures 15 ins., ending row on wrong side.

Detail of stitch of blouse front.

Break off wool. Using crochet cotton and working in k. 1, p. 1 rib:—

Shape Neck thus:—

Next row.—Rib 56, cast off 38 sts., rib to end.

Continue in rib on 56 sts., dec. 1 st. at neck edge on every alternate row until 42 sts. remain.

Continue without shaping until work measures 18 ins., ending side edge.

Shape Shoulder thus:—

Next row.—Cast off 10 sts., work to end.

Next row.—Rib to end.

Rep. last 2 rows twice.

Cast off remaining sts.

Rejoin wool to other set of 56 sts. and work to match.

The Neck Band.—Using crochet cotton cast on 10 sts., work in k. 1, p. 1 rib for 13 ins. Cast off.

The Bow.—Using crochet cotton cast on 8 sts., work in k. 1, p. 1 rib for 8 ins. Cast off.

Make-up.—Press work lightly on wrong side with hot iron over damp cloth.

Cut a piece of net about 19½ ins. by 15 ins. for back.

Make a ½-in. hem along lower edge and each side edge.

Shape shoulders and sew to front shoulders.

Cut a 4½-in. opening down centre back, bind or hem the edges neatly. Sew neck band round neck edge.

Make a small bow with bow strip and sew to centre front of neck band.

Fasten back opening with buttons and small button loops or press fasteners.

Press seams.

The Rosette Motif

SHOWN ON PAGE 7 ADAPTS ITSELF TO A NECKLET

MATERIALS

1 ball of size 20 crochet cotton.
Crochet hook, size 2.
Small button.

TENSION

Largest flower measures about 2 ins. across.

The Large Rosette.—Make 6 ch. and join in ring with sl.st.

1st round.—5 ch., 1 tr. into ring (2 ch., 1 tr.) 6 times into ring, 2 ch., join to 3rd of 5 ch. with sl.st. (8 holes).

2nd round.—Into each 2 ch., hole put 1 d.c., 1 tr., 1 d.tr., 1 tr. 1 d.c.

3rd round.—4 ch., 1 d.c. into the trs. of 1st round, holding petals of 2nd round

For the woman who has neither the time nor the patience to knit a whole jumper—here is a smart substitute, a blouse front. It is knitted in alternate bands of cotton and wool and is worn with a suit.

*A single flower motif of the necklet
on page 78.*

under thumb and putting the 4 ch.
behind them.

4th round.—Into each 4 ch. put 1 d.c.,
2 trs., 3 d.trs., 2 trs., 1 d.c.

5th round.—5 ch., 1 d.c. into each d.c.
of 3rd row, behind 4th row.

6th round.—Into each 5 ch. put 1 d.c.,
2 trs., 5 d.trs., 2 trs., 1 d.c.

7th round.—6 ch., 1 d.c. into each d.c.
of 5th round, behind 6th round.

8th round.—Into each 6 ch. put 1 d.c.,
2 trs., 2 d.trs., 3 trip trs., 2 d.trs., 2 trs.,
1 d.c. Break cotton, leaving end to sew
tog.

The Medium Rosettes.—Make two
rosettes as above, but ending at 6th round.

The Small Rosettes.—Make two rosettes
as above but ending at 4th round.

Neatly sew the tips of petals tog. as
shown in the illustration.

Unwind about a yd. of thread and join
to the petals of small rosettes (as shown)
and using double cotton, work a length
of ch. sufficient to reach back of neck,
allowing about 2 in. extra for the knots.

Join another double length to next
petal and work same length of ch.

Tie knots at intervals. Work other
side to match.

Sew a small button to left end, and
make a loop on the other.

Coloured Snood

FOR CASUAL WEAR

MATERIALS

1 oz. wool, cotton or yarn.
Pair knitting needles size 0.
Medium crochet hook.
Round elastic to fit back of head.

TENSION

About 1 patt. to 1 in.

Cast on 42 sts.
1st row.—K.
2nd row.—K. 1, * (k. 1, p. 1, k. 1) all in
same st., p. 3 tog.; rep. from * to last st.,
k. 1.
3rd row.—P.

4th row.—K. 1, * p. 3 tog., (k. 1, p. 1,
k. 1) all in same st.; rep. from * to last st.,
k. 1.

5th row.—P.

The last 4 rows form the patt. and are
repeated until work measures 14 ins. (or
suitable length). Cast off, but do not
break off yarn.

Make-up.—Holding the elastic against
the knitting, work d.c. over it into the
edge of the knitting. Work round three
sides, leaving the cast-off edge plain for
front of head. Draw up the elastic to a
suitable length and sew neatly to beg. and
end of d.c.

Practical and gay, the coloured snood will always find favour, especially with the woman who is "growing her hair"! It is so quickly and easily made you can have one to match every frock.

Mesh Stockings

THAT FLATTER AND LEND ELEGANCE

MATERIALS

10 small balls of mercerized cotton No. 8.
2 No. 12 and 2 No. 14 needles.

MEASUREMENTS

Length from top of leg to bottom of heel, 27 ins.
Length of foot, 9½ ins. (adjustable).

TENSION

8 sts. to 1 in. on No. 12 needles.

With No. 12 needles cast on 99 sts. using double thread. Work in k. 1, p. 1 rib for 2 ins. (Do not work into back of sts. of 1st row.) Break off 1 strand of thread. Continue in the following patt.:—

Next row.—K. 2, * m. 1, k. 3, sl. the first of these 3 sts. over the other 2 sts. (it will be found easier to sl. the sts. from behind). Rep. from * to last st., k. 1.

Rep. this row until work measures 14 ins. Shape leg thus: Continue in patt., dec. 1 st. both ends of the next row and every following 4th row until 63 sts. remain. Continue without further shaping until work measures 24½ ins. from cast-on edge.

Divide for heel and instep thus:—

1st row.—Patt. 48, turn.

2nd row.—Patt. 33, turn.

Continue in patt. on these 33 sts. for the instep for 6 ins. (for a longer or shorter foot work more or less at this point). Change to No. 14 needles.

Shape Toe thus: K. 1, k. 2 tog., k. to last 3 sts., k. 2 tog., k. 1.

2nd row.—K. 1, p. to last st., k. 1; rep. these 2 rows until 11 sts. remain. Leave on spare needle.

Return to heel sts. and sl. the 2 sets of sts. on to one needle with the side edges to the centre to form the back seam. Change to No. 14 needles.

Next row.—(K. 2, k. twice into next st.) 10 times (40 sts.). Work 33 rows of st.st. (1 row plain, 1 row purl) commencing with a p. row. Turn the heel:—

1st row.—K. 26, k. 2 tog., turn.

2nd row.—P. 13, p. 2 tog., turn.

3rd row.—K. 14, k. 2 tog., turn.

4th row.—P. 15, p. 2 tog., turn. Continue in this manner until all side sts. are worked off and 26 sts. remain.

Next row.—With wrong side of work facing, pick up and p. 17 sts. down heel flap. Turn.

2nd row.—K. 43, then pick up and k. 17 sts. along other side of heel flap (60 sts.). P. 1 row.

Shape Instep thus:—

1st row.—K. 2, k. 2 tog., k. to last 4 sts., sl. 1, k. 1, p.s.s.o., k. 2.

2nd row.—K. 1, p. to last st., k. 1.

Rep. these 2 rows until 40 sts. remain. Continue in st.st. until foot measures the same as top part to commencement of toe shaping, ending with a k. row.

Next row.—(P. 3, p. 2 tog.) 7 times, p. 5 (33 sts.)

Now work toe as given for top of foot, then graft 2 sets of sts. tog.

Work a second stocking to match.

Make-up.—Press work carefully under a damp cloth with a hot iron. Join foot and leg seams neatly. Press the seams.

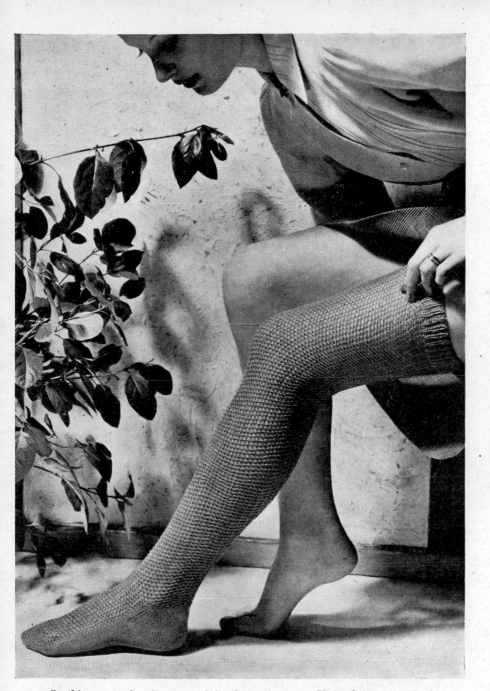

Stockings can be elegant and hardwearing too. Knitted in mercerized cotton, you will find these stockings good companions to low-heeled brogues for country wear, yet they look well to wear with town shoes.

For Shirt Design—

Smart
Cardigan—

—Lacy Bedjacket

A Trio of Alternative Stitches

Alternative Stitches

TO USE FOR GARMENTS IN THE WOMEN'S SECTION

"Shirt" Stitch

Number of stitches divisible by 7, plus 3.

1st row.—P. 1, k. 1, p. 1, * w.o.n. (to make a st.), k. 2 tog., w.fd., w.o.n. (to make a st.), sl. 1, k. 1, p.s.s.o., w.r.n., p. 1, k. 1, p. 1; rep. from *.

2nd row.—P. 1, k. 1, p. 1, * k. into back of next st., p. 1, w.r.n., sl. 1 p.w., p. 1, k. into back of next st., p. 1, k. 1. p. 1; rep. from *.

3rd row.—P. 1, k. 1, p. 1, * k. 2 tog., (k. into back of next st.) twice, sl. 1, k. 1. p.s.s.o., p. 1, k. 1, p. 1; rep. from *.

4th row.—P. 1, k. 1, p. 1, * p. 4, p. 1. k. 1, p. 1; rep. from *.

Rep. these 4 rows.

"Cardigan" Stitch

Number of stitches divisible by 5, plus 2.

1st row.—K. 1, * k. 2 tog., p. 1, sl. 1, k. 1, p.s.s.o.; rep. from * to the last st. k. 1.

2nd row.—K. 1, p. 1, k. 1, * p. 2, k. 1; rep. from * to the last 2 sts., p. 1, k. 1.

3rd row.—K. 2, * pick up and k. the wool 2 rows below between the last st. and the next, p. 1, pick up and k. the wool 2 rows below between the last st. and the next, k. 2; rep. from * to the end.

4th row.—K. 1, p. 2, * k. 1, p. 4; rep. from * to the last 4 sts., k. 1, p. 2, k. 1.

Rep. these 4 rows.

"Bedjacket" Stitch

Number of stitches divisible by 6, plus 3.

1st row.—K. 2, * m. 1, sl. 1, k. 1. p.s.s.o., k. 1, k. 2 tog., m. 1, k. 1; rep. from *, k. 1.

2nd row.—P. to end.

3rd row.—K. 3, * m. 1, sl. 1, k. 2 tog., p.s.s.o., m. 1, k. 3; rep. from * to end.

4th row.—P. to end.

Rep. these 4 rows.

"Bouquet" Stitch Number One

Number of stitches divisible by 7, plus 4.

1st row.—K. 1, p. 1, * w.r.n. twice in knitting next st., p. 2, k. 1, p. 2, w.r.n twice in knitting next st.; rep. from * ending p. 1, k. 1.

2nd row.—K. 2, * w.fd., sl. 1 p.w., dropping extra loop, w.b., k. 2, p. 1, k. 2, w.fd., sl. 1 p.w., dropping extra loop, rep. from *, ending with k. 2.

3rd row.—K. 1, p. 1, * sl. long st. off left-hand needle, leave it at front of work. p. next 2 sts., then sl. dropped st. on to right-hand needle, k. next st., leaving it on left-hand needle, p.s.s.o., w.fd., k. 1 again into st. just worked and sl.st. off, drop next 3 sts. off left-hand needle replacing the p. sts. first and then the long st., now return last st. on right-hand needle back to left-hand needle, pass long st. over and replace on to right-hand needle, p. 2; rep. from *, ending p. 1, k. 1.

4th row.—K. 5, * p. 1, k. 6; rep. from * to last 6 sts., p. 1, k. 5. Rep. these 4 rows.

"Bouquet" Stitch Number Two

Number of stitches divisible by 5, plus 4.

1st row.—K. to end.

2nd row. P. to end.

3rd row.—* K. 4, p. 1; rep. from * to last 4 sts., k. 4.

4th row.—* P. 4, k. into previous row of next st., then k. the st. itself; rep. from * to last 4 sts., p. 4.

5th row.—* K. 4, p. 2; rep. from * to last 4 sts., k. 4.

6th row.—* P. 4, k. 1, k. into the previous row of next st., k. the st. itself; rep. from * to last 4 sts., p. 4.

7th row.—* K. 4, p. 3; rep. from * to last 4 sts., k. 4.

8th row.—* P. 4, k. 2, k. into the previous row of next st., k. the st. itself; rep. from * to last 4 sts., p. 4

9th row.—* K. 4, p. 4; rep. from * to last 4 sts., k. 4.

10th row.—* P. 4, k. 4 tog.; rep. from * to last 4 sts., p. 4.

11th row.—K. 1, * k. 2, w.r.n. twice in knitting next st., k. 1, w.r.n. twice in knitting next st.; rep. from * to last 3 sts., k. 3.

12th row.—P. 1, * p. 2, w.b., sl. 1 p.w., dropping extra loop, w.fd., p. 1, w.bk., sl. 1 p.w., dropping extra loop; rep. from * to last 3 sts., p. 3.

13th row.—K. 1, * k. 2, w.fd., sl. long loop, w.bk., k. 1, w.fd., sl. long loop, w.bk.; rep. from * to last 3 sts., k. 3.

14th row.—P. 2, * sl. next st. off needle, keeping it at back of work, and k. the dropped st., put p. st. on left-hand needle, p. 2, sl. dropped st. off needle, p. 1, then k. dropped st.; rep. from *, ending with p. 2.

Rep. rows 3 to 14.

"Bouquet" Stitch Number Three

Any odd number of stitches.

1st row.—P. 2, * sl. 1 p.w., w.r.n., p. 1; rep. from * to last st. p. 1.

2nd row.—K. 2, * p. 1 into loop of previous row, bringing loop to front of work, k. next st. at the back of this loop, then p. 1 again into the loop and sl. off in usual way; k. 1; rep. from * to last st., k. 1

3rd row.—P. 2, * k. 3 tog. through back of loops, p. 1; rep. from * to last st., p. 1.

4th row.—K. 2, * w.fd., sl. 1 p.w., w.o.n., k. 1; rep. from * to last st., k. 1.

5th row.—P. 2, * k. 1 into loop of previous row and sl. off at back of work, k. next st., then k. 1 again into the loop, p. 1; rep. from * to last st., p. 1.

6th row.—K. 2 * p. 3 tog., k. 1; rep. from * to last st., k. 1.

Rep. these 6 rows.

"Bouquet" Stitch Number Four

Number of stitches divisible by 3, plus 2.

1st row.—K. 2, * m. 1, sl. 1, k. 2, p.s.s.o. the last 2 sts.; rep. from * to end.

2nd row.—P. to end.

3rd row.—K. 1, * sl. 1, k. 2, p.s.s.o. the last 2 sts., m. 1; rep. from * to last st., k. 1.

4th row.—P. to end. Rep. these 4 rows.

"Bouquet" Stitch Number Five

Number of stitches divisible by 4, plus 3.

1st row.—K. 1, p. 1, * m. 1, sl. 1, k. 1 into next st., leaving the st. on left-hand needle, p.s.s.o., k. 2 tog. using this st. again and next st. (this will be referred to as "dec. twice in next 3 sts."), m. 1, p. 1; rep. from * to last st., k. 1.

2nd row.—K. 2, * k. into back of loop, p. 2, k. into back of loop, k. 1; rep. from * to last st., k. 1.

3rd row.—K. 1, p. 1, * k. 2 tog., m. 1, sl. 1, k. 1, p.s.s.o., p. 1; rep. from * to last st., k. 1.

4th row.—K. 2, * p. 3, k. 1; rep. from * to last st., k. 1.

5th row.—K. 1, k. 2 tog. * m. 1, k. 1, m. 1, dec. twice in next 3 sts.; rep. from * to last 4 sts., m. 1, k. 1, m. 1, sl. 1, k. 1, p.s.s.o., k. 1.

6th row.—P.

7th row.—K. 2, * m. 1, sl. 1, k. 2 tog., p.s.s.o., m. 1, k. 2; rep. from * to end.

8th row.—P.

9th row.—K. 1, m. 1, * sl. 1, k. 1, p.s.s.o., k. 1, k. 2 tog. m. 1; rep. from * to last st., k. 1.

10th row.—K. 1, k. into back of loop, * p. 3, k. into back of loop; rep. from * to last st., k. 1.

Rep. these 10 rows.

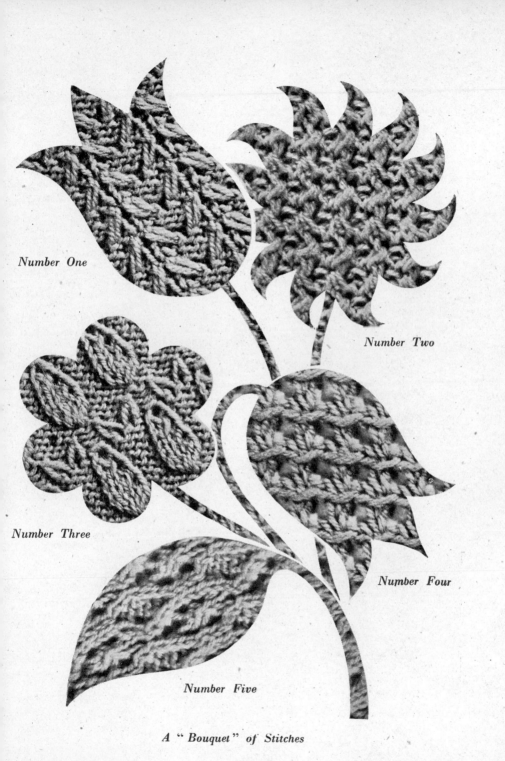

Number One

Number Two

Number Three

Number Four

Number Five

A " Bouquet " of Stitches

Two More Stitches

DESIGNED FOR WOMEN'S GARMENTS

"Cat's-paw" Stitch (below)

Number of stitches divisible by 9, plus 3.

1st row.—P. 4, * k. 4, p. 5; rep. from * to last 8 sts., k. 4, p. 4.

2nd row.—K. 4, * p. 4, k. 5; rep. from * to last 8 sts., p. 4, k. 4.

3rd row.—P. 3, * k. 2 tog., k. 1, w.fd., k. 1, sl. 1, k. 1, p.s.s.o., p. 3; rep. from * to end.

4th row.—K. 3, * p. 2, (p. 1, k. 1) into next st., p. 2, k. 3; rep. from * to end.

5th row.—P. 2, * k. 2 tog., k. 1, w.r.n., p. 2, w.o.n., k. 1, sl. 1, k. 1, p.s.s.o., p. 1; rep. from * to last st., p. 1.

6th row.—K. 2, * p. 2, k. 4, p. 2, k. 1; rep. from * to last st., k. 1.

7th row.—P. 1, k. 2 tog., w.fd., sl. 1, k. 1, p.s.s.o., * p. 2, k. 2 tog., w.fd., sl. 1, k. 2 tog., p.s.s.o., w.fd., sl. 1, k. 1, p.s.s.o.; rep. from * to last 7 sts., p. 2, k. 2 tog., w.fd., sl. 1, k. 1, p.s.s.o., p. 1.

8th row.—K. 1, p. 3, * k. 2, p. 5; rep. from * to last 6 sts., k. 2, p. 3, k. 1.

9th row.—P. 1, k. 2, w.fd., k. 1, * p. 2, k. 1, w.fd., k. 3, w.fd., k. 1; rep. from * to last 6 sts., p. 2, k. 1, w.fd., k. 2, p. 1.

10th row.—K. 1, p. 4, * k. 2, p. 7; rep. from * to last 7 sts., k. 2, p. 4, k. 1.

11th row.—P. 1, k. 2 tog., w.fd., k. 2 tog., * w.r.n., p. 2, w.o.n., sl. 1, k. 1, p.s.s.o., w.fd., sl. 1, k. 2 tog., p.s.s.o., w.fd., k. 2 tog.; rep. from * to last 7 sts., w.r.n., p. 2, w.o.n., sl. 1, k. 1, p.s.s.o., w.fd., sl. 1, k. 1, p.s.s.o., p. 1.

12th row.—K. 1, p. 3, * k. t.b.l., k. 2, k. t.b.l., p. 5; rep. from * to last 8 sts., k. t.b.l., k. 2, k. t.b.l., p. 3, k. 1.

13th row.—P. 1, k. 1, k. 2 tog., * w.r.n., p. 1, k. 2, p. 1, w.o.n., sl. 1, k. 1, p.s.s.o.; k. 1, k. 2 tog.; rep. from * to last 8 sts., w.r.n., p. 1, k. 2, p. 1, w.o.n., sl 1, k. 1, p.s.s.o., k. 1, p. 1.

14th row.—K. 1, p. 2, * k. t.b.l., k. 1, p. 2, k. 1, k. t.b.l., p. 3; rep. from * to end, ending p. 2, k. 1 instead of p. 3.

15th row.—P. 1, k. 2 tog., * w.r.n., p. 1, k. 4, p. 1, w.o.n., sl. 1, k. 2 tog., p.s.s.o.; rep. from * to end, ending sl. 1, k. 1, p.s.s.o., p. 1 instead of sl. 1, k. 2 tog., p.s.s.o.

16th row.—K. 1, p. 1, * k. t.b.l., k. 1, p. 4, k. 1, k. t.b.l., p. 1; rep. from * to last st., k. 1. Rep. last 14 rows.

Detail of "cat's-paw" stitch.

"Outfit" Stitch (opposite page)

Number of stitches divisible by 2.

1st row.—K. to end.

2nd row.—P. to end.

3rd row.—K. 1, * sl. 1, k. 1, pass the slipped st. back on to the left-hand needle and k. into the back of it. This will be referred to as cross; rep. from * to the last st., k. 1.

4th row.—P. to end.

Rep. last 2 rows, i.e. the 3rd and 4th.

A stitch suitable for the complete outfit shown here.

This sweater is no fair weather friend! Based on a traditional fisherman's jersey with a handsome cabled yoke and polo neck— it will prove an invaluable companion for winter outdoor activities.

Men's Garments

Heavy Sweater

FOR REAL WINTER WEATHER

MATERIALS

16 oz. 4-ply wool.

5 No. 10 needles with points both ends.

MEASUREMENTS

Length, 22 ins.

Chest, 38 ins.

Sleeve seam, 19 ins.

TENSION

7 sts. to 1 in.

Cast on 272 sts. (68 on each of 4 needles) and work 2½ ins. in rounds of k. 2, p. 2 rib, finishing end of round.

Next round.—P. to end.

Next round. 1st needle.—K.

2nd needle.—K. 67, p. 1.

3rd needle.—K.

4th needle.—K. 67, p. 1.

Rep. last round until work measures 12½ ins., finishing end of round.

Next round. 1st needle.—K. 1, p. 1, k. 66.

2nd needle.—K. 65, p. 1, k. 1, p. 1.

3rd needle.—K. 1, p. 1, k. 66.

4th needle.—K. 65, p. 1, k. 1, p. 1.

Next round. 1st needle.—K. twice into 1st st., p. 1, k. 66.

2nd needle.—K. 65, p. 1, k. twice into next st., p. 1.

3rd needle.—As 1st needle.

4th needle.—As 2nd needle.

Next round. 1st needle.—K. 2, p. 1, k. 66.

2nd needle.—K. 65, p. 1, k. 2, p. 1.

3rd needle.—As 1st needle.

4th needle.—As 2nd needle.

Rep. last round twice more.

Next round. 1st needle.—K. twice into 1st st., k. 1, p. 1, k. 66.

2nd needle.—K. 65, p. 1, k. twice into next st., k. 1, p. 1.

3rd needle.—As 1st needle.

4th needle.—As 2nd needle.

Next round. 1st needle.—K. 3, p. 1, k. 66.

2nd needle.—K. 65, p. 1, k. 3, p. 1.

3rd needle.—As 1st needle.

4th needle.—As 2nd needle.

Rep. last round twice more.

Next round. 1st needle.—K. 1 k. twice into next st., k. 1, p. 1, k. 66.

2nd needle.—K. 65, p. 1, k. twice into next st., k. 2, p. 1.

3rd needle.—As 1st needle.

4th needle.—As 2nd needle.

Work 3 rounds without shaping.

Continue to inc. in this way on next round and every following 4th round until there are 304 sts. in round (8 sts. extra on each needle).

Work 4 rounds after last inc. round.

Shape Armholes thus:—

Next round. 1st needle.—Sl. first 10 sts. of round on to a safety pin, k. 66.

2nd needle.—K. 65, sl. last 11 sts. on to a safety pin, turn.

Now sl. sts. from first and second needles on to one needle and continue to work on these 131 sts. in rows as follows:—

1st row.—P. to end.

2nd row.—K. 3, (p. 2, k. 6) twice, p. 2, k. 89, p. 2, (k. 6, p. 2) twice, k. 3.

3rd row.—P. 3, (k. 2, p. 6) twice, k. 2, p. 89, k. 2, (p. 6, k. 2) twice, p. 3.

4th and 5th rows.—Rep. 2nd and 3rd rows.

6th row.—K. 3, p. 2, (sl. next 3 sts. on to spare needle, leave at back of work, k. 3, then k. 3 sts. from spare needle, p. 2) twice, k. 89, p. 2, (twist next 6 sts. p. 2) twice, k. 3.

7th row.—As 5th row.

8th to 11th rows.—Rep. 1st and 2nd rows twice.

The last 10 rows, i.e. rows 2 to 11 inclusive, form patt.

Continue in patt. until work measures 22 ins. from cast-on edge, finishing row on wrong side.

Next row.—Cast off 43 sts., k. to last 43 sts., cast off 43.

Leave remaining 45 sts. on a safety pin.

Now rejoin wool to 3rd and 4th needles with right side of work facing and work exactly as given for first side, beg. from 1st round of armhole shaping.

The Shoulder Yokes.—With 2 No. 10 needles cast on 24 sts.

1st row.—K. 3, p. 2, (k. 6, p. 2) twice, k. 3.

2nd row.—P. 3, k. 2, (p. 6, k. 2) twice, p. 3.

3rd and 4th rows.—Rep. 1st and 2nd rows once.

5th row.—K. 3, p. 2, (twist next 6 sts., p. 2) twice, k. 3.

6th row.—As 2nd row.

7th to 10th rows.—Rep. 1st and 2nd rows twice.

These 10 rows form patt. Continue in patt. until work measures 6¾ ins., finishing row on wrong side.

Now sl. first 10 sts. from 45 sts. left for front neck on to end of this needle, then sl. last 10 sts. from 45 sts. left for back neck on to the empty right-hand needle and work as follows:—

1st row.—Patt. 24, k. 1, turn.

2nd row.—P. 1, patt. 24, p. 1, turn.

3rd row.—K. 1, patt. 24, k. 2, turn.

4th row.—P. 2, patt. 24, p. 2, turn.

5th row.—K. 2, patt. 24, k. 3, turn.

6th row.—P. 3, patt. 24, p. 3, turn.

Continue in this way, taking up 1 st. extra on every row, keeping these extra sts. in st.st. until all sts. are worked on to 1 needle.

Leave these 44 sts. on a safety pin.

Now work a second yoke piece in exactly the same way, reversing the order of front and back neck sts. when picking up extra sts.

The Collar.—Now sl. neck sts. on to 2 needles and yoke sts. on to 2 other needles and work in rounds of k. 2, p. 2 rib thus, beg. at neck sts.:—

1st needle.—K. 2 tog., k. 1, * p. 2, k. 2; rep. from * to last 2 sts., p. 2.

2nd needle.—* K. 2, p. 2; rep. from * to end.

3rd needle.—As 1st needle.

4th needle.—As 2nd needle.

Continue in rounds of k. 2, p. 2 rib for 3½ ins.

Cast off loosely in rib.

Sew side edges of yokes along cast-off shoulder edges.

The Sleeves.—With right side of work facing, sl. a set of 10 sts. from safety pin on to a No. 10 needle, k. these 10 sts., then k. up 100 sts. evenly round armhole

Detail of the cable stitch panel.

This sweater is knitted in 4-ply wool. It has a polo neck, and "short" long sleeves which are both comfortable and practical for working.

edge, then k. 11 sts. from other safety pin.

Arrange these sts. on 4 needles (30, 30, 30, 31) and work 3 rounds in smooth fabric, with the 10th, 111th and the last st. in p.

Shape thus:—

Next round.—K. 7, k. 2 tog., p. 1, k. 100, p. 1, k. 2 tog., k. 7, p. 1.

Work 3 rounds in smooth fabric with p. sts.

Next round.—K. 6, k. 2 tog., p. 1, k. 100, p. 1, k. 2 tog., k. 6, p. 1.

Work 3 rounds in smooth fabric with p. sts.

Next round.—K. 5, k. 2 tog., p. 1, k. 100, p. 1, k. 2 tog., k. 5, p. 1.

Continue dec. in this way on every 4th round until 105 sts. remain.

Work 3 rounds without shaping.

Next round.—K. 2 tog., k. 100, k. 2 tog., p. 1.

Next round.—K. 102, p. 1.

Rep. last round 5 times.

Next round.—K. 1, k. 2 tog., k. 96, k. 2 tog., k. 1, p. 1.

Work 5 rounds without shaping with p. st.

Next round.—K. 1, k. 2 tog., k. 94, k. 2 tog., k. 1, p. 1.

Continue dec. in this way on every 6th round until 69 sts. remain.

Continue without shaping until work measures 14 ins. from picked-up armhole sts., finishing end of round.

Next round.—K. to last 2 sts., k. 2 tog.

Work 5 ins. in k. 2, p. 2 rib.

Cast off loosely in rib.

Work other sleeve in same way.

Press work lightly on wrong side with hot iron over damp cloth.

Cable Stitch Cardigan

INTERESTING TO KNIT—PRACTICAL TO WEAR

MATERIALS

17 oz. of 4-ply mixture yarn.
1 pair each of No. 9 and No. 12 needles.
8 buttons.

MEASUREMENTS

Length, 24 ins.
Chest, 38 ins. to 40 ins.
Sleeve seam, 20 ins.

TENSION

Using No. 9 needles, about 7 sts. to 1 in.

The Back.—Using No. 9 needles cast on 131 sts. and work in k. 1, p. 1 rib for 1 in.

Now change to patt. as follows:—

1st row.—K. 1, p. 2, k. 2, * k. 2 tog., inc. in next st. thus: K. 1, then k. again into the back of the st. before slipping it off the needle. p. 2, k. 1, p. 2, k. 2; rep. from * to last 6 sts., k. 2 tog., inc. in next st., p. 2, k. 1.

2nd and every alternate row.—K. 3, * p. 5, k. 5; rep. from * to last 8 sts., p. 5, k. 3.

3rd row.—K. 1, p. 2, k. 1, * k. 2 tog., inc. in next st. (as in 1st row), k. 1, p. 2, k. 1, p. 2, k. 1; rep. from * to last 7 sts., k. 2 tog., inc. in next st., k. 1, p. 2, k. 1.

5th row.—K. 1, p. 2, * k. 2 tog., inc. in next st., k. 2, p. 2, k. 1, p. 2; rep. from * to last 8 sts., k. 2 tog., inc. in next st., k. 2, p. 2, k. 1.

6th row.—As 2nd row.

These 6 rows form the patt.

Continue in patt. until work measures 15½ ins., ending with row on wrong side; then shape armholes.

Cast off 10 sts. at the beg. of the next 2 rows, then dec. 1 st. at both ends of every row until 91 sts. remain.

Continue without further dec. until work measures 24 ins., ending with row on wrong side, then shape shoulders.

Cast off 7 sts. at the beg. of the next 8 rows.

Cast off remaining 35 sts. for back of neck.

Before commencing fronts, make 2 pocket linings as follows:—

Using No. 9 needles cast on 35 sts and work in st.st. for 4 ins.

Leave on spare needle.

The Right Front.—Using No. 9 needles cast on 71 sts. and work as follows:—

1st row.—K. 10, work in k. 1, p. 1 to end.

2nd row.—K. 1, p. 1 rib until 10 sts. remain, k. 10.

Rep. these 2 rows until work measures 1 in. ending with row on wrong side of work.

Now work in patt. as for back, keeping the 10 g.sts. for front border

Continue in this way until work measures 5 ins., ending with row on wrong side.

Next row.—K. 10, patt. 13 sts., sl. the next 35 sts. on to a safety pin, slip the sts. of one pocket lining on to left-hand needle continue across these sts. in patt.; patt. to end.

Continue in patt. until work measures 15½ ins., ending with row on wrong side of work, then shape neck and armholes.

Next row.—K. 10, work 2 tog., patt. to end.

The cardigan—the garment that belongs to all ages of man! It is the most useful of all knitted garments, and if you choose this mock cable design, you will find it as much fun to work as it is practical to wear.

Next row.—Cast off 10 sts., patt. to last 10 sts., k. 10.

Next row.—K. 10 work in patt. to last 2 sts., work 2 tog.

Next row.—Work 2 tog., patt. to last 10 sts., k. 10.

Next row.—K. 10, work 2 tog., patt. to last 2 sts., work 2 tog.

Next row.—Work 2 tog., patt. to last 10 sts., k. 10.

Rep. the last 4 rows until 10 sts. have been dec. at underarm.

Then continue dec. at neck edge only on every 4th row, until there are 38 sts. left on needle.

Continue without further dec. until work measures 24 ins., ending with row on right side of work. then shape shoulders.

Cast off 7 sts. at the beg. of next 4 rows from armhole edge.

Now work in g.st. on the remaining 10 sts. for 2½ ins., for half back of neck.

Cast off.

The Pocket Top.—Slip the 35 sts. left for pocket top on to a No. 9 needle, join on wool and work in k. 1, p. 1 rib for 1 in. Cast off fairly loosely in ribbing.

The Left Front.—Using No. 9 needles, cast on 71 sts. and work as follows:—

The original cardigan was knitted in a mixture yarn of a medium brown colour. The mock cable detail is on the left.

1st row.—Rib in k. 1, p. 1 to last 10 sts., k. 10.

2nd row.—K. 10, rib to end.

Rep. these 2 rows for 1 in.

Change to patt. and make a buttonhole as follows:—

1st row.—Patt. to last 10 sts., k. 3, cast off 4, k. 3.

2nd row.—K. 3, cast on 4, k. 3, patt. to end.

Continue in patt. and g.st. border, making 7 more buttonholes in the same way at intervals of 3 ins. (measured from commencement of last buttonhole).

When front measures 5 ins., insert pocket lining in the same way as on first front.

Continue in patt. and g.st. border until work measures 15½ ins., ending with row on right side of work, then shape for armhole and front edge and complete to correspond with right front.

The Pocket Top.—Slip the 35 sts. from safety pin on to a No. 9 needle and work in rib to match right front pocket.

The Sleeves.—Using No. 12 needles cast on 70 sts. and work 3 ins. in k. 1, p. 1 rib, inc. 1 st. at end of last row.

Change to No. 9 needles and patt. as for back, inc. 1 st. at each end of 5th and every following 6th row until there are 111 sts. on needle.

Continue without further shaping until work measures 20 ins., ending with row on wrong side of work, then shape top.

Continue in patt., dec. 1 st. at both ends of every row until 21 sts. remain.

Cast off.

Make-up.—Press work lightly on the wrong side, using a hot iron over a damp cloth.

Join side, shoulder and sleeve seams with a narrow backstitch.

Pin sleeves into armholes, matching seams to side seams, backstitch into position.

Sew down pocket linings on the wrong side of work, and stitch ends of pocket tops in place on the right side as neatly as possible.

Oversew ends of neck border and place at centre of back of neck; sew into position.

Sew on buttons to correspond with buttonholes.

Press all seams.

Striped Shirt

FOR SUMMER SPORTS WEAR

MATERIALS

5 oz. 3-ply wool.
4 oz. fine knitting cotton.
2 No. 9 knitting needles pointed at both ends and 2 No. 12 knitting needles.
3 buttons.

MEASUREMENTS

Chest, 40 ins.
Length, 27 ins.
Sleeve seam, 6 ins.

TENS.ON

7 sts. to 1 in.

The main part of garment is worked in st.st. stripes of 1 row wool, 1 row cotton.

Work the stripes as follows to avoid unnecessary ends: K. 1 row in wool, sl. sts. back again to other end of needle and k. 1 row in cotton; now p. 1 row in wool, then sl. sts. back again to other end of needle and p. 1 row in cotton.

Continue in this way throughout except for shoulder shapings and last 8 rows of top of sleeve shaping; work these in usual way, breaking off thread at end of rows, or use 2 balls of wool and 2 balls of cotton.

The Back.—With No. 9 needles and wool cast on 140 sts. Work ¾ in. in k. 1, p. 1 rib.

Join in cotton and continue in st.st. stripes (as above) until work measures 19 ins., finishing with 1 k. row.

Shape Armholes thus: Continue in stripes, cast off 6 sts. beg. of next 2 rows, then dec. 1 st. both ends of every row until 104 sts. remain.

Continue straight until work measures 27 ins., finishing p. rows.

Shape Shoulders thus:—

Cast off 9 sts. beg. of next 6 rows, cast off 8 sts. beg. of next 2 rows.

Cast off remaining sts.

The Front. The Pocket Lining.—With No. 9 needles and wool cast on 28 sts. Join in cotton and work in st.st. stripes for 4 ins., finishing 2 k. rows.

Leave sts. on spare needle.

Now work for front exactly as given for back until work measures 19 ins., finishing with 1 k. row.

Detail of the stripe stitch.

Shape Armholes and Divide for Opening thus: Continue in stripes, cast off 6 sts. beg. of next 2 rows, then dec. 1 st. both ends of next 5 rows, thus finishing with 2 p. rows.

Next row.—K. 2 tog., k. 54, turn. Leave remaining sts. on spare needle.

Continue in st.st. stripes on these 55 sts., dec. 1 st. at armhole edge on every row until 49 sts. remain.

Continue straight until work measures 21¼ ins., finishing with 1 k. row.

Next row.—K. 10, cast off 28 sts. for pocket, k. to end.

Next row.—P. 11, p. 28 sts. for pocket lining, p. 10.

Continue straight on 49 sts. until work measures 25 ins., finishing front opening edge.

Shape Neck and Shoulder thus:—Cast off 3 sts. beg. of next row, then dec. 1 st. both ends of every row until 38 sts. remain, then dec. on every alternate row until 35 sts. remain.

Continue straight until work measures 27 ins., finishing armhole edge.

Next row.—Cast off 9, work to end.

Next row.—Work to end.

Rep. last 2 rows twice.

Cast off remaining sts.

Return to remaining sts., sl. centre 6 sts. on to a safety-pin and leave for front border, rejoin wool and continue in stripes on remaining 56 sts., dec. 1 st. at armhole edge on every row until 49 sts. remain.

Continue straight until work measures 25 ins., finishing front opening edge.

Shape Neck and Shoulder as for first side.

The Left-front Border.—Slip the 6 sts. from safety-pin on to a No. 12 needle and with right side of work facing and using wool throughout, work thus:—

1st row.—K. twice into first st., k. 1, p. 1, k. twice into next st., k. 1, p. 1.

Work ¾ in. in rib on 8 sts., finishing row on wrong side.

Cotton and wool in two colours combine to make a striped shirt that, with short sleeves and adaptable neckline, is perfect for summer sportswear.

Next row.—Rib 3, cast off 3 sts. for a buttonhole, rib to end.

Next row.—Rib 2, cast on 3, rib 3.

* Continue in rib for 2 ins., then make another buttonhole in next 2 rows.

Rep. from * once, then continue in rib until border is same length as front edge when slightly stretched. Cast off in rib.

The Right Front Border.—With No. 12 needles and wool k. up 8 sts. at back of left front border at lower edge.

Work in k. 1, p. 1 rib until this border is same length as first. Cast off in rib.

The Sleeves.—With No. 9 needles and

The shirt is worked in stocking stitch of 1 row wool and 1 row cotton. Navy and natural were the colours used for the original.

wool cast on 106 sts. and work ¾ in. in k. 1, p. 1 rib. Join in cotton and continue in st.st. stripes until work measures 6 ins., finishing with 1 k. row.

Shape Top thus: Cast off 6 sts. beg. of next 2 rows, dec. 1 st. both ends of every row until 74 sts. remain.

Cast off 8 sts. beg. of next 8 rows.

Cast off remaining sts.

The Collar.—With No. 12 needles and wool cast on 189 sts.

Work 2 rows in k. 1, p. 1 rib, beg. and finishing 1st row with k. 1.

3rd row.—K. 1, p. 1, sl. 1, k. 1, p.s.s.o., work in rib to last 4 sts., k. 2 tog., p. 1, k. 1.

4th row.—Work in rib.

Rep. last 2 rows until work measures 2½ ins.

Cast off 30 sts. beg. of next 2 rows, then cast off 6 sts. beg. of next 4 rows.

Cast off remaining sts.

The Pocket Border.—With No. 12 needles and wool and with right side of work facing, k. up 32 sts. evenly along cast-off edge of pocket.

Work ¾ in. in k. 1, p. 1 rib.

Cast off loosely in rib.

Make-up.—Press work lightly on wrong side with hot iron over damp cloth.

Join side, shoulder and sleeve seams.

Backstitch sleeves into armholes, matching seams.

Sew front borders to front edges.

Sew round pocket lining on wrong side and down side edges of pocket border.

Pin centre of cast-off edge of collar, to centre back of neck and sew collar round neck edge, finishing in centre of front border.

Sew on buttons to match buttonholes.

Press seams.

Sleeveless Pullover

FEATURING A ROUND NECK

MATERIALS

6 oz. of 4-ply wool.

2 No. 8 and 2 No. 12 knitting needles.

MEASUREMENTS

Length, 23 ins.

Across chest, 13 ins.

Under arms, 38 ins.

TENSION

About 7 sts. to 1 in. on No. 8 needles.

The Back.—With No. 12 needles cast on 112 sts. and work as follows:—

1st row.—K. 1, * p. 1, k. 2, p. 4, k. 2, p. 1; rep. from * to last st., k. 1.

2nd row.—K. 2, * p. 2, k. 4, p. 2, k. 2; rep. from * to end of row.

Rep. these 2 rows for 4 ins., ending with a 2nd row of rib.

Change to No. 8 needles and continue in patt. thus:—

1st row.—K. 1, * p. 1, k. 2, p. 4, k. 2, p. 1; rep. from * to last st., k. 1.

2nd row.—K. 2, * p. 2, k. 4, p. 2, k. 2; rep. from * to end of row.

3rd to 8th rows.—Rep. 1st and 2nd rows 3 times.

9th row.—K. 1, * p. 1, k. 1, k. into back of second st. on left-hand needle, then k. first st., sl. both sts. off needle tog., p. 2, k. into front of second st. on left-hand needle, then k. first st. and sl. both sts. off needle tog., k. 1, p. 1; rep. from * to last st., k. 1.

10th row.—K. 2, * p. 3, k. 2; rep. from * to end of row.

11th row.—K. 1, * p. 1, k. 3, p. 2, k. 3,

p. 1; rep. from * to last st., k. 1.

12th row.—As 10th row.

13th and 14th row.—Rep. 11th and 12th rows.

15th row.—K. 1, * p. 1, k. 2, k. into back of second st. on left-hand needle, then k. first st. and sl. both sts. off needle tog., k. into front of second st. on left-hand needle, then k. first st. and sl. both sts. off needle tog., k. 2, p. 1; rep. from * to last st., k. 1.

16th row.—K. 2, * p. 8, k. 2; rep. from * to end of row.

17th row.—K. 1, * p. 1, k. 8, p. 1; rep. from * to last st., k. 1.

18th row.—As 16th row.

Detail of pullover stitch.

Lazy days call for comfortable clothes, and that is the cue for the sleeveless pullover's entry. It is an informal garment, ideal for slipping on over sports shirts, yet not bulky when worn under a jacket.

Rep. these 18 rows, inc. 1 st. at each end of next and every following 3rd row until there are 136 sts. on needle (working inc. sts. into patt.), continuing without shaping until work measures 15 ins. from commencement.

Shape Armholes thus: Continue in patt., cast off 8 sts. at beg. of next 2 rows, then dec. 1 st. at both ends of next 8 rows, 104 sts. remain, continue without shaping until work measures 22½ ins. from commencement.

Shape Neck thus: Patt. 31 sts., cast off 42 sts., continue in patt. on last 31 sts. until work measures 23 ins., cast off 10 sts. at armhole edge on next 2 alternate rows.

Cast off remaining sts. Join wool to remaining 31 sts. and work to match other shoulder.

The Front.—Work as back until work measures 19 ins. from commencement and there are 104 sts. on needle.

Shape Neck thus: Continue in patt., work 41 sts., cast off 22 sts., work on last 41 sts. as follows: dec. 1 st. at neck edge on next 10 rows (31 sts.), continue without shaping until work measures 23 ins.

Cast off 10 sts. at armhole edge on next 2 alternate rows.

Cast off remaining sts. Work remaining 41 sts. to match.

The Neck Band.—With No. 12 needles cast on 164 sts. and work in k. 2, p. 2 rib until band is 1 in. in depth.

Cast off loosely.

The Armhole Bands (both alike).—With No. 12 needles cast on 132 sts. and work in k. 2, p. 2 rib until work is 1 in. in depth. Cast off loosely.

Make-up.—Pin work out to measurements stated and press under a damp cloth with hot iron.

Join shoulder and side seams. Oversew neck band round neck and armhole bands round armholes.

Press all seams.

The round neck is a popular feature of this pullover, and the stitch is new and effective. The original was knitted in soft grey, in 4-ply wool.

Lightweight Sweater

KNITTED IN STOCKING STITCH

MATERIALS

11 oz. of 3-ply wool.
1 pair each No. 11, 12 and 14 needles.

MEASUREMENTS

Length, 23 ins.
Chest, 42 ins.
Sleeve seam, 21 ins.

TENSION

Using No. 11 needles about 17 sts. to 2 ins.

The Back.—Using No. 12 needles cast on 152 sts. and work in k. 1, p. 1 rib for 4 ins.

Change to No. 11 needles and work in st.st. (k. 1 row, p. 1 row), inc. 1 st. at the beg. and end of 1st and every following 6th row until there are 176 sts. on needle.

Continue without further shaping until work measures 15 ins., ending with row on wrong side of work, then shape armholes thus:—

Cast off 12 sts. at the beg. of the next 2 rows, then dec. 1 st. at both ends of every row until 118 sts. remain.

Continue without further shaping until work measures 23 ins., ending with a row on the wrong side, then shape neck and shoulders thus:—

Cast off 9 sts. at beg. of next 6 rows and 10 sts. at beg. of following 2 rows.

Cast off remaining sts.

The Front.—Work exactly as given for back until armhole shapings are completed and 118 sts. remain, then divide for neck thus:—

With right side of work facing k. 57, cast off 4 sts., k. 57.

Now work on the last set of sts. for right side of front, dec. 1 st. at neck edge on the 2nd and every 3rd following row until there are 37 sts. left.

Continue without shaping until work measures 23 ins., ending at armhole edge, then shape shoulder.

1st row.—Cast off 9 sts., work to end.

2nd row.—Work to end.

Rep. these 2 rows twice more. Cast off remaining 10 sts.

Rejoin wool to 2nd

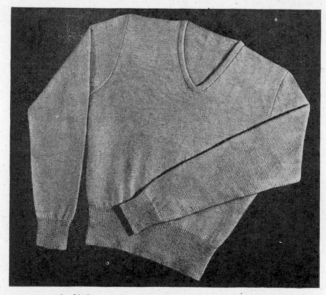

A lightweight sweater in 3-ply wool.

Every beginner can knit this sweater, and be thought the world of for doing so! Of classic style, it is knitted throughout in stocking stitch, and is a practical all-purpose garment. Notice the neat V neckline.

set of sts. at neck edge and work to match 1st side.

The Sleeves.—Using No. 12 needles cast on 76 sts. and work in k. 1, p. 1 rib for 3 ins.

Change to No. 11 needles and work in st.st., inc. 1 st. at both ends of 1st and every 6th row until there are 128 sts. on needles.

Continue without shaping until work measures 21 ins., ending with row on wrong side, then shape top thus:—

Dec. 1 st. at both ends of every row until 28 sts. remain. Cast off.

The Neck Border.—Using No. 14 needles cast on 10 sts. and work in g.st. (k. every row) for about 21 ins. Cast off.

Make-up.—Press the work lightly on the wrong side, using a hot iron over a damp cloth.

Join side, shoulder and sleeve seams with a narrow backstitch. Backstitch sleeves into armholes, matching seam to underarm seam.

Stitch the garter stitch border to neck edge, stretching border slightly.

Then fold border in half and hem down neatly on wrong side. Press all seams.

Long-sleeved Pullover

DESIGNED WITH A STRAIGHT NECKLINE

MATERIALS
12 oz. 3-ply wool.
2 No. 10 and 2 No. 12 knitting needles.
A short spare needle, pointed each end.

MEASUREMENTS
Length 23 ins.
Chest, 38 ins.
Sleeve seam, 20 ins.

TENSION
About 10 sts. to 1 in. measured over slightly stretched patt.
$7\frac{1}{2}$ sts. to 1 in. over st.st.

The Front and Back Alike.—Using No. 12 needles cast on with double wool by cable method 160 sts.

Work 4 ins. in k. 1, p. 1 rib using single wool.

Change to No. 10 needles and continue in patt. thus:—

1st row.—K. 2, * p. 6, k. 4; rep. from * to last 8 sts., p. 6, k. 2.

2nd row.—K. 1, p. 1, * k. 6, p. 4; rep. from * to last 8 sts., k. 6, p. 1, k. 1.

3rd row.—As 1st row.

4th row and all alternate rows.—As 2nd row.

5th row.—K. 2, * p. 6, sl. next 2 sts. on to spare needle, leave at back of work, k. next 2 sts., k. 2 sts. from spare needle; rep. from * to last 8 sts., p. 6, k. 2.

7th row.—As 1st row.

Detail of cable pattern.

A sweater of outstanding design is pictured here. The small cable rib gives a neatness of appearance that cannot help but be popular. A straight neckline adds an original touch and is very easy to knit.

9th row.—As 5th row.

11th row.—As 1st row.

13th row.—As 5th row.

15th to 20th rows.—Rep. 1st and 2nd rows 3 times.

Rep. these 20 rows, inc. 1 st. each end of every 8th row until there are 188 sts. on needle, working extra sts. into patt.

Continue straight in patt. until work measures 16 ins.

Shape Armholes thus: Continuing in patt., cast off 6 sts. at beg. of next 6 rows, dec. 1 st. each end of next 6 rows. Continue on 140 sts. until work measures 21¾ ins.

Change to k. 1, p. 1 rib, work 1¼ ins.

Next row.—Rib to last 10 sts., turn.

Rep. this row 7 times, leaving 60 sts. in centre.

Cast off 60 sts. loosely in rib. Work across each shoulder once to get even row for grafting.

Work another piece in same way, then graft shoulders.

The Sleeves.—With No. 12 needles cast on 90 sts. Work 3 ins. in k. 1, p. 1 rib.

Change to No. 10 needles. Continue in patt. as given for front, inc. 1 st. each end of every 5th row until there are 160 sts. on needle, working extra sts. into patt. Continue straight until work measures 20 ins.

Shape Top thus: Continue in patt., dec. 1 st. each end of every row until 44 sts. remain.

Cast off.

Make-up.—Press work lightly on wrong side with hot iron and damp cloth.

Join side and sleeve seams. Sew sleeves into armholes matching seams. Press.

Knitted in 3-ply wool, this jersey is lightweight and comfortably loose fitting. The straight neckline is wide enough to slip over the head easily.

Gloves and Scarf

IN SIMPLE COLOUR KNITTING

MATERIALS

3 oz. 3-ply wool dark shade.
3 oz. 3-ply wool light shade.
4 No. 13 and 4 No. 10 knitting needles.
To make separately: 1 oz. in dark and
½ oz. in light with No. 13 needles for
gloves; 2 oz. in dark and 2½ oz. in light
with No. 10 needles for scarf.

MEASUREMENTS

The Gloves: To fit average size.
The Scarf: Length, 40 ins.
Width, 7½ ins.

TENSION

With No. 13 needles, 9 sts. to 1 in.
With No. 10 needles, 7½ sts. to 1 in.

ADDITIONAL ABBREVIATIONS

Dk. = dark; lt. = light; m. 1 = make
1 st. by picking up thread between st.
just worked and next st. and k. 1 st.
into back of loop.

THE GLOVES

The Right-hand Glove.—With No. 13
needles and dk. wool cast on 64 sts. (20,
20, 24).

Work in rounds of k. 2, p. 2 rib for
2½ ins., finishing end of round.

Continue in patt., taking wool very
loosely across back of work when working
the Fair Isle.

1st round.—* K. 1 dk., k. 3 lt.; rep.
from * to end.

2nd round.—As 1st round.

3rd round.—Beg. thumb gusset: (K. 1
dk., k. 3 lt.) 8 times, k. 1 dk., k. 1 lt., m.
1, k. 1, m. 1 dk., k. 1 lt., (k. 1 dk., k. 3 lt.)
7 times.

4th round.—With dk. k. to end.

5th round.—(K. 1 dk., k. 1 lt.) 17 times,
k. 3 dk., k. 1 lt., (k. 1 dk., k. 1 lt.) 14 times.

6th round.—(K. 1 lt., k. 1 dk.) 17 times,
k. 3 dk., (k. 1 dk., k. 1 lt.) 14 times, k. 1 dk.

7th round.—With dk. k. 34, m. 1, k. 3,
m. 1, k. 29.

8th round.—(K. 2 lt., k. 1 dk., k. 1 lt.)
8 times. k. 2 lt., k. 5 dk., (k. 3 lt., k. 1 dk.)
7 times, k. 1 lt.

9th round.—As 8th round.

10th round.—As 8th round.
One patt. is now completed.

11th round.—(K. 1 dk., k. 3 lt.) 8 times,
k. 1 dk., k. 1 lt., m. 1, k. 5, m. 1 dk., k. 1
lt., (k. 1 dk., k. 3 lt.) 7 times.

Continue in this way, keeping continuity of patt. for main part with thumb
gusset in dk. wool, inc. 1 st. each side of
gusset on every 4th round until 82 sts.
are on needle. Work 1 round after last
inc. round.

Next round.—Patt. 34, sl. next 19 sts.
on to a short length of wool and leave
for thumb, cast on 5 sts., patt. to end.

Work 10 rounds in patt. on 68 sts.,
finishing end of round.

Next round.—Patt. 9, sl. these sts. on
to a safety-pin for fourth finger, patt. to
last 9 sts., sl. these 9 sts. on to a second
safety-pin, cast on 2 sts.

Work 2 more rounds in patt., thus
finishing with a 10th patt. round.

Break off lt. wool. With dk. k. 1 round.

Begin Fingers (work with dk. wool
throughout fingers and thumb):—

The First Finger. Next round.—K. 34,
sl. next 18 sts. on to a short length of
wool, then sl. first 16 sts. of round on to
same piece of wool, cast on 4 sts.

Arrange sts. on 3 needles.

Continue in smooth fabric on 22 sts. for 3 ins., finishing end of round.

Shape Top thus:—

Next round.—* K. 1, k. 2 tog.; rep. from * to last st., k. 1.

Next round.—K. to end.

Next round.—* K. 2 tog.; rep. from * to last st. k. 1.

Break off wool, thread through remaining sts., draw up and fasten off.

The Second Finger.—Return to main sts., sl. first 8 sts. back and front of hand on to 2 needles, rejoin wool and work thus:—

1st round.—K. up 4 sts. at base of first finger k. 8, cast on 4.

Arrange 24 sts. on 3 needles and work in rounds of smooth fabric for 3½ ins., finishing end of round.

Shape Top thus:—

Next round.—* K. 1, k. 2 tog.; rep. from * to end.

Next round.—K. to end.

Next round.—* K. 2 tog.; rep. from * to end.

Break off wool and complete to match first finger.

The Third Finger.—Sl. remaining 18 sts. on to needles, rejoin wool and work

Detail of two-colour pattern.

thus:—

1st round.—K. up 4 sts. at base of second finger, k. 9.

Arrange sts. on 3 needles and work in rounds of smooth fabric for 3 ins., finishing end of round.

Shape Top and complete as for first finger.

The Fourth Finger.—Sl. 18 sts. from wool on to needles, rejoin wool and work thus:—

1st round.—K. up 2 sts. at base of third finger, k. to end.

Arrange 20 sts. on 3 needles and work in rounds of smooth fabric for 2½ ins., finishing end of round.

Shape Top thus:—

Next round.—* K. 2 tog., k. 1; rep. from * to last 2 sts., k. 2 tog.

Next round.—K. to end.

Next round.—* K. 2 tog.; rep. from * to last st., k. 1.

Break off wool and complete to match first finger.

The Thumb.—Sl. 19 sts. on to needles, rejoin wool and work thus:—

1st round.—K. to end, k. up 5 sts. at cast-on edge.

Arrange 24 sts. on 3 needles and work in smooth fabric for 2½ ins., finishing end of round.

Shape Top as for second finger.

The Left-hand Glove.—Work ribbing as for right-hand glove, then begin patt.:

1st round.—* K. 3 lt., k. 1 dk.; rep. from * to end.

2nd round.—As 1st round.

3rd round.—(K. 3 lt., k. 1 dk.) 7 times, k. 1 lt., m. 1, k. 1, m. 1 dk., k. 1 lt., k. 1 dk., (k. 3 lt., k. 1 dk.) 8 times.

4th round.—With dk. k. to end.

5th round.—(K. 1 lt., k. 1 dk.) 14 times, k. 1 lt., k. 3 dk., (k. 1 lt., k. 1 dk.) 17 times.

6th round.—(K. 1 dk., k. 1 lt.) 14 times, k. 4 dk., (k. 1 dk., k. 1 lt.) 17 times.

7th round.—With dk. k. 29, m. 1, k. 3, m. 1, k. 34.

A simple two-colour pattern worked in dark red and grey, was used for the matching scarf and gloves. The same instructions can, of course, be adapted to a plain set, but the gay colour scheme would please most men.

The scarf and gloves are knitted on four needles in 3-ply wool.

Now complete hand, fingers and thumb exactly as given for right-hand glove.

Press work lightly with hot iron over damp cloth.

THE SCARF

With No. 10 needles and dk. wool cast on 112 sts. (36, 36, 40).

Work in patt., taking wool not in use loosely across back of work:—

1st round.—* K. 1 dk., k. 3 lt.; rep. from * to end.

2nd round.—As 1st round.

3rd round.—As 1st round.

4th round.—With dk. k. to end.

5th round.—* K. 1 dk., k. 1 lt.; rep. from * to end.

6th round.—* K. 1 lt., k. 1 dk.; rep. from * to end.

7th round.—With dk. k. to end.

8th round.—* K. 2 lt., k. 1 dk., k. 1 lt.; rep. from * to end.

9th round.—As 8th round.

10th round.—As 8th round.

Rep. these 10 rounds until work measures approximately 40 ins., finishing with a 10th patt. round.

Cast off with dk. wool.

Fold work flat, making beg. of the round one side edge, and press with a hot iron over damp cloth.

Slip stitch open ends and add fringe. (Instructions given on page 242.)

8th round.—(K. 1 lt., k. 1 dk., k. 2 lt.) 7 times, k. 1 lt., k. 5 dk., (k. 3 lt., k. 1 dk.) 8 times, k. 2 lt.

9th round.—As 8th round.

10th round.—As 8th round.

11th round.—(K. 3 lt., k. 1 dk.) 7 times, k. 1 lt., m. 1, k. 5, m. 1 dk., k. 1 lt., k. 1 dk., (k. 3 lt., k. 1 dk.) 8 times.

Continue in patt. as given for right-hand glove until 82 sts are on needle, finishing with 1 round after last inc. round.

Next round.—Patt. 29, sl. next 19 sts. on to a short length of wool and leave for thumb, cast on 5 sts., patt. to end.

Plain Socks

WITH THREE DIFFERENT TOES AND HEELS

No. 1. With Common Heel and Flat Toe

MATERIALS

4 oz. 3-ply wool.
4 No. 13 needles.

MEASUREMENTS

Length of leg to top of heel, 11 ins.
Length of foot, 11 ins. (adjustable).

TENSION

$9\frac{1}{2}$ sts. to 1 in.

Cast on 80 sts. (28, 28, 24).
Work 4 ins. in k. 2, p. 2 rib in rounds.
Work in smooth fabric (every round k.) for a further 4 ins.

Shape Leg thus:—

1st round.—K. 2 tog., k. to last 2 sts. of round, sl. 1, k. 1, p.s.s.o.

Work 6 rounds without shaping.

Rep. the last 7 rounds until 70 sts. remain.

Continue without shaping until work measures 11 ins. from cast-on edge, finishing end of round.

Divide sts. for heel thus:—

K. 18 sts. on to one needle, then sl. the last 18 sts. of the round on to other end of same needle. (These 36 sts. are for the heel.)

Divide the remaining sts. on two needles and leave for instep.

Work 39 rows on the heel sts. in st.st. starting with a p. row.

Next row.—K. 18, break wool, then graft the two sets of 18 sts. tog.

Rejoin wool and with right side of work facing pick up and k. 21 sts. along heel flap to bottom of heel, then with 2nd needle pick up 21 sts. along other side of heel flap.

Place instep sts. on to one needle, then k. across these sts. (76).

Work 1 round without shaping.

Next round. 1st needle.—K. 1, k. 2 tog., k. to end.

2nd needle.—K. to last 3 sts., k. 2 tog., k. 1.

3rd needle.—K. to end.

Work 2 rounds without shaping. Rep. the last 3 rounds until 68 sts. remain.

Continue without shaping until work measures $8\frac{1}{2}$ ins. (or length required) from back of heel.

Shape Toe thus:—

1st needle.—K. 1, k. 2 tog., k. to end.

2nd needle.—K. to last 3 sts., k. 2 tog., k. 1.

3rd needle.—K. 1, k. 2 tog., k. to last 3 sts., k. 2 tog., k. 1.

Work 1 round without shaping.

Rep. these 2 rounds until 20 sts. remain.

Slip sts. from 1st and 2nd needles on to one needle, place two sets sts. tog. and graft. (Instructions on page 243.)

No. 2. With Dutch or Horseshoe Heel and Wide Toe

Work as given for sock No. 1 until heel is reached.

Divide for heel as given and work 35 rows in st.st.

Turn Heel thus:—

1st row.—K. 22, sl. 1, k. 1, p.s.s.o., turn.

2nd row.—P. 9, p. 2 tog., turn.

3rd row.—K. 9, sl. 1, k. 1, p.s.s.o., turn.

Rep. these 2 rows until all side sts. are worked off and 10 sts. remain, ending with a p. row.

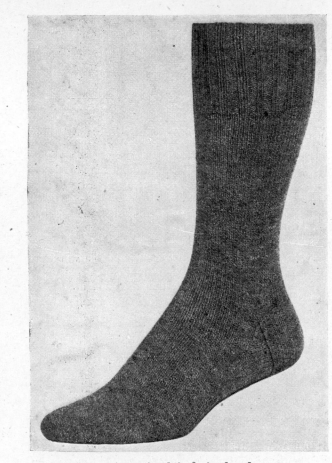

A man's plain knitted sock.

Shape Toe thus:—

1st round. 1st needle. —K. to last 6 sts., k. 2 tog., k. 4.

2nd needle.—K. 4, k. 2 tog., k. to last 6 sts., k. 2 tog., k. 4.

3rd needle.—K. 4, k. 2 tog., k. to end.

Work 3 rounds without shaping.

5th round. — As 1st round.

Work 2 rounds without shaping.

8th round. — As 1st round.

Work 1 round without shaping.

10th round. — As 1st round.

Work 1 round without shaping.

12th round. — As 1st round.

13th round. — Work without shaping.

Rep. rounds 12 and 13 until 26 sts. remain. Slip sts. from 1st and 3rd needles on to one needle. Place 2 sets of sts. tog. and graft. (Instructions on page 243.)

K. 10 sts., then on to this same needle pick up and k. 18 sts. along side of heel flap, then with 2nd needle k. across instep, then with 3rd needle pick up and k. 18 sts. down other side of heel flap, then 5 sts. from 1st needle.

Work 1 round without shaping.

1st needle.—K. to last 3 sts., k. 2 tog., k. 1.

2nd needle.—Work to end.

3rd needle.—K. 1, k. 2 tog., k. to end.

Rep. these 2 rounds until 68 sts. remain.

Continue without shaping until work measures 9 ins. from back of heel, finishing end of round.

No. 3. With Balbriggan Heel and Round Toe

Work as given for sock No. 1 until heel is reached.

Divide for heel thus: K. 20, turn.

Sl. 20 sts. from 3rd needle on to end of same needle.

These 40 sts. are for the heel.

Divide the remaining sts. on to 2 needles and leave for instep.

Work 35 rows in st.st. starting with a p. row.

36th row.—(K. 8, k. 2 tog.) twice, (k. 2 tog., k. 8) twice.

37th row.—P.

38th row.—K. 8, k. 2 tog. k. 6, k. 2 tog., k. 2 tog., k. 6, k. 2 tog., k. 8.

39th row.—P.

40th row.—K. 8, k. 2 tog., k. 4, k. 2 tog., k. 2 tog., k. 4, k. 2 tog., k. 8

41st row.—P.

42nd row.—K. 8, k. 2 tog., k. 2, k. 2 tog., k. 2 tog., k. 2, k. 2 tog., k. 8.

43rd row.—P.

44th row.—K. 8, k. 2 tog., k. 2 tog., k. 2 tog., k. 2 tog., k. 8.

45th row.—P. 10.

Graft the 2 sets of 10 sts. tog.

Continue as given for sock No. 1, but pick up 23 sts. each side of heel flap instead of 21. Dec. down to 64 instead of 68.

Continue without shaping until foot measures 8½ ins. Shape thus:—

1st round.—* K. 6, k. 2 tog.; rep. from * to end. Work 6 rounds without shaping.

8th round.—* K. 5, k. 2 tog.; rep. from * to end.

Work 5 rounds without shaping.

14th round.—* K. 4, k. 2 tog.; rep. from * to end.

Work 4 rounds without shaping.

19th round.—* K. 3, k. 2 tog.; rep. from * to end.

Work 3 rounds without shaping.

23rd round.—* K. 2, k. 2 tog.; rep. from * to end.

Work 2 rounds without shaping.

26th round.—* K. 1, k. 2 tog.; rep. from * to end.

27th round.—K. all round.

K. 2 tog. all round. Thread end through remaining sts. Draw up and fasten off.

*Top line, from left to right: Round Toe, Wide Toe, and Flat Toe.
Below, left to right: Common Heel, Dutch Heel, Balbriggan Heel.*

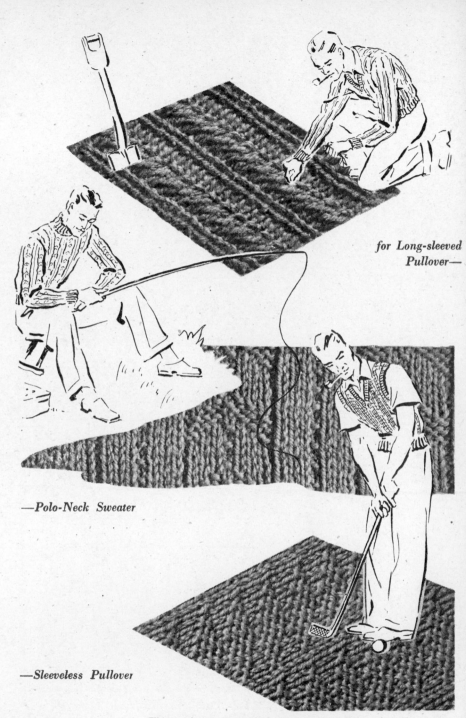

for Long-sleeved Pullover—

—Polo-Neck Sweater

—Sleeveless Pullover

Three alternative stitch suggestions.

Alternative Stitches

SUGGESTED FOR MEN'S GARMENTS

SIMPLE stitches that give a closely knitted fabric are best for men's garments. On the opposite page are three suggestions for stitches that would meet with any man's approval. The "Gardening" stitch would be an ideal alternative for the long-sleeved pullover shown on page 112; the "Fishing" stitch is suggested for the polo-necked sweater on page 115; the "Golfing" stitch for the sleeveless V-necked pullover pictured on page 110.

The time spent on making hand-knitted garments for the menfolk is repaid by long wear if you have taken care in choosing your materials and tools. Learn to discriminate between knitting yarns and choose the right kind for the purpose, tough wiry wool for hard wear and outdoor garments, soft, evenly spun yarns for indoor and underwear. Good needles, too, are essential for smooth knitting and comfort in working. Composition-covered steel needles, although more expensive, last longer and give better service than any other type.

Plastic needles that become bent should be placed in a jug of hot water and straightened when the heat has softened them.

"Gardening" Stitch

Number of stitches divisible by 6, plus 2.

1st row.—K. 1, * k. 1, p. 1; rep. from * to last st., k. 1.

2nd row.—K. 1, * sl. next 2 sts. on to spare needle and leave at front of work, k. 1, p. 1 on next 2 sts., then k. 1, p. 1 on sts. from spare needle, k. 1, p. 1; rep. from * to last st., k. 1. Rep. these 2 rows.

"Fishing" Stitch

Number of stitches divisible by 16, plus 1.

1st row.—K. 1, * p. 3, k. 1; rep. from * to end.

2nd row.—K. 4, p. 2, k. 5, p. 2, * k. 7, p. 2, k. 5, p. 2; rep. from *, ending with k. 4.

3rd row.—K. 1, * p. 3, k. 3, p. 1, k. 1, p. 1, k. 3, p. 3, k. 1; rep. from * to end.

4th row.—K. 4, p. 4, k. 1, p. 4, * k. 7, p. 4, k. 1, p. 4; rep. from *, ending with k. 4.

5th row.—K. 1, * p. 3, k. 1, p. 1, k. 5, p. 1, k. 1, p. 3, k. 1; rep. from * to end.

6th row.—K. 4, p. 1, k. 2, p. 1, k. 1, p. 1, k. 2, p. 1, * k. 7, p. 1, k. 2, p. 1, k. 1, p. 1, k. 2, p. 1; rep. from * and k. last 4 sts.

7th row.—K. 1, * p. 3, k. 1; rep. from * to end.

8th row.—K. 4, p. 1, * k. 7, p. 1; rep. from * and k. last 4 sts.

Rep. these 8 rows.

"Golfing" Stitch

Number of stitches divisible by 8.

1st row.—* P. 4, k. 4; rep. from * to end.

2nd row.—P. 3, * k. 4, p. 4; rep. from * to last 5 sts., k. 4, p. 1.

3rd row.—K. 2, * p. 4, k. 4; rep. from * to last 6 sts., p. 4, k. 2.

4th row.—P. 1, * k. 4, p. 4; rep. from * to last 7 sts., k. 4, p. 3.

Rep. these 4 rows.

The stitches pictured opposite, like those on page 124, are suitable for most of the men's garments shown in this book. Before beginning your garment, knit up a sample of the stitch you have chosen so that you can see how it is worked, and can then adapt it to the garment you have selected.

"Yacht" Stitch Number One

Number of stitches divisible by 4, plus 2.

1st row.—K. 1, p. 1, * k. 2, p. 2; rep. from * to end.

2nd row.—K. 2, * p. 2, k. 2; rep. from * to end.

3rd row.—K. 1, p. 1, * k. 1 into row below of next st., k. next st. in usual way, k. 1, k. 1 again into this same st. in row below, p. 2; rep. from * to end.

4th row.—K. 2, * p. 4, k. 2; rep. from * to end.

5th row.—K. 1, * k. 2 tog., p. 2, sl. 1, k. 1, p.s.s.o.; rep. from * to last st., k. 1.

6th row.—As 1st row.

Rep. these 6 rows.

"Yacht" Stitch Number Two

Number of stitches divisible by 16.

1st row.—* K. 6, p. 2; rep. from * to end.

2nd row.—* K. 2, p. 6; rep. from *.

3rd row.—* K. 1, p. 1, k. 4, p. 2, k. 4, p 1, k. 1, p. 2; rep. from *.

4th row.—* K. 2, p. 1, k. 2, p. 3, k. 2, p. 3, k. 2, p. 1; rep. from *.

5th row.—* K. 2, p. 2; rep. from *.

6th row.—* K. 2, p. 3, k. 2, p. 1, k. 2, p. 1, k. 2, p. 3; rep. from *.

7th row.—* K. 4, p. 1, k. 1, p. 2, k. 1, p. 1, k. 4, p. 2; rep. from *.

8th row.—As 2nd row.

Rep. these 8 rows.

"Yacht" Stitch Number Three

Number of stitches divisible by 8, plus 1.

1st row.—P. 4, * k. 1, p. 7; rep. from * to last 5 sts., k. 1, p. 4.

2nd row.—K. 3, * p. 3, k. 5; rep. from * to last 6 sts., p. 3, k. 3.

3rd row.—P. 2, * k. 5, p. 3; rep. from * to last 7 sts., k. 5, p. 2.

4th row.—K. 1, * p. 7, k. 1; rep. from * to end.

5th row.—K. to end.

6th row.—As 4th row.

7th row.—As 3rd row.

8th row.—As 2nd row.

Rep. these 8 rows.

"Yacht" Stitch Number Four

Number of stitches divisible by 4, plus 3.

1st row.—K. 1, * p. 1, k. 3; rep. from * to last 2 sts., p. 1, k. 1.

2nd row.—K. 1, * p. 1, k. 1; rep. from * to end of row.

Rep. these 2 rows.

"Yacht" Stitch Number Five

Number of stitches divisible by 8, plus 2.

1st row.—* K. 2, p. 2; rep. from * to last 2 sts., k. 2.

2nd row.—K. 1, p. 1, * k. 2, p. 2; rep. from * to last 4 sts., k. 2, p. 1, k. 1.

Rep. these 2 rows for 2 ins., ending with a 2nd row of rib

Continue in following patt:—

1st row.—K. 2, * p. 2, k. 2nd st. on left-hand needle and sl. off over the 1st st., w.fd., then k. the 1st st., p. 2, k. 2; rep. from * to end.

2nd row.—P. 2, * k. 2, p. 1, k. twice into next loop (by working in front and back of loop), p. 1, k. 2, p. 2; rep. from * to end.

3rd row.—K. 2, * p. 2, k. 1, p. 2, k. 1, p. 2, k. 2; rep. from * to end.

4th row.—P. 2, * k. 2, p. 1, k. 2, p. 1, k. 2, p. 2; rep. from * to end.

5th row.—As 3rd row.

6th row.—As 4th row.

7th row.—K. 2, * p. 2, sl. 1, k. 1, p.s.s.o., k. 2 tog., p. 2, k. 2; rep. from * to end.

8th row.—P. 2, * k. 2, p. 2; rep. from * to end.

Rep. these 8 rows.

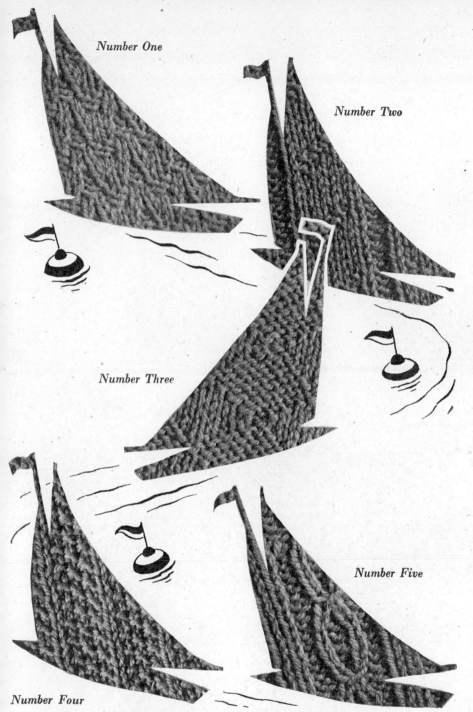

Number One

Number Two

Number Three

Number Four

Number Five

Five stitches race for popularity.

Distinctive Stitches

ONE FOR SWEATERS, THE OTHER FOR GARMENTS AND ACCESSORIES ON OPPOSITE PAGE

"Mock Cable" Rib (below

Number of stitches divisible by 10 plus 1.

1st row.—K. 1, p. 2, k. 2, * k. 2 tog., inc. in next st. thus: K. 1, then k. again into the back of the st. before slipping it off the needle, p. 2, k. 1, p. 2, k. 2; rep. from * to last 6 sts., k. 2 tog., inc. in next st., p. 2, k. 1.

2nd and each alternate row.—K. 3, * p. 5, k. 5; rep. from * to last 8 sts., p. 5, k. 3.

Detail of "mock cable" rib stitch suitable for men's sweater.

3rd row.—K. 1, p. 2, k. 1, * k. 2 tog., inc. in next st. (as in 1st row), k. 1, p. 2, k. 1, p. 2, k. 1; rep. from * to last 7 sts., k. 2 tog., inc. in next st., k. 1, p. 2, k. 1.

5th row.—K. 1, p. 2, * k. 2 tog., inc. in next st., k. 2, p. 2, k. 1, p. 2; rep. from * to last 8 sts., k. 2 tog., inc. in next st., k. 2, p. 2, k. 1.

6th row.—As 2nd row.

Rep. these 6 rows.

"Honeycomb" Stitch (opposite page)

Number of stitches divisible by 4, plus 2.

1st row.—K. 1, p. 1, * k. 2, p. 2; rep. from * to end.

2nd row.—K. 2, * p. 2, k. 2; rep. from * to end.

3rd row.—K. 1, p. 1, * k. 1 into row below of next st., k. next st. in usual way, k. 1, k. 1 again into this same st. in row below, p. 2; rep. from * to end.

4th row.—K. 2, * p. 4, k. 2; rep. from * to end.

5th row.—K. 1, * k. 2 tog., p. 2, sl. 1, k. 1, p.s.s.o.; rep. from * to last st., k. 1.

6th row.—As 1st row.

7th row.—As 2nd row.

8th row.—As 1st row.

9th row.—K. 1, * k. 1, k. again into this same st. in row below, p. 2, k. 1 into row below of next st., k. next st. in usual way; rep. from * to last st., k. 1.

10th row.—K. 1, p. 2, * k. 2, p. 4; rep. from * to last 5 sts., k. 2, p. 3.

11th row.—K. 1, p. 1, * sl. 1, k. 1, p.s.s.o., k. 2 tog., p. 2; rep. from * to end.

12th row.—As 2nd row.

Rep. these 12 rows.

An attractive " Honeycomb " Stitch in which to make this outfit.

Children's Garments

Baby Wear

DAINTY KNITTED DRESS AND
MATCHING MATINÉE JACKET

DRESS

MATERIALS

3½ oz. 3-ply wool.
2 No. 9 and 2 No. 12 knitting needles.
A fine crochet hook.
6 small buttons.

MEASUREMENTS

Length, 16 ins.
Chest, 18 ins.
Sleeve seam, 2 ins.

TENSION

7 sts. to 1 in. measured over moss st.

The Front.—With No. 9 needles cast on 147 sts. Work 1 in. in moss st.
Continue in patt.:—
1st row.—(Wrong side of work facing) k. 3, * p. 3, k. 3; rep. from * to end.
2nd row.—P. 2, * k. 2 tog., k. 1, sl. 1, k. 1, p.s.s.o., p. 1; rep. from * to last st., p. 1.
3rd row.—K. 2, * p. 3, k. 1; rep. from * to last st., k. 1.
4th row.—P. 1, k. 2 tog., * pick up and k. 1 st. into thread between st. just worked and next st., drop next st. down 1 row and work (k. 1, w.fd. k. 1) into double loops, pick up and k. 1 st. into thread between st. just worked and next st., sl. 1, k. 2 tog., p.s.s.o.; rep. from * to end, ending sl. 1, k. 1, p.s.s.o., p. 1,

instead of sl. 1, k. 2 tog., p.s.s.o.
These 4 rows form patt.
Continue in patt. until work measures 12 ins., finishing with a 4th patt. row.
Change to No. 12 needles and dec. for waist:—
Next row.—(P. 3 tog.) 7 times, * p. 2 tog.; rep. from * to last 18 sts., (p. 3 tog.) 6 times (67 sts.).
Work 1 in. in moss st., finishing row on right side.
Change to No. 9 needles and work bodice in moss st. with patt. centre panel:—
1st row.—Moss st. 23, (k. 3, p. 3) 3 times, k. 3, moss st. 23.
Work 3 rows in moss st. with patt. panel, beg. at 2nd row, on centre sts.
Shape Armholes thus: Continue in moss st. and patt., cast off 3 sts. at beg. of next 2 rows, dec. 1 st. both ends of next 4 rows. (53 sts. at end of a 4th patt. row on centre sts.)
Continue straight until work measures 15 ins., finishing with a 4th patt. row in centre panel.
Shape Neck thus:—
Next row.—Moss st. 14, cast off 25 sts., moss st. to end.
Work 1 in. in moss st. on last set of 14 sts. Cast off.
Work other side to match.

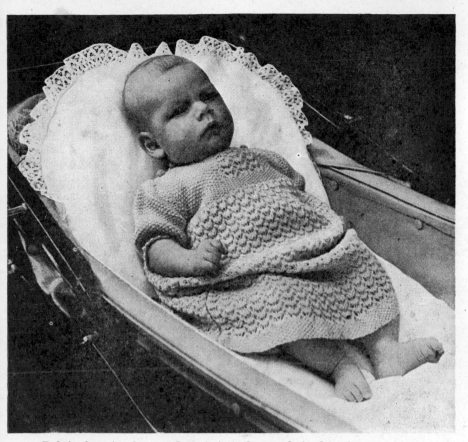

Baby's first-size dress and matinée jacket are knitted in the same pretty stitch. Blue, pink, or white are the best colours to choose for them.

The Back.—Work as for front to end of armhole shapings.

Continue straight on 53 sts. until work measures 16 ins., finishing with 4th patt. row in centre panel.

Cast off right across.

The Sleeves.—With No. 12 needles cast on 39 sts. Work ½ in. in moss st.

Next row.—Moss st. 7, (work 3 times into next st., moss st. 4) 6 times, moss st. 2 (51 sts.).

Change to No. 9 needles and continue in moss st. until work measures 2 ins.

Shape Top thus.—Continue in moss st., cast off 3 sts. at beg. of next 2 rows, dec.

1 st. at beg. of every row until 21 sts. remain.

Cast off 7 sts. at beg. of next 2 rows. Cast off 7 sts.

Make-up.—Press work lightly with a hot iron over damp cloth.

Join shoulder seams at armhole edges only.

Join side and sleeve seams.

Sew in sleeves matching seams.

Work a row of d.c. along neck and shoulder edges, then make 3 small chain button loops on each front shoulder.

Sew on buttons to match loops.

Work a row of picot edge round neck and sleeves. Press seams

MATINÉE JACKET

MATERIALS

2 oz. 3-ply wool.
2 No. 9 knitting needles.
4 small buttons.
A fine crochet hook.

MEASUREMENTS

Length, 10½ ins.
Chest, 22 ins.
Sleeve seam, 6 ins.

TENSION

About 8 sts. to 1 in. measured over unstretched patt.

The Back.—With No. 9 needles cast on 87 sts. Work 1 in. in moss st.

Continue in patt.:—

1st row (wrong side of work facing):—k. 3, * p. 3, k. 3; rep. from * to end.

2nd row.—P. 2, * k. 2 tog., k. 1, sl. 1, k. 1, p.s.s.o., p. 1; rep. from * to last st., p. 1.

3rd row.—K. 2, * p. 3, k. 1; rep. from * to last st., k. 1.

4th row.—P. 1, k. 2 tog., * pick up and k. 1 st. into thread between st. just

Detail of dress and jacket stitch.

worked and next st., drop next st. down 1 row and work (k. 1, w.fd., k. 1) into double loops, pick up and k. 1 st. into thread between st. just worked and next st., sl. 1, k. 2 tog., p.s.s.o.; rep. from * to end, ending sl. 1, k. 1, p.s.s.o., p. 1, instead of sl. 1, k. 2 tog., p.s.s.o.

These 4 rows form patt.

Continue in patt. until work measures 7 ins., finishing 4th patt. row.

Shape Armholes thus: Cast off 6 sts. at beg. of next 2 rows, dec. 1 st. both ends of next 6 rows, keeping patt. correct throughout (63 sts. at end of a 4th patt. row).

Continue straight until work measures 9¾ ins., finishing with a 4th patt. row.

Begin Neck Border thus:—

Next row.—Patt. 15, (k. 1, p. 1) 16 times, k. 1, patt. 15.

Rep. this row until work measures 10½ ins.

Cast off.

The Left Front.—With No. 9 needles cast on 46 sts. Work 1 in. in moss st.

Continue in patt. with moss st. border:—

1st row.—Moss st. 7, k. 3, * p. 3, k. 3; rep. from * to end.

Continue in patt., beg. at 2nd patt. row on 39 sts. with moss st. border of 7 sts. at front edge until work measures 7 ins., ending with a 1st patt. row at side edge.

Shape Armhole thus: Keeping patt. and moss st. correct, cast off 6 sts. at beg. of next row, dec. 1 st. at same edge on next 6 rows.

Continue straight on 34 sts. until work measures 9¼ ins., finishing with a 4th patt. row at front edge.

Begin Neck Border thus:—

Next row.—Moss st. 19, patt. to end.

Next row.—Patt. to last 19 sts., moss st. 19.

Rep. these 2 rows until work measures 10 ins., finishing front edge.

Cast off 13 sts. at beg. of next row.

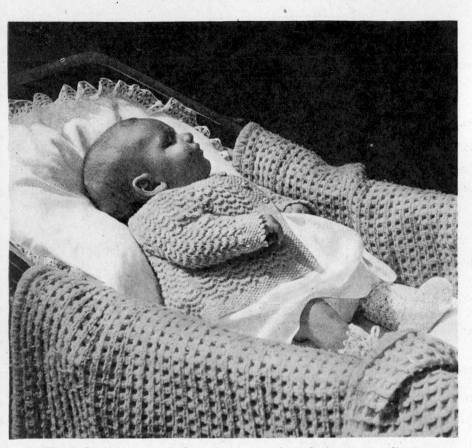

The jacket is as practical as it is attractive. It is easy to slip on and off, and fastens prettily but securely with four small buttons.

Continue straight on remaining sts. until work measures 10½ ins.

Cast off.

The Right Front.—With No. 9 needles cast on 46 sts. Work 1 in. in moss st.

Continue in patt. with moss st. border :—

1st row.—K.3, * .p. 3, k. 3; rep. from * to last 7 sts., moss st. 7.

Continue in patt., beg. at 2nd patt. row on 39 sts., with moss st. border of 7 sts. at front edge until work measures 6 ins. finishing front edge.

Make a Buttonhole thus:—

Next row.—Moss st. 2, cast off 2 sts.,

moss st. to end of border, patt. to end of row.

Next row.—Patt. to last 5 sts., moss st. 3, cast on 2 sts., moss st. 2.

Continue in patt. and moss st. until work measures 7 ins., finishing side edge with a 4th patt. row.

Shape Armhole as for left front, making a second buttonhole 1¼ ins. from first.

Continue on 34 sts. until work measures 8½ ins.; make a 3rd buttonhole in next 2 rows, then continue until work measures 9¼ ins., finishing with a 4th patt. row at armhole edge.

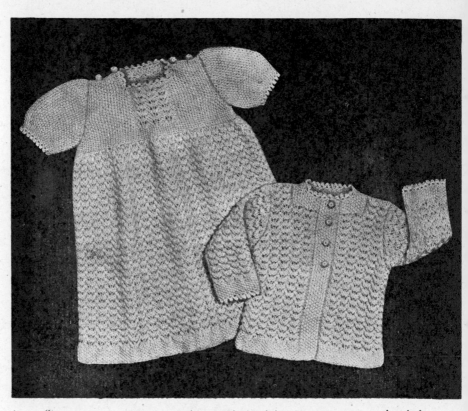

The frock and matinee jacket are knitted in an easy open-work stitch, with yokes of moss stitch. You will enjoy making these pretty garments.

Begin Neck Border thus:—

Next row.—Patt. to last 19 sts., moss st. 19.

Next row.—Moss st. 19, patt. to end.

Rep. last 2 rows until work measures 9½ ins., make a 4th buttonhole in next 2 rows, then continue until work measures 10 ins., finishing front edge.

Cast off 13 sts. at beg. of next row.

Continue straight until work measures 10½ ins. Cast off.

The Sleeves.—With No. 9 needles cast on 41 sts. Work 1 in. in moss st.

Next row.—Moss st. 5, * work twice into next st., moss st. 2; rep. from * to last 6 sts.; moss st. 6 (51 sts.).

Continue in patt., inc. 1 st. both ends of 5th row and every following 6th row until 69 sts. are on needle, working extra sts. gradually into patt.

Continue straight in patt. until work measures 6½ ins., finishing with a 4th patt. row.

Shape Top thus: Keeping continuity of patt., dec. 1 st. both ends of every row until 57 sts. remain (counting at end of a 4th patt. row); cast off 6 sts. at beg. of next 6 rows.

Cast off remaining sts.

Make-up.—Press work lightly with hot iron and damp cloth.

Join side and sleeve seams.

Sew in sleeves, matching seams.

Sew on buttons to match buttonholes.

Press seams. Picot round sleeves and neck.

Outdoor Set

BONNET, MITTENS, BOOTEES AND SHAWL

THE BONNET

MATERIALS

1 oz. 3-ply wool.
2 No. 9 and 2 No. 12 knitting needles.
A crochet hook.
A button.

MEASUREMENTS

All round face, 11¼ ins.
Front to back. 5½ ins.

TENSION

7 sts. to 1 in. over moss st. on No. 9 needles.

With No. 9 needles cast on 81 sts.
Change to No. 12 needles, work ½ in. in moss st.
Change to No. 9 needles and patt.:—
1st row (wrong side of work facing).—K. 3, * p. 3, k. 3; rep. from * to end.
2nd row.—P. 2, * k. 2 tog., k. 1, sl. 1 k. 1, p.s.s.o., p. 1; rep. from * to last st., p. 1.
3rd row.—K. 2, * p. 3, k. 1; rep. from * to last st., k. 1.
4th row.—P. 1, k. 2 tog., * pick up and k. 1 st. into thread between st. just worked and next st., drop next st. down 1 row and work (k. 1, w.fd., k. 1) into double loops, pick up and k. 1 st. into thread between st. just worked and next st., sl. 1, k. 2 tog., p.s.s.o.; rep. from * to end, ending sl. 1, k. 1, p.s.s.o., k. 1 instead of sl. 1, k. 2 tog., p.s.s.o.

Rep. these 4 rows until work measures 3¾ ins., finishing with a 4th patt. row.
Next row.—Cast off 27, p. to last 27 sts., cast off 27.
Rejoin wool at needle point and continue in moss st. on 27 sts. for about 3½ ins. or until back panel is same length as cast-off sts. on each side, ending with a row on right side, p. 2 tog. right across next row.
Cast off.
Sew cast-off edges along side edges of back panel.
The Neck Border.—Using No. 12 needles cast on 12 sts., then on to same needle k. up about 51 sts. evenly round lower edge of bonnet with right side of work facing, now cast on 12 sts.
Work in moss st. for ½ in.
Cast off in moss st.
Make-up.—Press lightly with hot iron over damp cloth.
Make a button loop on end of one strap for fastening and sew button on opposite end.
Press seams.
Work a picot edge round front edge of bonnet.

THE MITTENS

MATERIALS

½ oz. 3-ply wool.
2 No. 9 and 2 No. 12 knitting needles.
1 yd. ribbon.
A fine crochet hook.

MEASUREMENTS

Width of hand, 2¼ ins.

TENSION

About 7 sts. to 1 in. over moss st. on No. 9 needles.

With No. 9 needles cast on 45 sts. Work ½ in. in moss st.

A carrying shawl is an essential item in Baby's trousseau. This one is made in a distinctive design. Bonnet and mittens are shown on page 139.

Continue in patt.:—

1st row (wrong side facing).—K. 3, * p. 3, k. 3; rep. from * to end.

2nd row.—P. 2, * k. 2 tog., k. 1, sl. 1, k. 1, p.s.s.o., p. 1; rep. from * to last st., p. 1.

3rd row.—K. 2, * p. 3, k. 1; rep. from * to last st., k. 1.

4th row.—P. 1, k. 2 tog., * pick up and k. 1 st. into thread between st. just worked and next st., drop next st. down 1 row and work (k. 1, w.fd., k. 1) into

double loops, pick up and k. 1 st. into thread between st. just worked and next st., sl. 1, k. 2 tog., p.s.s.o.; rep. from * to end, ending sl. 1, k. 1, p.s.s.o., p. 1 instead of sl. 1, k. 2 tog., p.s.s.o.

Rep. these 4 rows until work measures about 2¼ ins., finishing 4th patt. row.

Next row.—P. 3, * p. 2 tog., p. 5; rep. from * to end (39 sts.).

Change to No. 12 needles, work 2 rows in moss st.

Next row.—* Moss st. 2, m. 1, work

2 tog.; rep. from * to last 3 sts., moss st. 1, m. 1, work 2 tog.

Continue in moss st. for $1\frac{3}{4}$ ins., finishing row on wrong side.

Shape Top thus:—

1st row.—Work 2 tog., moss st. 16, work 3 tog., moss st. 16, work 2 tog.

2nd and alternate rows.—Moss st. to end.

3rd row.—Work 2 tog., moss st. 14, work 3 tog., moss st. 14, work 2 tog.

5th row.—Work 2 tog., moss st. 12, work 3 tog., moss st. 12, work 2 tog.

7th row.—Work 2 tog., moss st. 10, work 3 tog., moss st. 10, work 2 tog.

9th row.—Work 2 tog., moss st. 8, work 3 tog., moss st. 8, work 2 tog.

11th row.—Work 2 tog., moss st. 6, work 3 tog., moss st. 6, work 2 tog.

13th row.—Work 2 tog., moss st. 4, work 3 tog., moss st. 4, work 2 tog.

Arrange sts. on 2 needles (6, 5) and graft or cast off tog.

Work second mitten in same way.

Make-up.—Press lightly with hot iron over damp cloth.

Join side seams. Press seams.

Thread ribbon through holes at wrist.

Work a picot edge round wrist edge.

THE BOOTEES

MATERIALS

$\frac{1}{2}$ oz. 3-ply wool.

2 No. 9 and 2 No. 12 knitting needles.

A crochet hook.

1 yd. narrow ribbon.

MEASUREMENTS

Length of leg to ankle, $2\frac{1}{2}$ ins.

Length of foot, $3\frac{1}{2}$ ins.

TENSION

About 8 sts. to 1 in. measured over patt.

With No. 9 needles cast on 39 sts. Work $\frac{1}{2}$ in. in moss st.

Continue in patt.:—

1st row (wrong side facing).—K. 3, * p. 3, k. 3; rep. from * to end.

2nd row.—P. 2, * k. 2 tog., k. 1, sl. 1, k. 1, p.s.s.o., p. 1; rep. from * to last st., p. 1.

3rd row.—K. 2, * p. 3, k. 1; rep. from * to last st., k. 1.

4th row.—P. 1, k. 2 tog., * pick up and k. 1 st. into thread between st. just worked and next st., drop next st. down 1 row and work (k. 1, w.fd., k. 1) into double loops, pick up and k. 1 st. into thread between st. just worked and next st., sl. 1, k. 2 tog., p.s.s.o.; rep. from * to end, ending sl. 1, k. 1, p.s.s.o., p. 1 instead of sl. 1, k. 2 tog., p.s.s.o.

Rep. these 4 rows until work measures $2\frac{1}{2}$ ins., finishing with a 4th patt. row.

Change to No. 12 needles, work 1 row in moss st.

Work for Foot thus:—

Next row.—Moss st. 26, turn.

Next row.—Moss st. 13, turn.

Work 20 rows in moss st. on centre 13 sts. Break off wool.

Rejoin wool to first set of 13 sts. with right side of work facing and k. up 12 sts. along side of instep flap, moss st. next 13 sts., k. up 12 sts. along other side of flap, moss st. next 13 sts.

Work 9 rows in moss st. on 63 sts.

Shape Foot thus:—

1st row.—Work 2 tog., moss st. 21, work 3 tog., moss st. 11, work 3 tog., moss st. 21, work 2 tog.

2nd and alternate rows.—Moss st. to end.

3rd row.—Work 2 tog., moss st. to last 2 sts., work 2 tog.

5th row.—Work 2 tog., moss st. 18, work 3 tog., moss st. 9, work 3 tog., moss st. 18, work 2 tog.

6th row.—Moss st.

Cast off.

Work second bootee in same way.

Make-up.—Press lightly with hot iron over damp cloth. Join foot and leg seams.

Thread ribbon through patt. at ankle.

Press seams.

Work a picot edge round top of bootees.

THE SHAWL

MATERIALS

8 oz. 3-ply wool.
1 pair knitting needles, size 6.
1 pair knitting needles, size 7.

MEASUREMENTS

About 40 ins. square.

TENSION

About 5 sts. to 1 in. measured over the g.st. on size 7 needles.

Commence with centre by casting on 148 sts. on No. 7 needles.

1st row.—K.

2nd row.—K.

3rd row.—K. 2, * wind wool over needle twice, k. 1; rep. from * to last 2 sts., k. 2.

4th row.—K. 2, * draw next 6 sts. on to right-hand needle, dropping the wool round and drawing the sts. out as long loops. Now pass the left-hand needle through the first 3 loops taken on right needle and draw them over the other 3. Put all 6 loops back on to left needle and k. them (they are knitted in this order: 4, 5, 6, 1, 2, 3). Rep. with each 6 sts. throughout the row, ending k. 2.

These 4 rows form the patt. and are repeated 36 times, or until a square is formed. K. 1 row. Cast off fairly loosely.

The Lace Border.—Commence at outer corner and cast on 2 sts. on No. 6 needles.

1st row.—K. 2.

2nd row.—K. 1, m. 1, k. 1.

3rd and all alternate rows.—K.

4th row.—K. 1, (m. 1, k. 1) twice.

6th row.—(K. 1, m. 1) twice, k. 2 tog., m. 1, k. 1.

8th row.—(K. 1, m. 1) twice, (k. 2 tog., m. 1) twice, k. 1.

10th row.—(K. 1, m. 1) twice, (k. 2 tog., m. 1) 3 times, k. 1.

12th row.—(K. 1, m. 1) twice, (k. 2 tog., m. 1) 4 times, k. 1.

14th row.—K. 1, m. 1, (k. 2 tog., m. 1) twice, k. 3, (m. 1, k. 2 tog.) twice, m. 1, k. 1.

16th row.—K. 1, m. 1 (k. 2 tog., m. 1) twice, k. 5, (m. 1, k. 2 tog.) twice, m. 1, k. 1.

18th row.—K. 1, m. 1, (k. 2 tog., m. 1) twice, k. 7, (m. 1, k. 2 tog.) twice, m. 1, k. 1.

20th row.—K. 1, m. 1, (k. 2 tog., m. 1) twice, k. 9, (m. 1, k. 2 tog.) twice, m. 1, k. 1.

22nd row.—K. 1, m. 1, (k. 2 tog., m. 1) twice, k. 11, (m. 1. k. 2 tog.) twice, m. 1, k. 1.

24th row.—K. 1, m. 1, (k. 2 tog., m. 1) twice, k. 13, (m. 1, k. 2 tog.) twice, m. 1, k. 1.

26th row.—K. 1, m. 1, (k. 2 tog., m. 1) twice, k. 15, (m. 1, k. 2 tog.) twice, m. 1, k. 1.

28th row.—K. twice in first st., k. 1, (m. 1, k. 2 tog.) 3 times, k. 11, k. 2 tog., (m. 1, k. 2 tog.) 3 times.

30th row.—K. twice in first st., k. 3, (m. 1, k. 2 tog.) 3 times, k. 9, k. 2 tog., (m. 1, k. 2 tog.) 3 times.

32nd row.—K. 1, m. 1, k. 2 tog., k. 3, (m. 1, k. 2 tog.) 3 times, k. 7, k. 2 tog., (m. 1, k. 2 tog.) 3 times.

34th row.—(K. 1, m. 1) twice, k. 2 tog., k. 3, (m. 1, k. 2 tog.) 3 times, k. 5, k. 2 tog., (m. 1, k. 2 tog.) 3 times.

36th row.—K. 1, m. 1, k. 1, (m. 1, k. 2 tog.) twice, k. 3, (m. 1, k. 2 tog.) 3 times, k. 3, k. 2 tog., (m. 1, k. 2 tog.) 3 times.

38th row.—K. twice in first st., k. 1, (m. 1, k. 2 tog.) 3 times, k. 3, (m. 1, k. 2 tog.) 3 times, k. 1, k. 2 tog., (m. 1, k. 2 tog.) 3 times.

40th row.—K. twice in first st., k. 3, (m. 1, k. 2 tog.) 3 times, k. 3, (m. 1, k. 2 tog.) twice, m. 1, k. 3 tog., (m. 1, k. 2 tog.) 3 times.

42nd row.—K. twice in first st., k. 2, (k. 2 tog., m. 1) 3 times, k. 3, (k. 2 tog., m. 1) 3 times, k. 3, (m. 1, k. 2 tog.) twice, m. 1, k. 1.

44th row.—K. twice in first st., k. 2, (k. 2 tog., m. 1) 3 times, k. 3, (k. 2 tog., m. 1)

The whole of this outfit for Baby is knitted in the same lacy pattern.
If you would like to make several sets in varying stitches, turn to page 155
where you will find a selection of equally attractive and suitable ones.

3 times, k. 5, (m. 1, k. 2 tog.) twice, m. 1, k. 1.

46th row.—K. twice in first st., k. 2, (k. 2 tog., m. 1) 3 times, k. 3; (k. 2 tog., m.

1) 3 times, k. 7, (m. 1, k. 2 tog.) twice, m. 1, k. 1.

48th row.—K. twice in first st., k. 2, (k. 2 tog., m. 1) 3 times, k. 3, (k. 2 tog.,

m. 1) 3 times, k. 9, (m. 1, k. 2 tog.) twice. m. 1, k. 1.

K. 1 row. This completes half the corner. The lace is continued as follows, keeping the inner edge straight.

1st row.—K. 3, (k. 2 tog., m. 1) 3 times, k. 3, (k. 2 tog., m. 1) 3 times, k. 11, (m. 1, k. 2 tog.) twice, m. 1, k. 1.

2nd and alternate rows.—K.

3rd row.—K. 2, (k. 2 tog., m. 1) 3 times, k. 3, (k. 2 tog., m. 1) 3 times, k. 13, (m. 1, k. 2 tog.) twice, m. 1, k. 1.

5th row.—K. 1, (k. 2 tog., m. 1) 3 times, k. 3, (k. 2 tog., m. 1) 3 times, k. 15, (m. 1, k. 2 tog.) twice, m. 1, k. 1.

7th row.—K. 3, (m. 1, k. 2 tog.) 3 times, k. 3, (m. 1, k. 2 tog.) 3 times, k. 11, k. 2 tog., (m. 1, k. 2 tog.) 3 times.

9th row.—K. 4, (m. 1, k. 2 tog.) 3 times, k. 3, (m. 1, k. 2 tog.) 3 times, k. 9, k. 2 tog., (m. 1, k. 2 tog.) 3 times.

11th row.—K. 5, (m. 1, k. 2 tog.) 3 times, k. 3, (m. 1, k. 2 tog.) 3 times, k. 7, k. 2 tog., (m. 1, k. 2 tog.) 3 times.

13th row.—K. 6, (m. 1, k. 2 tog.) 3 times, k. 3, (m. 1, k. 2 tog.) 3 times, k. 5, k. 2 tog., (m. 1, k. 2 tog.) 3 times.

15th row.—K. 7, (m. 1, k. 2 tog.) 3 times, k. 3, (m. 1, k. 2 tog.) 3 times, k. 3, k. 2 tog., (m. 1, k. 2 tog.) 3 times.

17th row.—K. 8, (m. 1, k. 2 tog.) 3 times, k. 3, (m. 1, k. 2 tog.) 3 times, k. 1, k. 2 tog., (m. 1, k. 2 tog.) 3 times.

19th row.—K. 9, (m. 1, k. 2 tog.) 3 times, k. 3, (m. 1, k. 2 tog.) twice, m. 1, k. 3 tog., (m. 1, k. 2 tog.) 3 times.

21st row.—K. 7, (k. 2 tog., m. 1) 3 times, k. 3, (k. 2 tog., m. 1) 3 times, k. 3, (m. 1, k. 2 tog.) twice, m. 1, k. 1.

23rd row.—K. 6, (k. 2 tog., m. 1) 3 times, k. 3, (k. 2 tog., m. 1) 3 times, k. 5, (m. 1, k. 2 tog.) twice, m. 1, k. 1.

25th row.—K. 5, (k. 2 tog., m. 1) 3 times, k. 3, (k. 2 tog., m. 1) 3 times, k. 7, (m. 1, k. 2 tog.) twice, m. 1, k. 1.

27th row.—K. 4, (k. 2 tog., m. 1) 3 times, k. 3, (k. 2 tog., m. 1) 3 times, k. 9, (m. 1, k. 2 tog.) twice, m. 1, k. 1.

28th row.—K. This completes one pattern of the lace and it should be repeated from 1st to 28th rows 7 times. Now k. from 1st row to the 13th row and k. back. Commence dec. for other corner.

1st row.—K. 2 tog., k. 5, (m. 1, k. 2 tog.) 3 times, k. 3, (m. 1, k. 2 tog.) 3 times, k. 3, (k. 2 tog., m. 1) 3 times, k. 2 tog.

2nd and alternate rows.—K.

3rd row.—K. 2 tog., k. 5, (m. 1, k. 2 tog.) 3 times, k. 3, (m. 1, k. 2 tog.) 3 times, k. 1, (k. 2 tog., m. 1) 3 times, k. 2 tog.

5th row.—K. 2 tog., k. 5, (m. 1, k. 2 tog.) 3 times, k. 3, (m. 1, k. 2 tog.) twice, m. 1, k. 3 tog., (m. 1, k. 2 tog.) 3 times.

7th row.—K. 2 tog., k. 2, (k. 2 tog., m. 1) 3 times, k. 3, (k. 2 tog., m. 1) 3 times, k. 3, (m. 1, k. 2 tog.) twice, m. 1, k. 1.

9th row.—K. 2 tog., (k. 2 tog., m. 1) 3 times, k. 3, (k. 2 tog., m. 1) 3 times, k. 5, (m. 1, k. 2 tog.) twice, m. 1, k. 1.

11th row.—(K. 2 tog.) twice, m. 1, k. 2 tog., m. 1, k. 3, (k. 2 tog., m. 1) 3 times, k. 7, (m. 1, k. 2 tog.) twice, m. 1, k. 1.

13th row.—(K. 2 tog.) twice, m. 1, k. 3, (k. 2 tog., m. 1) 3 times, k. 9, (m. 1, k. 2 tog.) twice, m. 1, k. 1.

15th row.—K. 2 tog., k. 3, (k. 2 tog., m. 1) 3 times, k. 11, (m. 1, k. 2 tog.) twice, m. 1, k. 1.

17th row.—K. 2 tog., k. 1, (k. 2 tog., m. 1) 3 times, k. 13, (m. 1, k. 2 tog.) twice, m. 1, k. 1.

19th row.—K. 3 tog., m. 1, (k. 2 tog., m. 1) twice, k. 15, (m. 1, k. 2 tog.) twice, m. 1, k. 1.

21st row.—K. 2 tog., (m. 1, k. 2 tog.) 3 times, k. 11, k. 2 tog., (m. 1, k. 2 tog.) 3 times.

23rd row.—(K. 2 tog., m. 1) 3 times, k. 2 tog., k. 9, k. 2 tog., (m. 1, k. 2 tog.) 3 times.

25th row.—(K. 2 tog., m. 1) 3 times, k. 2 tog., k. 7, k. 2 tog., (m. 1, k. 2 tog.) 3 times.

27th row.—(K. 2 tog., m. 1) 3 times, k. 2 tog.. k. 5, k. 2 tog., (m. 1, k. 2 tog.) 3 times.

29th row.—(K. 2 tog., m. 1) 3 times, k. 2 tog., k. 3, k. 2 tog., (m. 1, k. 2 tog.) 3 times.

31st row.—(K. 2 tog., m. 1) 3 times, k. 2 tog., k. 1, k. 2 tog., (m. 1, k. 2 tog.) 3 times.

33rd row.—(K. 2 tog., m. 1) 3 times, k. 3 tog., (m. 1, k. 2 tog.) 3 times.

35th row.—(K. 2 tog., m. 1) twice, k. 3 tog., (m. 1, k. 2 tog.) 3 times.

37th row.—K. 2 tog., m. 1. k. 3 tog., (m. 1, k. 2 tog.) 3 times.

39th row.—K. 3 tog., (m. 1, k. 2 tog.) 3 times.

41st row.—K. 3 tog.. (m. 1, k. 2 tog.) twice.

43rd row.—K. 3 tog., m. 1, k. 2 tog.

45th row.—Cast off 3.

K. 3 more pieces exactly the same.

Make-up.—Press carefully under a damp cloth.

Sew the sides to the centre. Join mitred corners neatly, matching pattern.

Vest and Pants

TO FIT A BABY UP TO THREE MONTHS

THE VEST

MATERIALS

2 oz. 3-ply wool.
2 No. 9 and 2 No. 12 knitting needles.
3 buttons.

MEASUREMENTS

Length, 10½ ins.
Chest, 17 ins. slightly stretched.
Sleeve, 5½ ins.

TENSION

7 sts. to 1 in.

The Front.—With No. 9 needles cast on 58 sts. Work 1 in. in g.st.

Continue in st.st. until work measures 7 ins., finishing p. row.

Divide for opening:—

Next row.—K. 27, turn.

Continue in st.st. on 27 sts. until work measures 7¾ ins., finishing side edge.

Shape Armhole thus:—

Next row.—K. 5, sl. these sts. on to a safety-pin, k. to end. P. 1 row, then begin yoke:—

Next row.—* K. 1, p. 1; rep. from * to end.

Next row.—P. to end.

Rep. these 2 rows until work measures 9¾ ins., finishing opening edge.

Shape Neck thus: Cast off 4 sts. at beg. of next row, dec. 1 st. at same edge on every row until 12 sts. remain.

Continue straight until work measures 10¾ ins. Cast off.

Return to main sts., sl. centre 4 sts. on to a safety-pin and leave for front border, with No. 9 needles k. to end.

Work on 27 sts. to match 1st side.

The Right Front Border: Sl. 4 sts. from safety-pin on to a No. 12 needle and work ½-in. in g.st.

Next row.—K. 2, m. 1, k. 2 tog.

Continue in g.st. for 1¼ ins., then make a second buttonhole in next row.

Now continue in g.st. until border is same length as right front opening edge.

Leave sts. on spare needle.

The Left Front Border: With No. 12

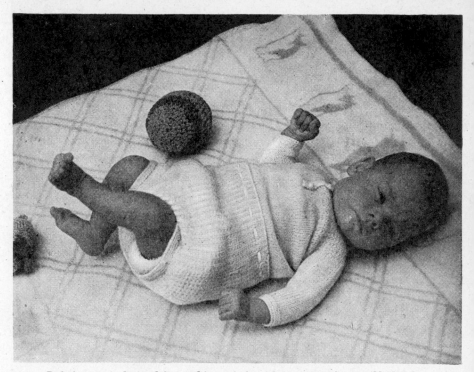

Baby's vest is knitted in stocking stitch with a pretty, fancy-ribbed yoke. It has a neat neck, fastening at the front with self-covered buttons.

needles k. up 4 sts. at back of buttonhole border. Work in g.st. until border is same length as first border.

Leave sts. on spare needle.

The Back.—Work as front, continuing in st.st. until work is 7¾ ins., finishing p. row (thus omitting opening).

Shape Armholes thus:—

Next row.—K. 5 sl. on to a safety-pin, k. to last 5 sts., sl. these sts. on to a second safety-pin.

P. 1 row, then continue in rib for yoke thus:—

1st row.—* K 1, p. 1; rep. from * to end.

2nd row.—P. to end.

Rep. these 2 rows until work measures 10½ ins.

Cast off.

The Sleeves.—Join shoulder seams.

With right side of work facing, using No. 9 needles, k. 5 sts. from safety-pin, k. up 40 sts. along armhole edge (20 each side of shoulder seam), k. 5 sts. from second safety-pin.

Next row.—P. to end.

Next row.—K. 4, sl. 1, k. 1, p.s.s.o., k. to last 6 sts., k. 2 tog., k. 4.

Rep. these 2 rows until 40 sts. remain.

Continue in st.st. dec. 1 st. at both ends of every 6th row until work measures 4½ ins. from picked-up armhole sts., finishing p. row.

Change to No. 12 needles and work 1 in. in g.st.

Cast off with a No. 9 needle.

The Neck Band.—Sl. 4 sts. for buttonhole band on to a No. 12 needle, then on to same needle k. up 44 sts. evenly round neck edge, k. 4 sts. for second border.

Work ½ in. in g.st., making a third buttonhole at front edge after about ¼ in.

Cast off loosely.

Make-up.—Press work lightly with hot iron over damp cloth.

Join side and sleeve seams.

Sew front borders to opening edges.

Sew on buttons to match buttonholes.

Press seams.

THE PANTS

MATERIALS

1 oz. 3-ply wool.

2 No. 9 and 2 No. 12 knitting needles.

½ yd. elastic.

MEASUREMENTS

Waist to crutch, 8½ ins.

Width all round, 19 ins.

TENSION

7 sts. to 1 in.

With No. 12 needles begin at front waist and cast on 69 sts.

Work in rib thus:—

1st row.—K. 1, * p. 1, k. 1; rep. from * to end.

2nd row.—P. to end.

Rep. these 2 rows twice.

7th row.—* K. 1, p. 1, m. 1, p. 2 tog.; rep. from * to last st., k. 1.

8th row.—P. to end.

Continue in patt. until work measures 2 ins.

Change to No. 9 needles and continue in patt. until work measures 6 ins., finishing p. row.

Shape Legs thus: Continue in patt., cast off 5 sts. at beg. of next 10 rows.

Continue straight in patt. on 19 sts. for gusset, for 3 ins., then cast on 5 sts. at beg. of next 10 rows.

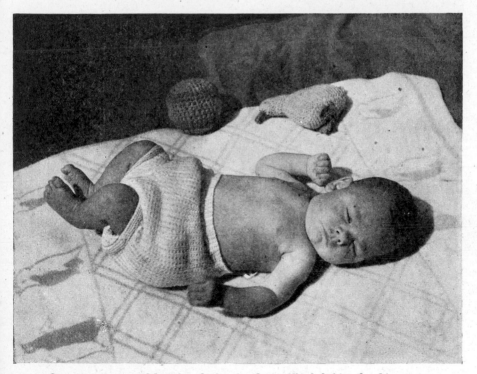

Our youngest model enjoyed the freedom afforded him by his smart pants, and kicked about freely! They are in rib to match the vest yoke.

Continue straight on 69 sts. for 4 ins., finishing p. row.

Shape Back thus:—

Next 2 rows.—Work to last 5 sts., turn.

Next 2 rows.—Work to last 10 sts., turn.

Next 2 rows.—Work to last 15 sts., turn.

Next 2 rows.—Work to last 20 sts., turn.

Next 2 rows.—Work to last 25 sts., turn.

Next 2 rows.—Work to end.

Change to No. 12 needles and continue in patt. until work measures at side edges same as front to elastic holes, finishing p. row.

Make elastic holes as for front, then work 5 rows in patt.

Cast off.

The Leg Borders.—With right side of work facing and using No. 12 needles, k. up 72 sts. evenly along shaped leg and gusset edges.

Work $\frac{1}{2}$ in. in g.st.

Cast off loosely with a No. 9 needle.

Make-up.—Press work lightly with hot iron over damp cloth.

Join side seams.

Thread elastic through holes at waist.

Press seams.

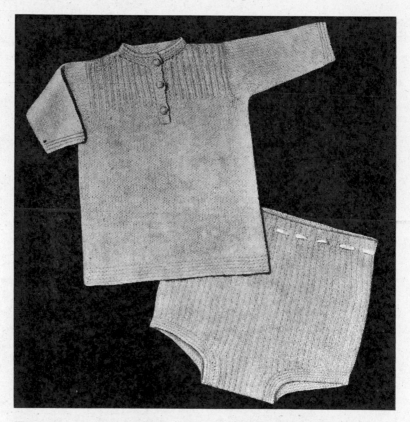

The vest and pants are made in 3-ply wool and you will require 3 oz. to make the set. The original garments were made in pale pink.

Carrying Coat

OR TODDLER'S DRESSING GOWN

MATERIALS

10 oz. bouclé wool or mixture yarn.
2 No. 8 and 2 No. 12 knitting needles.
1 yd. ribbon about 1 in. wide.
A crochet hook.
A small ball of coloured silk for smocking and crochet edges.

MEASUREMENTS

Length, 24 ins.
Chest, 22 ins.
Sleeve seam, 6 ins.

TENSION

6 sts. to 1 in. measured over st.st.

The Back.—Using No. 8 needles cast on 115 sts. Work in moss st.:—

1st row.—K. 1, * p. 1, k. 1; rep. from * to end. Rep. this row for 1½ ins.

Continue in st.st. for 1½ ins., finishing p. row, then begin shaping:—

Next row.—K. 2 tog., k. 38, sl. 1, k. 1, p.s.s.o., k. 31, k. 2 tog., k. 38, k. 2 tog.

Work 1¼ ins. in st.st., finishing p. row.

Next row.—K. 38, sl. 1. k. 1, p.s.s.o.. k. 31, k. 2 tog. k. 38.

Work 1¼ ins. in st.st., finishing p. row.

Next row.—K. 2 tog., k. 35, sl. 1, k. 1, p.s.s.o., k. 31, k. 2 tog., k. 35, k. 2 tog.

Work 1¼ ins. in st.st., finishing p. row.

Next row.—K. 35, sl. 1, k. 1, p.s.s.o., k. 31, k. 2 tog., k. 35.

Work 1¼ ins. in st.st., finishing p. row.

Next row.—K. 2 tog., k. 32, sl. 1, k. 1. p.s.s.o., k. 31, k. 2 tog., k. 32, k. 2 tog.

Continue in this way, working in st.st. and dec. 1 st. on each side of centre panel at intervals of 1¼ ins. and dec. at each end of row at intervals of 2½ ins. until

79 sts. remain.

Continue straight until work measures 18 ins., finishing p. row.

Next row. K. 9, * k. 2 tog., k. 5; rep. from * to end.

Continue in st.st. on 69 sts. until work measures 20 ins., finishing p. row.

Shape Armholes thus: Cast off 4 sts. at beg. of next 2 rows, dec. 1 st. at both ends of every row until 51 sts. remain.

Continue straight until work measures 24 ins., finishing p. row.

Cast off.

The Right Front.—With No. 8 needles cast on 82 sts. Work 1½ ins. in moss st.

Continue in st.st. with moss st. front border:—

Next row.—Moss st. 9, k. to end.

Next row.—P. to last 9 sts., moss st. 9.

Rep. these 2 rows for 1½ ins., finishing row on wrong side.

Next row.—Moss st. 9, k. 31, k. 2 tog., k. 38, k. 2 tog.

Work 1¼ ins. in st.st. with moss st. border, finishing p. row.

Next row.—Moss st. 9, k. 31, k. 2 tog., k. to end.

Work 1¼ ins. in st.st. with moss st. border, finishing p. row.

Next row.—Moss st. 9, k. 31, k. 2 tog., k. to last 2 sts., k. 2 tog.

Work 1¼ ins. in st.st. with moss st. border, finishing p. row.

Next row.—Moss st. 9, k. 31, k. 2 tog., k. to end.

Continue in this way, working in st.st. with moss-st. border, dec. 1 st. after front panel of 31 sts. at intervals of 1¼ ins. and 1 st. at end of row at intervals of 2½ ins. until 69 sts. remain

This novelty carrying coat is sometimes more useful than a shawl is;
it is made in a fine white bouclé wool, trimmed with smocking.

Continue straight until work measures 18 ins., finishing p. row.

Next row.—Moss st. 9, * k. 4, k. 2 tog.; rep. from * to end (59 sts.).

Next row.—P. 10, turn.

Continue in st.st. on these 10 sts. for 1 in., finishing p. row.

Break off wool.

Rejoin wool to 49 sts. and work in rib thus:—

Next row.—P. 1, * k. 3, p. 1; rep. from * to end.

Next row.—K. 1, * p. 3, k. 1; rep. from * to end.

Rep. these 2 rows for 1 in., finishing row on wrong side.

Work 2 rows in st.st. across all sts., then dec. for front edge thus:—

Next row.—K. 3, sl. 1, k. 1, p.s.s.o., k. to end.

Next row.—P. to last 5 sts., p. 2 tog., p. 3.

Rep. these 2 rows · until work measures 20 ins. at front edge, finishing side edge.

Shape Armhole thus: Continue to dec. inside first 3 sts. at front edge on every row at the same time, cast off 4 sts. beg. of next row, then dec. 1 st. at side edge on next 5 rows. Now work with armhole edge straight and continue to dec. at front edge until 16 sts. remain.

Continue without shaping until work measures 24 ins., finishing p. row. Cast off.

The Left Front.—With No. 8 needles cast on 82 sts.

Work 1½ ins. in moss st.

Continue in st.st. with moss-st. front border:—

Next row.—K. to last 9 sts., moss st. 9.

Next row.—Moss st. 9, p. to end.

Rep. these 2 rows for 1½ ins. finishing row on wrong side.

Next row.—K. 2 tog., k. 38, sl. 1, k. 1, p.s.s.o., k. 31, moss st. 9.

Work 1¼ ins. in st.st. with moss-st. border, finishing p. row.

Next row.—K. 38, sl. 1, k. 1, p.s.s.o., k. 31, moss st. 9.

Work 1¼ ins. in st.st. with moss-st.

The coat is made to fasten with coloured ribbons which thread through slots at the side and tie in a bow at the back; it is designed with reversible fronts for boy or girl.

border, finishing p. row.

Next row.—K. 2 tog., k. 35, sl. 1, k. 1, p.s.s.o., k. 31, moss st. 9.

Continue in this way, working in st.st. with moss-st. border, dec. 1 st. before front panel of 31 sts. at intervals of 1¼ ins. and 1 st at beg. of row at intervals of 2½ ins. until 69 sts. remain.

Continue straight until work measures 18 ins., finishing p. row.

Next row.—* K. 2 tog., k. 4; rep. from * to last 9 sts., moss st. 9 (59 sts.).

Next row.—P. 1, * k. 3, p. 1; rep. from * to last 10 sts., turn.

Next row.—K. 1, * p. 3, k. 1; rep. from * to end.

When Baby has grown a little and can stand on his or her own feet, the carrying coat becomes a dressing gown! This garment is the same as the one that Baby wears on page 146.   It ties at the back with ribbons.

Continue in rib on these 49 sts. tor 1 in., finishing row on wrong side.

Break off wool. Rejoin wool to remaining 10 sts. and work 1 in. in st.st., finishing p. row.

Work 2 rows in st.st. across all sts., then dec. for front edge thus:—

Next row.—K. to last 5 sts., k. 2 tog., k. 3.

Next row.—P. 3, p. 2 tog., p. to end. Rep. these 2 rows until work measures 20 ins., finishing side edge.

Shape Armhole and complete front to match right front.

The Sleeves.—With No. 8 needles cast on 36 sts.

Work in st.st. for 1 in., finishing p. row, then inc. 1 st. both ends of next row and every 6th row until 50 sts. are on the needle.

Continue straight until work measures 5½ ins., finishing p. row.

Shape Top thus: Dec. 1 st. both ends of every alternate row until 34 sts. remain.

Cast off 4 sts. beg. of next 6 rows.

Cast off remaining sts.

Make-up.—Press work lightly on wrong side with hot iron over damp cloth.

Join side and shoulder seams.

Join sleeve seams and sew sleeves into armholes, matching seams.

With the coloured silk work 2 rows of d.c. round neck and front edges of bodice and round sleeve edges.

Still using the coloured silk work any simple smocking pattern across the waist ribbing, using the plain ribs as a guide.

Cut ribbon in half and sew one piece to each front edge at the waist, thread one end through waist slot and tie at back (only one slot is used, but the two slots make the fronts reversible).

Press seams.

Little Boy's Suit

JERSEY AND KNICKERS

MATERIALS

5 oz. 3-ply wool.

2 No. 12 and 2 No. 9 knitting needles.

3 buttons for jersey.

2 large buttons for knickers.

MEASUREMENTS

The Jersey: Length from shoulder, 13 ins.

Chest, 21 ins.

Sleeve seam, 8½ ins.

The Knickers: Waist to crutch, 8½ins.

All round above gusset, 24 ins.

TENSION

Using No. 9 needles, about 7½ sts. to 1 in.

THE JERSEY

The Front.—Using No. 12 needles cast on 80 sts. and work in k. 1, p. 1 rib for 1 in., inc. 1 st. at the end of the last row.

Change to No. 9 needles and work in the following patt.:—

1st row.—K. 4, * k. 2 tog., inc. in next st. thus: k. 1, then k. again into the back of the st. before slipping off the needle, k. 6; rep. from * to end, ending k. 2 instead of k. 6.

2nd and every alternate row.—P.

3rd row.—K. 3, * k. 2 tog., inc. in next st. (as in 1st row), k. 6; rep. from * to end, ending k. 3 instead of k. 6.

5th row.—K. 2, * k. 2 tog., inc. in next st., k. 6; rep. from * to end, ending k. 4 instead of k. 6.

6th row.—P. to end.

These 6 rows form patt.

Rep. them until work measures 7½ ins. from cast on edge, divide for front opening.

With right side of work facing, work in patt. over 36 sts. leaving the remaining 45 sts. on a spare needle.

Continue in patt. on the first 36 sts. until front measures 9 ins.

Shape Armholes thus: With right side of work facing, cast off 4 sts. at the beg. of next row, then dec. 1 st. at armhole edge on each of the next 5 rows.

Continue in patt. without shaping until work measures 11½ ins., then with the right side facing you, shape for the neck.

Next row.—Work in patt. to neck edge.

Next row.—Cast off 3 sts. and p. to end of row.

Now dec. 1 st. at neck edge on every row until there are 20 sts. on needle. Work should now measure 13 ins. With the right side of the work facing, shape shoulders thus:—

Cast off 10 sts., work to neck edge, turn, p. to end.

Cast off.

Slip the centre 9 sts. on to a stitch-holder.

Rejoin wool to second set of 36 sts. and work to match first side, reversing shapings.

The Front Band.—Using No. 12 needles pick up the 9 sts. left on stitch-holder and inc. 1 st. at beg. and end of 1st row (11 sts.).

Work in k. 1, p. 1 rib for ¾ in.

Make a buttonhole thus:—

With right side facing, rib 4 sts., cast off 3, rib to end.

In the following row cast on 3 sts. to replace those cast off in previous row. Make 2 more buttonholes at intervals of 1½ ins.

Work 2 rows in rib after the last buttonhole.

Cast off.

Using No. 12 needles cast on 11 sts. and work in k. 1, p. 1 rib for 4 ins. for an underwrap of right side.

Cast off.

The Back.—Work as given for front for 7½ ins.

Continue in patt. until work measures 9 ins., then shape armholes.

Cast off 4 sts. at beg. of next 2 rows, then dec. 1 st. at both ends of next 5 rows.

Continue on 63 sts. until work measures 13 ins., shape shoulders.

Cast off 10 sts. at beg. of next 4 rows.

Cast off remaining 23 sts. for back of neck.

The Sleeves.—With No. 12 needles cast on 44 sts. and work 1½ ins. in k. 1, p. 1 rib., inc. 1 st. at end of last row.

Change to No. 9 needles and continue in patt. inc. 1 st. at both ends of 7th and every following 6th row until there are 63 sts. on needle.

Work without shaping until sleeve measures 8½ ins., then shape top.

Dec. 1 st. at each end of every alternate row until 53 sts. remain, then dec. 1 st. at both ends of every row until 19 sts. remain.

Cast off.

The Collar.—With No. 12 needles cast on 103 sts., work 4 rows in g.st. (k. every row).

5th row.—K. 3, * p. 1, k. 1; rep. from * until 2 sts. remain, k. 2.

6th row.—K. 2, p. 1, * k. 1, p. 1; rep. from * until 2 sts. remain, k. 2.

7th row.—K. 2, sl. 1, k. 1, p.s.s.o., work in rib until 4 sts. remain, k. 2 tog., k. 2.

8th row.—K. 2 rib to last 2 sts., k. 2.

Rep. the last 4 rows until collar measures 1½ ins.

Now cast off 10 sts. at beg. of next 6 rows.

Cast off remaining sts.

Your son's first suit! Very practical and tailored; the jersey is knitted in a simple mock cable stitch. The trousers have a single strip of pattern on each leg, and have " braces " buttoning at the front for easy dressing.

THE KNICKERS

The Front. The Right Leg.—With No. 12 needles cast on 48 sts. and work in k. 1, p. 1 rib for 1 in., leave sts. on a spare needle.

The Left Leg.—Work as given for right leg, then change to No. 9 needles and join legs and start gusset thus:—

With right side of work facing, k. 20. Work in cable patt. as for jersey on the following 9 sts., k. 19, cast on 21 sts. for gusset.

Work over sts. for right leg, k. 19, cable patt. on next 9 sts., k. 20.

Next row.—P.

Shape Gusset thus:—

1st row.—K. 20, cable patt. on 9 sts., k. 19, sl. 1, k. 1, p.s.s.o., k. until 50 sts. remain, k. 2 tog., k. 19, cable patt. 9, k. 20.

2nd row.—P.•

Rep. the last 2 rows until 99 sts. remain

Detail of the mock cable stitch.

(keeping cable patt. correct up centre of each leg) and ending with a p. row.

Next row.—Work on 48 sts., sl. 1, k. 2 tog., p.s.s.o., work to end.

Next row.—P. 48, k. 1, p. 48.

Next row.—Work in st.st. and patt. to centre, p. 1, work to end.

Work 3 more rows thus, then shape as follows on next and every following 6th row.

Work to within 2 sts. of centre p. st., sl. 1, k. 1, p.s.s.o., p. 1, k. 2 tog., work to end.

Continue in this way until 8 dec. rows have been worked (81 sts.), then continue without shaping until front measures 7½ ins. from cast-on gusset sts., ending with a p. row.

Change to No. 12 needles and work ½ in. in k. 1, p. 1 rib.

Next row.—Rib 21, cast off 3, rib 33, cast off 3, rib 21.

Next row.—Work in rib, casting on 3 sts. for each buttonhole to replace those cast off.

Continue in rib until ribbing measures 1 in.

Cast off loosely in rib using No. 10 needles.

The Back.—Work as given for front until work measures 7½ ins. from cast-on gusset sts., ending with a p. row, then work back shaping.

Next 2 rows.—Work to last 7 sts., turn.

Next 2 rows.—Work to last 14 sts., turn.

Next 2 rows.—Work to last 21 sts., turn.

Next 2 rows.—Work to last 28 sts., turn.

Next 2 rows.—Work to end.

Change to No. 12 needles and work 1 in. rib as for front, omitting buttonholes.

Continue thus:—

Next row.—Cast off 19 sts., rib across 10 sts., cast off 23 sts., rib 10, cast off 19. Break off wool.

Here you can see clearly the straps which go over his shoulder to keep up his trousers. The jumper can be worn over the knickers or tucked in. The trousers are in stocking stitch, with a strip of mock cable.

Rejoin wool to first set of 10 sts. and work in k. 1, p. 1 rib for 15 ins.

Cast off.

Rejoin wool to other set of 10 sts. and work to match.

Make-up, Jersey.—Press work lightly with hot iron over damp cloth.

Backstitch shoulder, side and sleeve seams.

Pin sleeves into armholes and backstitch.

Oversew ribbed bands to edges of front opening, neaten placket.

Sew collar to neck edge to within about ½ in. of front edges.

Sew buttons on to right side of front opening to correspond with buttonholes.

Make-up, Knickers.—Backstitch side and leg seams.

Oversew gusset seams.

Sew a button to each end of the straps and fasten to buttonholes in front.

Press seams.

"Ark" Stitch

"Mr. and Mrs. Noah" Stitch

"Elephant" Stitch

Enchanting Stitches for Baby's Trousseau

Alternative Stitches

FOR VARIETY, KNIT THE BABY DESIGNS ON THE PREVIOUS PAGES IN THESE STITCHES

THESE simple knitting stitches are especially suitable for baby garments as they are small and neat.

The vest and pants on page 141, knitted in either " Elephant " or " Mr. and Mrs. Noah " stitch would make a charming baby boy's suit especially if a second colour is used for the edges.

" Ark " stitch is good for matinée coats and cardigans. Try bands of these stitches alternated with moss stitch or stocking stitch for skirts of dresses and carrying coats.

A good way of using up odd amounts of wool is to use one colour for the plain band and various contrasting colours for the patterned bands. Very interesting results can be obtained if the colours are chosen carefully.

The toddler's suit on page 149 could be knitted in " Elephant " stitch instead of cable stitch, and here again contrasting straps and knickers would be good.

Try " Noah " stitch for the Baby Accessories on page 135, keeping the moss-stitch borders and " Ark " stitch for the skirt of the carrying coat on page 145, with stocking-stitch bodice and sleeves.

"Ark" Stitch

Cast on a number of stitches divisible by 6.

1st row.—* P. 3, pass wool over needle to make a st., k. 2 tog., k. 1; rep. from *.

2nd row.—* P. 3, k. 3; rep. from *.

3rd row.—* P. 3, k. 1, m. 1, k. 2 tog.; rep. from *.

4th row.—As 2nd row.

Rep. these 4 rows.

"Mr. and Mrs. Noah" Stitch

Number of stitches divisible by 3, plus 2.

1st row.—Sl. 1, * wl. fwd., sl. 1, k. 2 tog., p.s.s.o., wl. fwd., k. 3; rep. from *

2nd row.—P.

3rd row.—Sl. 1, * k. 3, wl. fwd., sl. 1, k. 2 tog., p.s.s.o., wl. fwd.; rep. from *.

4th row.—P. Rep. these 4 rows.

"Elephant" Stitch

Number of stitches divisible by 3, plus 2.

1st row.—K. 1, * wl. twd., sl. 1, k. 2, p.s.s.o. the 2 k. sts.; rep. from * to last st., k. 1.

2nd row.—P.

3rd row.—K.

4th row.—P.

5th row.—K. 3, * wl. fwd., sl. 1, k. 2, p.s.s.o. the 2 k. sts.; rep. from * to last 2 sts., k. 2.

6th-8th rows.—Rep. 2nd to 4th rows.

9th row.—K. 2, * wl. fwd., sl. 1, k. 2, p.s.s.o. the 2 k. sts.; rep. from * to end.

10th-12th rows.—Rep. 2nd to 4th rows.

Rep. these 12 rows.

"Carrying Coat" Stitch

Number of stitches divisible by 7.

1st row.— * P. 1, k. 2 tog., m. 1, k. 1, m. 1, sl. 1, k. 1, p.s.s.o., p. 1 ; rep. from * to end.

2nd row.— * k. 1, p. 5, k. 1 ; rep. from * to end.

3rd row.— * p. 1, k. 5, p. 1 ; rep. from * to end.

4th row.— As 2nd row. Rep. these 4 rows.

"Shawl" Stitch

Cast on a number of stitches divisible by 8, plus 1 for edge st.

1st row.— Sl. 1, k. 1, * m. 1, k. 2 tog. Rep. from * to last st., k. 1.

2nd row.— P.

3rd row.— Sl. 1, p. 1, * m. 1, p. 2 tog., p. 2 ; rep. from * to last 3 sts., m. 1, p. 2 tog., p. 1.

4th row.— K. 2, p. 1, * k. 3, p. 1 ; rep. from * to last 2 sts., k. 2.

5th row.— Same as 3rd row.

6th row.— P. Rep. these 6 rows.

"Matinée Jacket" Stitch

Number of stitches divisible by 6.

1st row.— K.

2nd row.— K.

3rd row.— * P. 1, k. 4, p. 1 ; rep. from * to end.

4th row.— * K. 1, p. 4, k. 1 ; rep. from * to end.

5th row.— As 3rd row.

6th row.— * K. 1, p. 2, wool over and round needle, p. 2, k. 1 ; rep. from * to end.

7th row.— * P. 1, k. 5, p. 1 ; rep. from * to end.

8th row.— * K. 1, p. 2, p. 2 tog., p. 1, k. 1 ; rep. from * to end. Rep. these 8 rows.

MEASUREMENTS

IF you want to design your own garments from any of the stitches given here, the following chart will be helpful in making the garments to the right proportion.

Of course, a good deal depends on the individual child, and some children at one year are as big as others at two, therefore base your garments on the chest measurement rather than the age. For cardigans and coats which have to be worn over other garments, allow an inch extra on the chest measurement, and about half an inch on the armhole depth, but keep the shoulder seams narrow so that the garment will hang well.

Age	Frock length	Chest	Sleeve seam	Shoulder seam	Armhole depth
Birth	16 or 22 ins.	18 ins.	6 ins.	2 ins.	3 ins.
6 months	16 ins.	19 ins.	6½ ins.	2 ins.	3¼ ins.
1 year	16 ins.	20 ins.	7½ ins.	2¼ ins.	3½ ins.
2 years	17 ins.	21 ins.	8½ ins.	2¼ ins.	3¾ ins.
3 years	18 ins.	22 ins.	10 ins.	2½ ins.	4 ins.
4 years	20 ins.	23 ins.	11 ins.	2½ ins.	4¼ ins.
5 years	22 ins.	24 ins.	12 ins.	2¾ ins.	4½ ins.
6 years	24 ins.	25 ins.	13 ins.	2¾ ins.	4¾ ins.
7 years	26 ins.	26 ins.	13½ ins.	3 ins.	5 ins.
8 years	28 ins.	26½ ins.	14 ins.	3 ins.	5¼ ins.
9 years	30 ins.	27 ins.	15 ins.	3¼ ins.	5½ ins.
10 years	32 ins.	28 ins.	15½ ins.	3¼ ins.	5¾ ins.
11 years	34 ins.	29 ins.	16 ins.	3½ ins.	6 ins.
12 years	36 ins.	30 ins.	16½ ins.	3½ ins.	6 ins.

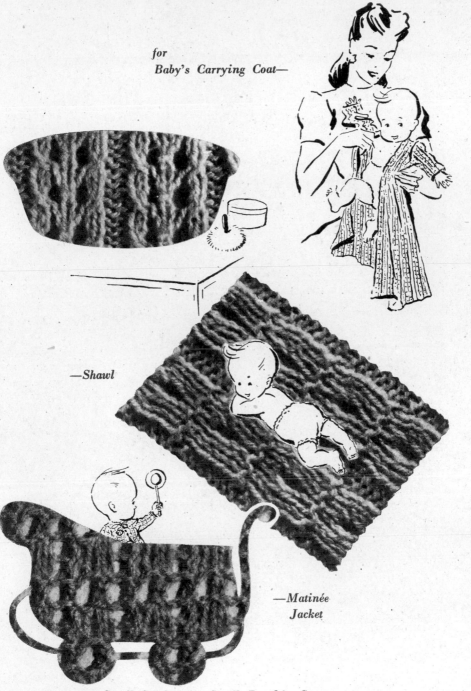

for
Baby's Carrying Coat—

—Shawl

—Matinée Jacket

Small Stitches for Small People's Garments

Dainty Stitches

WHICH ARE SUITABLE FOR THE BABY GARMENTS ON THE PRECEDING PAGES

Detail of the "Feather" Stitch.

"Feather" Stitch

Number of stitches divisible by 2.
Rows 1 to 5.—K.
Row 6.—K. 1, * sl. 1, k. 1, p.s.s. back on to left-hand needle and k. into back of it; this will be referred to as cross; rep. from * to last st., k. 1.
Rep. these 6 rows.

"Butterfly" Stitch

Number of stitches divisible by 8, plus 3 sts.

1st row.—* P. 3, k. 5; rep. from * to last 3 sts., p. 3.
2nd and alternate rows.—P.
3rd row.—* P. 3, wool to front, sl. 5, rep. from * to last 3 sts., p. 3.
5th and 7th rows.—As 3rd row.

9th row.—* P. 3, k. 2, k. 1 inserting needle upwards through the 3 loose sts. and next st., k. 2; rep. from * to last 3 sts., p. 3.
10th row.—P.
Rep. these 10 rows.

Detail of the "Butterfly" Stitch.

"Outfit" Stitch
(See opposite page)

Number of stitches divisible by 2.
1st row.—K. to end.
2nd row.—P. to end.
3rd row.—K. 1, * sl. 1, k. 1, p.s.s. back on to left hand needle and k. into the back of it; this will be referred to as cross. Rep. from * to last st., k. 1.
4th row.—P. to end.
5th row.—K. 2, * sl. 1, k. 1, cross; rep. from * to last 2 sts., k. 2.
Rep. last 4, i.e. rows 2-5.

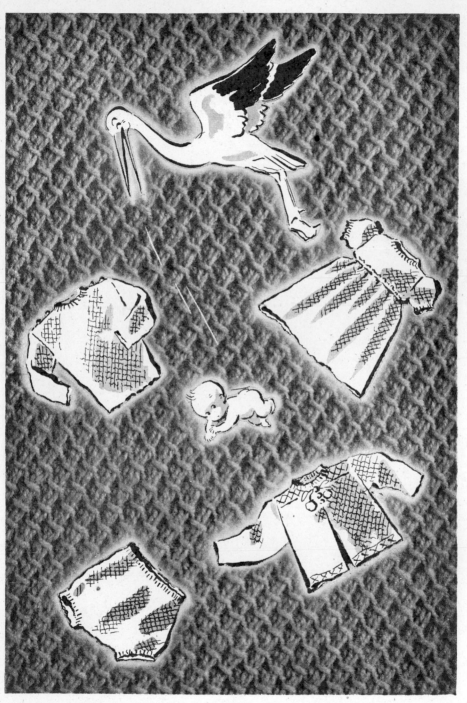

An attractive stitch in which to make a whole outfit.

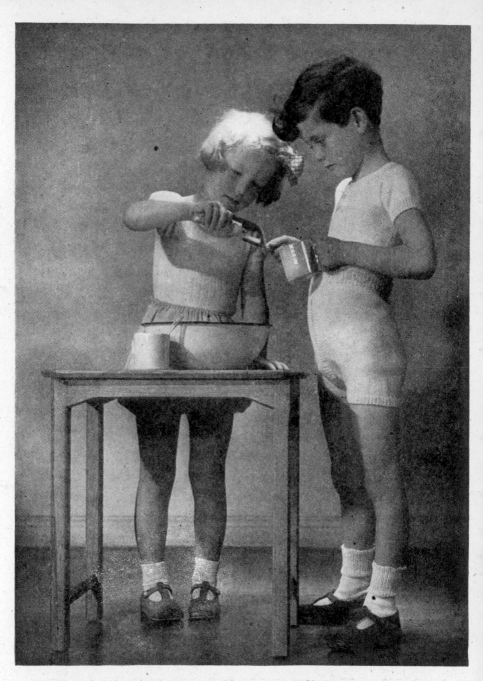

Mutual aid and admiration! Margaret and Christopher have a great regard for mother's insistence on this tooth-cleaning business— and her habit of dressing them both in hand-knitted underwear.

Boy's Vest and Pants

IN TWO SIZES FOR THE UNDER ELEVENS

SIZE 1

MATERIALS

5 oz. 3-ply wool (3 oz. vest, 2 oz. pants).
2 No. 10 and 2 No. 12 knitting needles.
A fine crochet hook.
3 small buttons for vest.
$\frac{3}{4}$ yd. elastic for pants.

MEASUREMENTS

The Vest.—Length, 18 ins.
Chest, 22 ins. (unstretched).
Sleeve seam, $3\frac{1}{2}$ ins.
Pants.—Waist to crutch, $9\frac{1}{2}$ ins.
Waist, 20 ins.

TENSION

$7\frac{1}{2}$ sts. to 1 in.

THE VEST

The Front.—With No. 10 needles cast on 80 sts., work 1 in. in k. 1, p. 1 rib.

Continue in st.st. until work measures 13 ins., finishing p. row.

Divide for Front opening thus:—

Next row.—K. 42, turn.

Next row.—K. 4, p. to end.

Continue in st.st. with front border in g.st. on these 42 sts. for left side of front as follows, leaving remaining 38 sts. on a spare needle for right front.

Next row.—K. to end.

Next row.—K. 4, p. to end.

Rep. these 2 rows until work measures $13\frac{3}{4}$ ins., finishing side edge.

Next row.—K. to last 4 sts., k. 1, m. 1, k. 2 tog. for a buttonhole, k. 1.

Work 2 more rows in st.st. and g.st. border, thus finishing front edge.

Shape for Armhole thus:—

Next row.—K. 4, p. to last 6 sts., sl. these 6 sts. on to a safety pin.

Continue on 36 sts., making a second buttonhole about 1 in. above first one, until work measures $15\frac{1}{2}$ ins., finishing front edge.

Shape for Neck thus:—

Next row.—K. 4, turn.

Continue in g.st. on these 4 sts. for $\frac{1}{2}$ in. making a third buttonhole 1 in. above second one. Cast off.

Rejoin wool to main sts. and continue in st.st. thus:—

Cast off 6 sts. beg. of next row, then dec. 1 st. at neck edge on every row until 18 sts. remain.

Continue straight until work measures 18 ins., finishing armhole edge.

Shape Shoulder thus: Cast off 6 sts. beg. of next 3 rows at armhole edge.

Rejoin wool to 38 sts. for right side of front at opening edge and work thus:—

1st row.—Cast on 4 sts. for underwrap, k. to end.

Continue in st.st. with 4 underwrap sts. in g.st. until work measures same as left side of front to armhole shaping, finishing front edge.

Shape Armhole as for left side, substituting k. row for p. row, then continue straight on 36 sts. until work measures $15\frac{1}{2}$ ins., finishing front edge.

Shape Neck and complete to match first side.

The Back.—With No. 10 needles cast on 80 sts., work 1 in. in k. 1, p. 1 rib.

Continue in st.st. until work measures same as front side edge to armhole shapings, finishing p. row.

Shape Armholes thus:—

Next row.—K. 6, sl. these sts. on to a safety-pin, k. to last 6 sts., sl. these 6 sts. on to a second safety-pin.

Continue in st.st. on 68 sts. until work measures 17¼ ins., finishing p. row.

Shape Neck thus:—

Next row.—K. 24, cast off 20 sts., k. to end.

Work 6 rows on last 24 sts., dec. 1 st. at neck edge on every row, finishing armhole edge.

Shape Shoulder as for front shoulder.

Rejoin wool to remaining 24 sts., work 1 row to armhole edge, then complete to match first side.

The Sleeves.—Join shoulder seams.

With right side of work facing and using No. 10 needles, work across 6 sts. from a safety-pin, k. up 60 sts. evenly along armhole edge, (30 sts. each side of shoulder seam), k. 6 sts. from second safety-pin (72 sts.).

Work as follows:—

1st row.—P.

2nd row.—K. 6, k. 2 tog., k. to last 8 sts., k. 2 tog., k. 6. Rep. these 2 rows until 60 sts. remain.

Continue in st.st., dec. 1 st. each end of every 6th row until work measures 2¾ ins. from picked-up armhole sts. finishing p. row.

Change to No. 12 needles, work ¾ in. in k. 1, p. 1 rib.

Cast off loosely in rib with a No. 10 needle.

The Neck Band.—With right side of work facing and using No. 12 needles, k. up 116 sts. evenly round neck edge, beg. and ending inside g.st. borders.

Work ½ in. in k. 1, p. 1 rib.

Cast off loosely in rib.

Make-up.—Press lightly. Join seams.

Sew inside edges of g.st. borders to front edges of neck band.

Sew underwrap at lower edge along back of left front border.

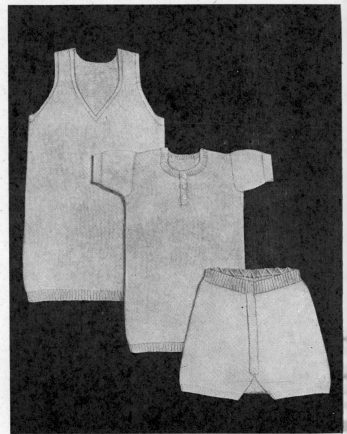

The boy's vest and pants can be worked in two sizes, with a variation in the vest design. All are knitted in stocking stitch.

Sew on buttons to match buttonholes. Press seams.

THE PANTS

The Right Leg.—With No. 10 needles cast on 92 sts., work ¾ in. in k. 1, p. 1 rib.

Continue in st.st., inc. 1 st. at both ends of next row and every following 4th row until 100 sts. are on needle.

Continue straight until work measures 2½ ins., finishing p. row at front edge.

Begin Front Border and Shapings thus:—

Next row.—Cast on 3 sts., k. these 3 sts., then k. next 3 sts., k. 2 tog., k. to last 3 sts., k. 2 tog., k. 1.

Next row.—P. to last 6 sts., k. 6.

Work 2 rows in st.st. with 6 sts. at front edge in g.st.

Next row.—K. 6, k. 2 tog., k. to last 3 sts., k. 2 tog., k. 1.

Work 3 rows in st.st. with 6 sts. in g.st.

Next row.—K. 6, k. 2 tog., k. to last 3 sts., k. 2 tog., k. 1.

Work 5 rows in st.st. with 6 sts. in g.st.

Rep. last 6 rows until 79 sts. remain.

Continue straight until work measures 9½ ins. from lower edge, finishing back edge.

Shape Back thus:—

Next 2 rows.—Work to last 36 sts., turn, work to end.

Next 2 rows.—Work to last 46 sts., turn, work to end.

Next 2 rows.—Work to last 56 sts., turn, work to end.

Next 2 rows.—Work to last 66 sts., turn, work to end.

Next row.—Work to front edge.

Next row.—Cast off 3, work to end.

Change to No. 12 needles, work 1 in. in k. 1, p. 1 rib.

Cast off loosely in rib.

The Left Leg.—Work as given for right leg until work measures 2½ ins., finishing with a p. row at back edge.

Begin Front Border and Shapings thus:—

Next row.—K. 1, k. 2 tog., k. to last 5 sts., k. 2 tog., k. 3, cast on 3.

Work 3 rows in st.st. with 6 sts. at front edge in g.st.

Next row.—K. 1, k. 2 tog., k. to last 8 sts., k. 2 tog., k. 6.

Work 3 rows in st.st. with 6 sts. in g.st.

Next row.—K. 1, k. 2 tog., k. to last 8 sts., k. 2 tog., k. 6.

Work 5 rows in st.st. with 6 sts. in g.st.

Rep. last 6 rows until 79 sts. remain.

Continue straight until work measures 9½ ins. from lower edge, finishing back edge.

Shape Back and complete as for right leg.

The Gusset.—With No. 10 needles cast on 2 sts.

1st row.—K. twice into 1st st., k. 1.

Continue in st.st., inc. 1 st. both ends of every k. row (by working twice into first st. and last st. but one) until 15 sts. are on needle, then dec. 1 st. both ends of every k. row until 3 sts. remain.

K. 3 tog. and fasten off.

Make-up.—Press lightly with hot iron over damp cloth.

Join centre back seam, then join centre front seam of waist ribbing.

Sew gusset into position along shaped leg edges, with points to end of back seam and beg. of front border.

Join remaining leg edges.

Sew left front border on right side of work across right front border at waist and lower edge, then stitch right front border on wrong side of work at back of left border.

Work an elastic casing round waist thus:—

With wrong side of work facing begin at a side seam with 1 s.c. into seam, * 6 ch., 1 s.c. into ribbing about ¾ in. down and ¾ in. along, 6 ch., 1 s.c. into top edge of ribbing about ¾ in. along.

Rep. from * all round.

Press seams.

Thread elastic through casing.

VEST AND PANTS. SIZE 2

MATERIALS

7 oz. 3-ply wool (4 oz. vest, 3 oz. pants).
2 No. 10 and 2 No. 12 knitting needles.
A fine crochet hook.
¾ yd. elastic for pants.

MEASUREMENTS

Vest: Length, 22 ins.
Chest, 26 ins. (unstretched).
Pants: Waist to crutch, 11 ins.
Waist, 24 ins.

TENSION

7½ sts. to 1 in

THE VEST

The Front.—With No. 10 needles cast on 94 sts., work 1 in. in k. 1, p. 1 rib.

Continue in st.st. until work measures 16 ins., finishing k. row.

Begin Armhole and Neck Bands and Shape thus:—

1st row.—K. 6, p. 40, k. 2, p. 40, k. 6.
2nd and alternate rows.—K. to end.
3rd row.—K. 7, p. 38, k. 4, p. 38, k. 7.
5th row.—K. 8, p. 36, k. 6, p. 36, k. 8.
6th row.—Cast off 6 sts., now 1 st. on right-hand needle, k. 35, k. 2 tog., k. 3, turn.

Leave remaining 47 sts. on spare needle.

Continue on these 40 sts. for left side of front thus:—

7th row.—K. 3, p. to last 3 sts., k. 3.
8th row.—K. 3, k. 2 tog., k. to last 5 sts., k. 2 tog., k. 3.
Rep. last 2 rows 11 times, finishing k. row.

This completes armhole shaping.

Work 3 rows in st.st. with g.st. border.

Next row.—K. to last 5 sts., k. 2 tog., k. 3.

Continue straight on 15 sts. until work measures 22 ins., finishing armhole edge.

Shape Shoulder thus: Cast off 5 sts. on next 3 rows beg. armhole edge.

Rejoin wool to second set of sts. at opening edge and work thus:—

1st row.—K. 3, k. 2 tog., k. to end.
2nd row.—Cast off 6, now 1 st. on right-hand needle, k. 2, p. to last 3 sts., k. 3.
3rd row.—K. 3, k. 2 tog., k. to last 5 sts., k. 2 tog., k. 3.
4th row.—K. 3, p. to last 3 sts., k. 3.
Rep. last 2 rows 11 times.

Work 2 rows in st.st. with g.st. borders.

Next row.—K. 3, k. 2 tog., k. to end.

Continue straight on 15 sts. to match with first side.

The Back.—With No. 10 needles cast on 94 sts., work 1 in. in k. 1, p. 1 rib.

Continue in st.st. until work measures 16 ins., finishing k. row.

Begin Armhole Bands and Shape Armholes thus:—

1st row.—K. 6, p. to last 6 sts., k. 6.
2nd and alternate rows.—K. to end.
3rd row.—K. 7, p. to last 7 sts., k. 7.
5th row.—K. 8, p. to last 8 sts., k. 8.
6th row.—Cast off 6, k. to end.
7th row.—Cast off 6, now 1 st. on right-hand needle, k. 2, p. to last 3 sts., k. 3.
8th row.—K. 3, k. 2 tog., k. to last 5 sts., k. 2 tog., k. 3.
9th row.—K. 3, p. to last 3 sts., k. 3.
Rep. last 2 rows 11 times.

Continue straight on 58 sts. until work measures 20½ ins., finishing p. row.

Shape Neck and Shoulders thus:—

1st and alternate rows.—K. to end.
2nd row.—K. 3, p. 18, k. 16, p. 18, k. 3.
4th row.—K. 3, p. 17, k. 18, p. 17, k. 3.
6th row.—K. 3, p. 16, k. 20, p. 16, k. 3.
8th row.—K. 3, p. 15, k. 22, p. 15, k. 3.
9th row.—K. 21, cast off 16, k. to end.

Work on last set of 21 sts., thus:—

Next row.—K. 3, p. to last 5 sts., p. 2 tog., k. 3.
Next row.—K. 3, k. 2 tog., k. to end.
Rep. last 2 rows twice.

Continue straight on 15 sts. until work measures 22 ins., finishing armhole edge.

Shape shoulder as for front shoulder.

Rejoin wool to remaining 21 sts. at

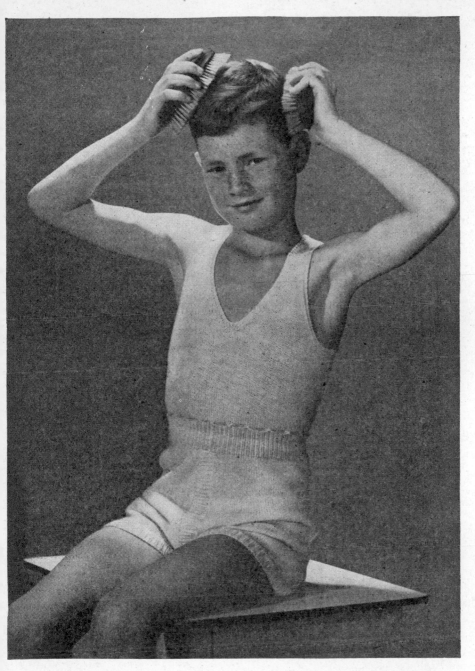

Thomas, who is ten, has outgrown the vest with sleeves that Christopher wears. He prefers his vest with a V neck and no sleeves. The pants are the same design as the smaller boy's, but knitted in a larger size.

neck edge and work thus:—

1st row.—K. 3, p. 2 tog., p. to last 3 sts., k. 3.

2nd row.—K. to last 5 sts., k. 2 tog., k. 3.

Rep. last 2 rows twice.

Continue straight on 15 sts. to match first side.

Make-up.—Press lightly on wrong side with hot iron over damp cloth.

Join side and shoulder seams.

Press seams.

THE PANTS

The Right Leg.—With No. 10 needles cast on 108 sts., work 1 in. in k. 1, p. 1 rib.

Continue in st.st. inc. 1 st. both ends of next row and every following 4th row until 116 sts. are on needle.

Continue straight until work measures 3½ ins., finishing p. row at front edge.

Begin Front Border and Shapings thus:—

Next row.—Cast on 4, k. these 4 sts., k. next 4 sts., k. 2 tog., k. to last 3 sts., k. 2 tog., k. 1.

Next row.—P. to last 8 sts., k. 8.

Work 4 rows in st.st. with 8 sts. at front edge in g.st.

Next row.—K. 8, k. 2 tog., k. to last 3 sts., k. 2 tog., k. 1.

Rep. last 6 rows until 96 sts. remain.

Continue straight until work measures 10½ ins. from lower edge., finishing back edge.

Shape Back thus:—

Next 2 rows.—Work to last 46 sts., turn, work to end.

Next 2 rows.—Work to last 56 sts., turn, work to end.

Next 2 rows.—Work to last 66 sts., turn, work to end.

Next 2 rows.—Work to last 76 sts., turn, work to end.

Next 2 rows.—Work to last 86 sts., turn, work to end.

Next row.—Work to front edge.

Next row.—Cast off 4 sts., work to end.

Change to No. 12 needles, work 1½ ins. in k. 1, p. 1 rib.

Cast off loosely in rib.

The Left Leg.—Work as given for right leg until work measures 3½ ins., finishing p. row at back edge.

Begin Front Border and Shapings thus:—

Next row.—K. 1, k. 2 tog., k. to last 6 sts., k. 2 tog., k. 4 cast on 4.

Next row.—K. 8, p. to end.

Work 4 rows in st.st. with 8 sts. at front edge in g.st.

Next row.—K. 1, k. 2 tog., k. to last 10 sts., k. 2 tog., k. 8.

Rep. last 6 rows until 96 sts. remain.

Continue straight until work measures 10½ ins. from lower edge, finishing back edge, then complete as for right leg.

The Gusset.—With No. 10 needles cast on 2 sts.

1st row.—K. twice into first st., k. 1.

Continue in st.st. inc. 1 st. both ends of every k. row (by working twice into first st. and last st. but one) until 21 sts. are on needle, then dec. at both ends of every k. row until 3 sts. remain.

K. 3 tog. and fasten off.

Make-up.—Press work lightly on wrong side with hot iron over damp cloth.

Join centre back seam, then join centre front seam of waist ribbing.

Sew gusset into position along shaped leg edges, with points to end of back seam and beg. of front border.

Join remaining leg edges.

Sew left front border on right side of work across right front border, at waist and crutch, then sew right front border at back of left front border.

Work an elastic casing round waist thus:—With wrong side of work facing begin with a s.c. into seam, * 6 ch., 1 s.c. into ribbing about ¾ in. down and ¾ in. along, 6 ch., 1 s.c. into top edge of ribbing about ¾ in. along; rep. from * all round.

Press seams.

Thread elastic through casing.

Three Piece Set

VEST, BODICE AND BUTTON-ON KNICKERS

MATERIALS

2 oz. 2-ply wool for the vest.
2 oz. 3-ply wool for the bodice.
2 oz. 3-ply wool for the knickers.
2 No. 10 and 2 No. 12 knitting needles.
A fine crochet hook.
4 small buttons for vest.
4 buttons and a piece of white tape about ½ to ¾ in. wide for bodice.
6 small buttons and a small piece of silk or thin cotton fabric for facing for knickers.

MEASUREMENTS

Vest: Length, 18 ins. Chest, 22 ins.
Bodice: Length, 13 ins. Chest, 23 ins.
Knickers: Waist to crutch, 10 ins. All round above gusset, 28 ins.

TENSION

With 2-ply wool, 8 sts. to 1 in.
With 3-ply wool, 7½ sts. to 1 in.

THE VEST

The Front.—Begin at shoulder edge with No. 10 needles and cast on 44 sts.

Work in g.st. rib with moss st. borders:

1st row.—(P. 1, k. 1) twice, p. 1, k. 34, p. 1, (k. 1, p. 1) twice.

2nd row.—P. 1, (k. 1, p. 1) twice, * p. 4, k. 1; rep. from * to last

9 sts., p. 4, (p. 1, k. 1) twice, p. 1.

Rep. these 2 rows until work measures 2½ ins., finishing row on wrong side.

Break off wool.

Work a second piece exactly the same for other shoulder, finishing row on wrong side, then join the two pieces thus:—

Next row.—Moss st. 5, k. 34, moss st. 5, cast on 35, moss st. 5, k. 34, moss st. 5 across first piece (123 sts.).

Next row.—Moss st. 5, (p. 4, k. 1) 6 times, p. 4, moss st. 45, (p. 4, k. 1) 6 times, p. 4, moss st. 5.

Next row.—Moss st. 5, k. 34, moss st. 45, k. 34, moss st. 5.

Rep. last 2 rows until work measures

Margaret's vest is knitted in a flat rib and fastens on the shoulders. The bodice can support both knickers and skirt.

¾ in. from cast-on edge of neck border, finishing row on wrong side.

Next row.—Moss st. 5, k. 34, k. twice into next st., k. to last 5 sts., moss st. 5 (124 sts.).

Next row.—Moss st. 5, * p. 4, k. 1; rep. from * to last 9 sts., p. 4, moss st. 5.

Next row.—Moss st. 5, k. to last 5 sts., moss st. 5. Rep. last 2 rows until work measures 4 ins. from shoulder edges.

Shape for Sleeves thus: Continue in g.st. rib, cast off 8 sts. beg. of next 2 rows, then dec. 1 st. both ends of every row until 84 sts. remain.

Continue without shaping until work measures 17½ ins. from shoulder edges, finishing row on wrong side.

Continue in moss st. across all sts. until work measures 18 ins.

Cast off loosely in moss st.

The Back.—Begin at shoulder edge with No. 10 needles, and cast on 44 sts. Work exactly as given for front in g.st. rib with moss st. borders but work for only 1 in. instead of 2½ ins.

Work a second piece in same way, then join as given for front (123 sts.).

Now continue across all sts. exactly as given for front.

THE BODICE

The Front.—Begin at lower edge with No. 10 needles and cast on 87 sts.

Work in moss st. for 1 in.

Continue in st.st. until work measures 7¾ ins., finishing p. row.

Begin Armhole Borders and Shape Armholes thus:—

Next row.—(P. 1, k. 1) 4 times, p. 1, k. to last 9 sts., (p. 1, k. 1) 4 times, p. 1

Next row.—P. 1, (k. 1, p. 1) 4 times, p. to last 9 sts., (p. 1, k. 1) 4 times, p. 1.

Rep. these 2 rows for ¾ in. finishing row on wrong side (8½ ins. from beg.).

Next row.—Cast off 4 sts., moss st. to end of border, work to end.

Rep. this row once.

Next row.—Moss st. 5, k. 2 tog., k. to

last 7 sts., k. 2 tog., moss st. 5.

Next row.—Moss st. 5, p. 2 tog., p. to last 7 sts., p. 2 tog., moss st. 5.

Rep. last 2 rows once.

Continue straight on 71 sts. until work measures 9¼ ins., finishing on wrong side.

Begin Neck Border and Shaping thus:—

Next row.—Moss st. 5, k. 10, (p. 1, k. 1) 20 times, p. 1, k. 10, moss st. 5.

Next row.—Moss st. 5, p. 10, (p. 1, k. 1) 20 times, p. 11, moss st. 5.

Rep. these 2 rows for ¾ in., finishing row on wrong side (10 ins. from beg.).

Next row.—Moss st. 5, k. 10, moss st. 5, cast off 31, moss st. to end of border, k. 10, moss st. 5.

Continue in st.st. and moss st. borders on 20 sts. for one shoulder until work measures 13 ins. Cast off.

Rejoin wool to other 20 sts. at neck edge and work to match.

The Back.—Work as given for front to end of armhole shapings.

Continue straight on 71 sts. until work measures 10¾ ins., finishing row on wrong side.

Work neck border as given for ¾ in. (11½ ins. from beg.), then cast off for neck and complete shoulders to match with front.

THE KNICKERS

The Front:—

Right Leg.—With No. 12 needles cast on 52 sts. loosely and work 1 in. in k. 1, p. 1 rib. Break off wool, leave sts. on spare needle.

The Left Leg.—Work another piece as for right leg, then join legs and begin gusset.

Change to No. 10 needles.

Next row.—K. 52, cast on 18 for gusset, k. 52 for right leg.

Next row.—P. to end.

Next row.—K. 52, k. 2 tog., k. to last 54 sts., k. 2 tog., k. 52.

Rep. last 2 rows until 106 sts. remain, finishing p. row.

Margaret is all for economy in effort. In winter she wears a knitted bodice over her vest, and buttons her knickers on to the bodice. Then she buttons her kilt on to the bodice too. The set is beautifully warm but not bulky.

Next row.—K. 52, k. 2 tog., k. 52 (105 sts.).

Work 3 rows in st.st., then shape thus:—

Next row.—K. 50, k. 2 tog., k. 1, k. 2 tog., k. 50.

Work 3 rows in st.st.

Next row.—K. 49, k. 2 tog., k. 1, k. 2 tog., k. 49.

Continue in this way, dec. 1 st. on each side of centre st. on every 4th row until work measures 5½ ins. from cast-on gusset sts., finishing with a p. row.

Begin moss st. borders, still dec. as before on every 4th row:—

Next row.—(K. 1, p. 1) twice, k. to last 4 sts., (p. 1, k. 1) twice.

Next row.—(K. 1, p. 1) twice, p. to last 4 sts., (p. 1, k. 1) twice.

Rep. these 2 rows, continuing to dec. on each side of centre st. on every 4th row for 1 in., finishing row on wrong side.

Next row.—K. 1, p. 1, w.r.n., p. 2 tog. for a buttonhole, work to last 4 sts., p. 2 tog., w.r.n., p. 1, k. 1

Continue in st.st. with moss st. borders, dec. on every 4th row until 83 sts. remain.

Continue without shaping until work measures 8 ins. from cast-on gusset sts. finishing p. row.

Next row.—K. 1, p. 1, w.r.n., p. 2 tog., * k. 1, p. 1; rep. from * to last 5 sts. k. 1, p. 2 tog., w.r.n., p. 1, k. 1.

Next row.—* K. 1, p. 1; rep. from * to last st., k. 1.

Rep. this last row for 1 in., finishing row on wrong side.

Next row.—Moss st. 19, turn.

Work ½ in. in moss st. on these 19 sts., finishing inside edge.

Break off wool. Rejoin to main sts., moss st. next 45 sts., turn.

Work ½ in. in moss st. on these 45 sts., finishing row on right side.

Break off wool. Rejoin to remaining 19 sts. and work ½ in. in moss st., finishing outside edge.

Work 1 row in moss st. across all sts.

Next row.—K. 1, p. 1, w.r.n., p. 2 tog., * k. 1, p. 1; rep. from * to last 5 sts., k. 1, p. 2 tog., w.r.n., p. 1, k. 1.

Continue in moss st. until work measures 10 ins. from cast-on gusset sts.

Cast off loosely in moss st.

The Back.—Continue as for front until work measures 5½ ins. from cast-on gusset sts., finishing p. row.

Begin moss st. underwraps thus, still dec. as before on every 4th row.

Next 2 rows.—Cast on 4 sts., work to end.

Next row.—(K. 1, p. 1) twice, k. to last 4 sts., (p. 1, k. 1) twice.

Next row.—(K. 1, p. 1) twice, p. to last 4 sts., (p. 1, k. 1) twice.

Continue thus, working in st.st. with moss st. borders and dec. on each side of centre st. on every 4th row until 91 sts. remain.

Continue straight until work measures 8 ins. from cast-on gusset sts., finishing p. row.

Shape for Back thus:—

1st row.—Moss st. 4, k. to last 10 sts., turn.

2nd row.—P. to last 10 sts., turn.

3rd row.—K. to last 20 sts., turn.

4th row.—P. to last 20 sts., turn.

Continue to work 10 sts. less on every row until 40 sts. are left at each side.

Work 2 rows across all sts., then continue in moss st. across all sts. for 1 in., finishing row on wrong side.

Next row.—Moss st. 23, turn.

Work ½ in. in moss st. on these 23 sts., finishing inside edge.

Break off wool. Rejoin to main sts., work ½ in. in moss st. on next 45 sts., finishing row on right side. Break off wool.

Rejoin to remaining 23 sts. and work ½ in. in moss st., finishing outside edge.

Continue in moss st. across all sts. until work measures 10 ins. from cast-on gusset sts. at side edge. Cast off.

Make-up.—Press all work lightly on wrong side with hot iron over damp cloth.

The Vest.—Join side seams.

Join shoulder seams beginning at sleeve edge and ending about 2 ins. from neck edge.

Work a row of d.c. along shoulder edges, making 2 small ch. button loops on front shoulders. Sew buttons on to back shoulders matching loops.

The Bodice.—Join side and shoulder seams. Press seams.

Sew a length of tape on wrong side down each side of front and back, beginning at shoulder edge and placing it in centre of shoulders.

Sew buttons on to tapes at required position from lower edge.

The Knickers.—Join leg and gusset seams. Join side seams as far as beginning of moss st. borders.

Cut cross-way strips of material about 2½ ins. to 3 ins. wide and with these face the moss st. waist band on wrong side.

Cut buttonholes neatly in this facing and buttonhole stitch round each one, working through double fabric.

Sew underwraps on wrong side at lower edge of moss st. front borders.

Sew buttons on to underwraps to match buttonhole.

Press all seams.

Boy's or Girl's Pullover

SLEEVELESS OR WITH LONG SLEEVES

MATERIALS

3 oz. 3-ply wool, for the sleeveless pullover.

5 oz. 3-ply wool for the long-sleeved style.

2 No. 10 and 2 No. 12 needles.

A medium size crochet hook.

6 buttons for the long-sleeved style.

MEASUREMENTS

Length, 14 ins.

Chest, 23 ins.

Sleeve seam, 12 ins.

TENSION

7½ sts. to 1 in. measured over moss st.

The Front.—With No. 10 needles cast on 96 sts. Change to No. 12 needles and work 2 ins. in k. 1, p. 1 rib.

Change to No. 10 needles and following patt.:—

1st row.—* P. 1, k. 1, p. 2, k. 4, p. 3, k. 1; rep. from * to end.

2nd row.—* K. 1, p. 1, k. 2, p. 4, k. 3, p. 1; rep. from * to end.

3rd row.—* Moss st. 2, p. 2, sl. next 2 sts. on to a spare needle and leave at back of work, k. next 2 sts., then k. 2 sts. from spare needle, p. 2, moss st. 2; rep. from * to end.

4th row.—As 2nd row.

These 4 rows form the patt.

Continue in patt. until work measures 9¼ ins., ending with row on wrong side.

Shape for Armholes thus: Cast off 5 sts. at beg. of next 2 rows, then dec. 1 st. at both ends of the next 4 rows. Now dec. 1 st. at both ends of every alternate row until 74 sts. remain.

Continue in patt. until work measures 12 ins., ending with a row on wrong side.

Shape for Neck thus:—

Next row.—Patt. across 28 sts., turn.

Christopher has beaten Margaret in the race to get dressed. He is wearing his cable-stitch sleeveless pullover over his shirt, for extra warmth, and begins the day well by seeing that the cat eats his breakfast properly.

Work 10 rows in patt. on this set of sts. only, dec. 1 st. at neck edge on every row (18 sts.).

Continue without shaping until work measures 14 ins., ending at armhole edge.

Shape Shoulders thus: Cast off 6 sts. on next 3 rows beg. at armhole edge.

Return to main set of sts., sl. the centre 18 sts. on to spare needle and leave for neck band, rejoin wool and work on remaining 28 sts. to match first side.

The Front Neck Border.—With right side of work facing and using No. 12 needles, K. up 24 sts. along neck edge,

Margaret has reached the skirt stage. She has buttoned it securely on to her knitted bodice, which has tape straps to take the strain of the buttons. Now she'll don the long-sleeved version of Christopher's pullover (page 175).

18 sts. from spare needle, 24 sts. along neck edge.

For sleeveless pullover, work ¾ ins. in k. 1, p. 1 rib. Cast off loosely in rib.

For the long-sleeved pullover proceed as above, but instead of casting off after the ¾ in. has been worked. dec. thus:—

K. 1, p. 1, k. 1, * p 3 tog., k. 1, p. 1, k. 1, p. 1, k. 1; rep. from * until 7 sts. remain, p. 3 tog., k. 1, p. 1, k. 1, p. 1. Work in rib for a further ½ in. Cast off.

The Back.—Proceed as given for front until armhole shapings are completed.

Continue in patt. on 74 sts. until work

measures 13½ ins., ending with a row on wrong side.

Shape Neck and Shoulders thus:—

Next row. — Patt. across 25 sts., turn. Work on these sts. only as follows:—

Work 3 rows in patt., dec. 1 st. at neck edge on every row.

Next row.—Cast off 6 sts., patt. to last 2 sts., k. 2 tog.

Next row.—K. 2 tog., patt. to end.

Rep. last 2 rows once. Cast off remaining sts.

Return to main set of sts., sl. centre 24 sts. on to a spare needle and leave for neck band.

Rejoin wool and work on remaining 25 sts. to match the first side.

The Back Neck Border.—With right side of work facing and using No. 12 needles, k. up 9 sts. along neck edge, 24 sts. from spare needle, 9 sts. along neck edge.

For sleeveless pullover, work ¾ in. in k. 1, p. 1 rib.

Cast off loosely in rib.

For long-sleeved pullover, proceed as above, but instead of casting off, dec. thus:—

K. 1, p. 1, k. 1, * p. 3 tog.. k. 1, p. 1, k. 1,

p. 1, k. 1; rep. from * until 7 sts. remain. P. 3 tog., k. 1, p. 1, k. 1, p. 1.

Work in rib for a further ½ in.

Cast off loosely in rib.

The Armhole Borders (for sleeveless pullover).—Backstitch shoulder seams, oversewing the neck borders.

With right side of work facing and using No. 12 needles, k. up 88 sts. along armhole edge, 44 sts. on each side of shoulder seam.

Work ¾ in. in k. 1, p. 1 rib.

Cast off loosely in rib.

The Sleeves.—With No. 12 needles cast on 48 sts. and work in k. 1, p. 1 rib for 2 ins.

Change to No. 10 needles and continue in patt. as for front, inc. 1 st. at both ends of next and every following 6th row until there are 72 sts. on needle.

Continue without further shaping until sleeve measures 12 ins.

Christopher's and Margaret's pullovers are made from the same pattern. The stitch is a combination of moss, purl and cable stitches.

At last she's dressed. Her pullover is like Christopher's except that it has long sleeves. Both versions of this pullover are suitable for a boy or girl.

Shape Top thus: Dec. 1 st. at both ends of every row until 16 sts. remain. Cast off.

Make-up. The Sleeveless Pullover.— Press work lightly on wrong side with a hot iron over a damp cloth. Join side and armhole border seams. Press all seams.

The Long-sleeved Pullover.—Join side and sleeve seams.

Join shoulders for about $\frac{1}{2}$ in. at armhole edges, then sew sleeves into armholes.

With a medium-size crochet hook work a row of d.c. on shoulder edges, making 3 button loops on each front shoulder.

Press all seams. Sew on buttons

Girl's Cardigan

IN A GAY, FEATHERY STITCH

MATERIALS

6 oz. 3-ply wool.
1 pair each No. 10 and No. 12 needles.
8 buttons.

MEASUREMENTS

Length, 16½ ins.
Chest, 28 ins.
Sleeve seam, 16 ins.

TENSION

8 sts. to 1 in. measured over patt.

The Back.—With No. 12 needles cast on 92 sts. and work in k. 1, p. 1 rib for 3 ins. Change to No. 10 needles and following patt.:—

1st row.—K. 4, * p. 4, k. 6; rep. from * to end, ending k. 4 instead of k. 6.

2nd row.—P. 4, * k. 4, p. 6; rep. from * to end, ending p. 4 instead of p. 6.

3rd row.—As 1st row.

4th row.—P. 4, * k. 1, m. 1, k. 2, m. 1, k. 1, p. 6; rep. from * to end, ending p. 4 instead of p. 6.

5th row.—K. 4, * p. 1, k. into back of loop, p. 2, k. into back of loop, p. 1, k. 6; rep. from * to end, ending k. 4. instead of k. 6.

6th row.—P. 3, * k. 2 tog., p. 1, m. 1, k. 2, m. 1, p. 1, sl. 1, k. 1, p.s.s.o., p. 4; rep. from * to end, ending p. 3 instead of p. 4.

7th row.—K. 3, * p. 1, k. 1, k. into back of loop, p. 2, k. into back of loop, k. 1, p. 1, k. 4; rep. from * to end. ending k. 3 instead of k. 4.

8th row.—K. 1, * k. 3 tog., p. 2, m. 1, k. 2, m. 1, p. 2, sl. 2, k. 1, p.s.sts.o.; rep. from * to last st., k. 1.

9th row.—K. 4, * k. into back of loop, p. 2, k. into back of loop, k. 6; rep. from * to end, ending k. 4 instead of k. 6.

The last 8 rows, i.e. rows 2 to 9 inclusive, form the patt.

Continue in patt., shaping as follows:—

Beg. again at 2nd row, work in patt. inc. 1 st. at both ends of the next and every following 4th row, 5 times, keeping the extra sts. at each side in the p. and k. fabric to fit in with patt.. ending with the 2nd patt. row (102 sts.).

Now work these extra sts. into patt. thus:—

27th row.—P. 3, * k. 6, p. 4; rep. from * to end, ending p. 3 instead of p. 4.

28th row.—K. 2, m. 1, k. 1, * p. 6, k. 1, m. 1, k. 2, m. 1, k. 1; rep. from * to last 9 sts., p. 6, k. 1, m. 1, k. 2.

29th row.—P. 2, k. into back of loop, p. 1, * k. 6, p. 1, k. into back of loop, p. 2, k. into back of loop, p. 1; rep. from * to last 10 sts., k. 6, p. 1, k. into back of loop, p. 2.

30th row.—K. twice into 1st st., k. 1, m. 1, p. 1, sl. 1, k. 1, p.s.s.o., * p. 4, k. 2 tog., p. 1, m. 1, k. 2, m. 1, p. 1, sl. 1, k. 1, p.s.s.o.; rep. from * to last 9 sts., p. 4, k. 2 tog., p. 1. m. 1, k. twice into next st., k. 1.

31st row.—P. 3, k. into back of loop, k. 1, p. 1, * k. 4, p. 1, k. 1, k. into back of loop, p. 2, k. into back of loop, k. 1, p. 1; rep. from * to last 10 sts., k. 4, p. 1, k. 1, k. into back of loop, p. 3.

32nd row.—K. 3, m. 1, k. 2, sl. 2, k. 1, p.s.sts.o. * k. 3 tog., p. 2, m. 1, k. 2, m. 1, p. 2, sl. 2, k. 1, p.s.sts.o.; rep. from * to last 8 sts., k. 3 tog., p. 2, m. 1, k. 3.

Ten-year-olds will like this gay and practical cardigan. It's pretty enough for feminine tastes, but will stand up to plenty of rough wear.

33rd row.—P. 3, k. into back of loop, * k. 6, k. into back of loop, p. 2, k. into back of loop, rep. from * to last 10 sts., k. 6, k. into back of loop, p. 3.

34th row.—K. twice into 1st st., k. 3. * p. 6, k. 4; rep. from * to last 10 sts.. p. 6, k. 2, k. twice into next st., k. 1.

35th row.—K. 1, p. 4, * k. 6, p. 4; rep. from * to last st., k. 1.

36th row.—P. 1, k. 3, m. 1, k. 1, * p. 6, k. 1, m. 1, k. 2, m. 1, k. 1; rep. from * to last 11 sts., p. 6, k. 1, m. 1, k. 3, p. 1.

37th row.—K. 1, p. 3, k. into back of loop, p. 1, * k. 6, p. 1, k. into back of loop, p. 2, k. into back of loop, p. 1; rep. from * to last 12 sts., k. 6, p. 1, k. into back of loop, p. 3, k. 1.

38th row.—P. twice into 1st st., k. 3, m. 1, p. 1, * sl. 1, k. 1, p.s.s.o., p. 4, k. 2 tog., p. 1, m. 1, k. 2, m. 1, p. 1; rep. from * to end, ending k. 3, p. twice into last st. instead of k. 2, m. 1, p. 1.

39th row.—K. 2, p. 3, * k. into back of loop, k. 1, p. 1, k. 4, p. 1, k. 1, k. into back of loop, p. 2; rep. from * to last 3 sts., p. 1, k. 2.

40th row.—P. 2, k. 3, * m. 1, p. 2, sl. 2, k. 1, p.s.sts.o., k. 3 tog., p. 2, m. 1, k. 2;

rep. from * to last 3 sts., k. 1, p. 2.

41st row.—K. 2, p. 1, * p. 2, k. into back of loop, k. 6, k. into back of loop; rep. from * to last 5 sts., p. 3, k. 2.

42nd row.—P. twice into first st., p. 1, * k. 4, p. 6; rep. from * to last 6 sts., k. 4, p. twice into next st., p. 1.

43rd row.—K. 3, * p. 4, k. 6; rep. from * to last 7 sts , p. 4, k. 3.

44th row.—P. 3, * k. 1. m. 1, k. 2, m. 1, k. 1, p. 6; rep. from * to end, ending p. 3 instead of p. 6.

45th row.—K. 3, * p. 1, k. into back of loop, p. 2, k. into back of loop, p. 1, k. 6; rep. from * to end, ending k. 3, instead of k. 6.

46th row.—P. twice into first st., p. 1, * k. 2 tog., p. 1, m. 1, k. 2, m. 1, p. 1, sl. 1, k. 1, p.s.s.o., p. 4; rep. from * to end, ending p. twice into next st., p. 1, instead of p. 4. This completes side shapings.

47th-49th rows.—Rep. patt. rows 7, 8 and 9 inclusive, once (112 sts. left).

Beg. at 2nd patt. row, continue in patt. without shaping until work measures 11 ins., ending with a 9th patt. row.

Shape Armholes thus: Keeping the continuity of the patt. cast off 6 sts. at beg. of next 2 rows, then dec. 1 st. at both ends of the next 4 alternate rows, working the extra sts. at both ends in the purl fabric (92 sts. remain).

Continue in patt. without shaping until work measures 16½ ins., ending with a 9th patt. row.

Shape Neck and Shoulders thus:—

Next row.—Work in patt. across 33 sts., cast off next 26 sts., work in patt. to end. Work on last set of 33 sts. thus:—

Next row.—Cast off 9 sts., work in patt. to last 2 sts., work 2 tog.

Next row.—Cast off 2 sts., work in patt. to end. Rep. the last 2 rows once.

Cast off remaining sts.

Rejoin wool to second set of sts. at neck edge and work to armhole edge.

Now shape to match first shoulder.

The Right Front.—With No. 12 needles cast on 42 sts. and work 3 ins. in k. 1, p. 1 rib.

Change to No. 10 needles and rep. patt. rows 1 to 9 inclusive as given for back once, ending at front edge.

Continue in patt., shaping side edge by inc. 1 st. at end of next and every following 4th row, 5 times, keeping the extra sts. in k. and p. fabric to fit in with patt. and ending with a second patt. row (47 sts.). Now work these extra sts. into patt. as in back, ending k. rows and beg. p. rows as for 27th to 49th rows inclusive.

Beg. at 2nd patt. row

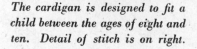

The cardigan is designed to fit a child between the ages of eight and ten. Detail of stitch is on right.

continue in patt. on these 52 sts. without further shaping until work measures 11 ins., ending with 2nd patt. row at side edge.

Shape Armhole thus: Keeping the continuity of the patt. cast off 6 sts. at beg. of next row, then dec. 1 st. at this same edge on the next 4 alternate rows, working the extra sts. at this edge in the p. fabric (42 sts. remain).

Continue in patt. without further shaping until work measures 15 ins. ending at front edge with a 9th patt. row.

Shape Neck thus:—

Next row.—Cast off 5 sts. from neck edge, work as 2nd patt. row to end.

Then dec. 1 st. on every row at neck edge until 27 sts. remain. Now work 5 more rows in patt. thus ending at armhole edge.

Shape Shoulder thus:—

Next row.—Cast off 9 sts. Patt. to end.

Next row.—Patt. to end. Rep. last 2 rows once. Cast off remaining sts.

The Left Front.—Proceed as given for right front until 47 sts. are on the needle at the end of a 2nd patt. row, shaping for side edge at the beg. of row.

Work these extra sts. into patt. as for back, beg. k. rows and ending p. rows as for 27th to 49th rows inclusive.

Beg. at 2nd patt. row, continue in patt. without shaping until work measures 11 ins. ending with a 9th patt. row at side edge. Shape armhole as given for right front, then continue on 42 sts. until work measures 15 ins., ending at front edge with a 2nd patt. row.

Shape Neck thus:—

Next row.—Cast off 5 sts., work as 3rd patt. row to end.

Now dec. 1 st. on every row at neck edge until 27 sts. remain.

Now work 4 more rows in patt. thus ending at armhole edge, then shape shoulder as given for right front.

The Sleeves.—With No. 12 needles, cast on 52 sts. and work 3 ins. in k. 1. p. 1 rib.

Change to No. 10 needles and rep. patt. rows 1 to 9 inclusive as given for back, once.

Then inc. 1 st. at beg. and end of next and every following 6th row (working extra sts. in k. and p. fabric, until there are sufficient sts. inc. to work into patt. as for back), until there are 92 sts. on needle. Continue in patt. without shaping until work measures 16 ins., ending with row on right side.

Shape Top thus: Keeping continuity of patt., dec. 1 st. at beg. and end of every row until 22 sts. remain. Cast off.

The Right Front Band.—With No. 12 needles cast on 10 sts. and work 4 rows in k. 1, p. 1 rib.

Next row.—Rib 3, cast off 4 sts. for a buttonhole, rib to end.

Next row.—Rib 3, cast on 4 sts., rib 3.

* Continue in rib until work measures 2 ins. from beg. of previous buttonhole; make another buttonhole in next 2 rows.

Rep. from * 5 times, then continue in rib until band measures the same as right front edge to beg. of neck shaping when slightly stretched.

Leave sts. on a spare needle.

The Left Front Band.—With No. 12 needles cast on 10 sts. and work in k. 1, p. 1 rib until band is the same length as right front band. Leave sts. on spare needle.

Make-up and Neck Band.—Press work lightly on wrong side. Join shoulder seams.

Stitch front bands to front edges.

Now with right side of work facing and using No. 12 needles, rib 10 sts. for right front band, k. up 84 sts. evenly round neck edge, rib 10 sts. for left front band.

Work ½ in. in k. 1, p. 1 rib, ending at right front edge, then make another buttonhole in next 2 rows.

Now continue in rib until neck band measures 1 in. Cast off loosely in rib.

Join side and sleeve seams. Sew sleeves into armholes, matching seams to side seams. Sew on buttons. Press seams.

Sun Suit

WITH SMART SIDE CABLE PANELS

MATERIALS

3 oz. 3-ply wool.
2 No. 10 and 2 No. 12 knitting needles.
A crochet hook.
4 button .

MEASUREMENTS

Waist to crutch, 9 ins.
All round above gusset, 25 ins.

TENSION

7½ sts. to 1 in. over st.st.

The Front. The Right Leg.—With No. 10 needles cast on 8 sts.

1st row.—K. to end, cast on 4 sts.
2nd row.—P. to end.
Rep. last 2 rows twice.
7th row.—K. to end, cast on 4 sts.
8th row.—K. 2, p. to end.
9th row.—K. 22, p. 2, cast on 4 sts.
10th row.—P 4, k. 2, p. 22.
11th row.—K. 22, p. 2, k. 4, cast on 4 sts.
12th row.—P. 8, k. 2, p. 22.
13th row.—K. 22, p. 2, k. 8, cast on 4 sts.
14th row.—P. 2, k. 2, p. 8, k. 2, p. 22.
15th row.—K. 22, p. 2, twist next 8 sts. thus: sl. next 4 sts. on to spare needle, leave at back of work, k. next 4 sts., k. 4 sts. from spare needle, p. 2, k. 2, cast on 4 sts.
16th row.—P. 6, k. 2, p. 8, k. 2, p. 22.
17th row.—K. 22, p. 2, k. 8, p. 2, k. 6, cast on 4 sts.
18th row.—P. 10, k. 2, p. 8, k. 2, p. 22.
19th row.—K. 22, p. 2, twist next 8 sts., p. 2, k. 10, cast on 4 sts.
20th row.—P. 14, k. 2, p. 8, k. 2, p. 22.

21st row.—K. 22, p. 2, k. 8, p. 2, k. 14, cast on 5 sts.
22nd row.—P. 19, k. 2, p. 8 k. 2, p. 22. Leave these sts. on spare needle.

The Left Leg.—With No. 10 needles cast on 8 sts.

1st row.—P. to end, cast on 4 sts.
2nd row.—K. to end.
Rep. last 2 rows twice, then 1st row.
8th row.—P. 2, k. to end.
9th row.—P. 22, k. 2, cast on 4 sts.
10th row.—K. 4, p. 2, k. 22.
11th row.—P. 22, k. 2, p. 4, cast on 4 sts.
12th row.—K. 8, p. 2, k. 22.
13th row.—P. 22, k. 2, p. 8, cast on 4 sts.
14th row.—K. 2, p. 2, k. 8, p. 2, k. 22.
15th row.—P. 22, k. 2, p. 8, k. 2, p. 2, cast on 4 sts.
16th row.—K. 6, p. 2, twist next 8 sts., p. 2, k. 22
17th row.—P. 22, k. 2, p. 8, k. 2, p. 6, cast on 4 sts.

The cable panel.

18th row.—K. 10, p. 2, k. 8, p. 2, k. 22.

19th row.—P. 22, k. 2, p. 8, k. 2, p. 10 cast on 4 sts.

20th row.—K. 14, p. 2, twist next 8 sts., p. 2, k. 22.

21st row.—P. 22, k. 2, p. 8, k. 2, p. 14, cast on 5 sts.

22nd row.—K. 19, p. 2, k. 8, p. 2, k. 22.

23rd row.—P. 22, k. 2, p. 8, k. 2, p. 19. Now join legs thus:—

24th row.—K. 19, p. 2, twist next 8 sts., p. 2, k. 22, now work across sts. for right leg thus: k. 22, p. 2, twist next 8 sts., p. 2, k. 19.

25th row.—P. 19, k. 2, p. 8, k. 2, p. 44, k. 2, p. 8, k. 2, p. 19.

26th row.—K. 19, p. 2, k. 8, p. 2, k. 44, p. 2, k. 8, p. 2, k. 19.

27th row.—As 25th row.

28th row.—K. 19, p. 2, twist next 8 sts.,

Simplicity is the keynote of this sun suit. It is knitted in stocking stitch with two decorative cable panels running up to form the shoulder straps.

p. 2, k. 44, p. 2, twist next 8 sts., p. 2, k. 19.

29th row.—As 25th row.

30th row.—As 26th row.

31st to 35th rows.—Rep. 29th and 30th rows twice, then 29th row again.

36th row.—K. 16, sl. 1, k. 1, p.s.s.o., k. 1, p. 2, k. 8, p. 2, k. 1, sl. 1, k. 1, p.s.s.o., k. 38, k. 2 tog., k. 1, p. 2, k. 8, p. 2, k. 1, k. 2 tog., k. 16.

37th row.—P. 18, k. 2, p. 8, k. 2, p. 42, k. 2, p. 8, k. 2, p. 18.

38th row.—K. 18, p. 2, k. 8, p. 2, k. 42, p. 2, k. 8, p. 2, k. 18.

39th row.—As 37th row.

(The last 24 rows, i.e. rows 16 to 39 inclusive, form the patt. of the cable panels. Keep this patt. correct throughout.)

40th row.—K. 18, p. 2, twist next 8 sts., p. 2, k. 42, p. 2, twist next 8 sts., p. 2, k. 18.

41st row.—As 37th row.

42nd row.—As 38th row.

43rd row.—As 37th row.

44th row.—As 40th row.

45th row.—As 37th row.

46th row.—K. to 3 sts. before cable panel, sl. 1, k. 1, p.s.s.o., k. 1, p. 2, k. 8, p. 2, k. 1, sl. 1, k. 1, p.s.s.o., k. to 3 sts. before cable panel, k. 2 tog., k. 1, p. 2, k. 8, p. 2, k. 1, k. 2 tog., k. to end.

Work 9 rows in st.st. with cable panels.

56th row.—As 46th row.

Work 9 rows in st.st. with cable panels.

66th row.—As 46th row (90 sts.).

Continue in st.st. with cable panels without shaping until work measures 8½ ins. from 8 cast-on sts., finishing row on wrong side.

Change to No. 12 needles and continue in st.st. and cable panels for 2 ins.

Change to No. 10 needles and continue in st.st. and cable panels until work measures 12½ ins., finishing row on right side.

Begin Armhole Borders thus:—

1st row.—K. 7, work in st.st. and cable panels to last 7 sts., k. 7.

2nd row.—As 1st row.

Rep. last 2 rows once, then 1st row again.

6th row.—Cast off 5 sts., work in st.st. and cable panels to last 5 sts., cast off 5.

7th row.—Rejoin wool, k. 2, p. 8, panel 12, p. 36, panel 12, p. 8, k. 2.

8th row.—K. 2, sl. 1, k. 1, p.s.s.o., k. 6, panel 12, k. 36, panel 12, k. 6, k. 2 tog., k. 2.

9th row.—K. 2, p. 7, panel 12, p. 36, panel 12, p. 7, k. 2.

10th row.—K. 2, sl. 1, k. 1, p.s.s.o., k. to cable panel, panel 12, k. 36, panel 12, k. to last 4 sts., k. 2 tog., k. 2.

11th row.—K. 2, p. to cable panel, panel 12, p. 36, panel 12, p. to last 2 sts., k. 2.

12th row.—As 10th row.

13th row.—K. 2, p. to cable panel, panel 12, k. 36, panel 12, p. to last 2 sts., k. 2.

Rep. last 2 rows twice.

18th row.—K. 2, sl. 1, k. 1, p.s.s.o.,

Make this sun suit in a bright colour.

k. 1, panel 12, k. 2, cast off 32 sts., k. 2 including st. already on needle after casting off, panel 12, k. 1, k. 2 tog., k. 2.

Work on last set of sts. thus:—

Next row.—K. 2, p. 2, panel 12, k. 2.

Next row.—K. 2, panel 12, k. 2 tog., k. 2.

Next row.—K. 2, p. 1, panel 12, k. 2.

Next row.—K. 2, panel 12, k. 2 tog., k. 1.

Next row.—K. 2, panel 12, k. 2.

Continue on 16 sts. until work measures 18½ ins. from 8 cast-on sts

Cast off.

Rejoin wool to remaining sts. and work thus:—

1st row.—K. 2, panel 12, p. 2, k. 2.

2nd row.—K. 2, sl. 1, k. 1, p.s.s.o., panel 12, k. 2.

3rd row.—K. 2, panel 12, p. 1, k. 2.

4th row.—K. 1, k. 2 tog., panel 12, k. 2.

5th row.—K. 2, panel 12, k. 2.

Cast off.

Continue on 16 sts. to match first side.

The Back.—Continue as front until work measures 8½ ins. from 8 cast-on sts., finishing row on wrong side.

Shape for Back thus:—

1st and 2nd rows.—Work to last 9 sts., turn.

3rd and 4th rows.—Work to last 17 sts., turn.

5th and 6th rows.—Work to last 25 sts., turn.

7th and 8th rows.—Work to last 33 sts., turn.

9th and 10th rows.—Work to end.

Change to No. 12 needles and continue in st.st. and cable panels for 2 ins.

Change to No. 10 needles and continue in st.st. and cable panels until work measures same as front at side edge to beg. of armhole borders, finishing row on right side.

Begin Armhole Borders thus: Rep. rows 1 to 12 inclusive as given for front once, then rep. 11th and 12th rows 3 times more, then 11th row once more.

Next row.—K. 2, sl. 1, k. 1, p.s.s.o., panel 12, k. 36, panel 12, k. 2 tog., k. 2.

Next row.—K. 2, p. 1, panel 12, p. 36, panel 12, p. 1, k. 2.

Next row.—K. 1, k. 2 tog., panel 12, k. 36, panel 12, k. 2 tog., k. 1.

Next row.—K. 2, panel 12, k. 36, panel 12, k. 2.

Rep. last row 4 times.

Next row.—K. 2, panel 12, k. 2, cast off 32 sts., k. 2 including st. already on needle after casting off, panel 12, k. 2.

Continue on last set of 16 sts. until work measures same as front at side edge.

Cast off.

Work on other set of sts. to match.

The Gusset.—With No. 10 needles cast on 2 sts.

1st row.—K. twice into first st., k. 1.

2nd row.—P. 3.

3rd row.—K. twice into first and second sts., k. 1.

4th row.—P. 5.

Continue in st.st., inc. 1 st. both ends of every k. row until 25 sts. are on needle. Work 1 in. in st.st. without shaping, then dec. 1 st. both ends of every k. row until 3 sts. remain.

Cast off.

The Leg Borders.—Sew gusset into position, arranging the shaped side edges of gusset to leg edges with the straight centre piece of gusset left free.

Now with right side of work facing and using No. 12 needles, k. up 52 sts. along shaped leg edge, 8 sts. along straight centre piece of gusset, 52 sts. along shaped leg edge.

Work ½ in. in g.st.

Cast off loosely.

Make-up.—Press work lightly with hot iron over damp cloth.

Join side seams. Press seams

Work 1 row d.c. all round armholes, shoulder straps and neck edges, making 2 button loops on edge of back shoulders.

Sew buttons to front shoulders according to length required for shoulder straps.

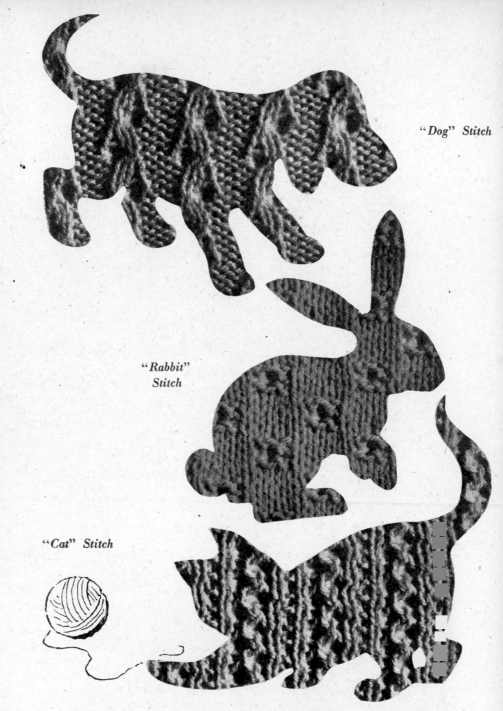

"Dog" Stitch

"Rabbit" Stitch

"Cat" Stitch

Three Openwork Stitches Designed for Simple Jumpers and Jackets.

Page 184

Alternative Stitches

THAT ARE SUITABLE FOR BOYS' AND GIRLS' UNDIES AND SCHOOL CLOTHES

HERE are some more easy stitches to give variety to plain jumpers, cardigans or underwear. All have a slightly open effect without being really lacy patterns, and all are quite simple to follow when working increasings or decreasings.

"Dog" stitch is ideal for underwear and can be substituted for stocking stitch or a plain rib without difficulty.

"Rabbit" stitch is good for girls' jumpers and cardigans, and could be attractively embroidered either around the holes or in the plain spaces between.

A plain stocking-stitch jersey or cardigan would look delightful with a yoke in this pattern with tiny flowers in pastel colours embroidered round the holes.

"Cat" stitch is an attractive zigzag rib, very easy to follow, and suitable for many garments. Try it for "best" underwear in 2-ply wool and for summer socks in cotton or silk; but when using a yarn other than that stated in the instructions, take the precaution of trying a tension sample first so that you can adjust your size of needles accordingly.

"Dog" Stitch

Number of stitches divisible by 5, plus 1 stitch.

1st row.—* P. 3, k. 2 tog., m. 1; rep. from * to last st., p. 1.

2nd row.—K. 1, * p. 2, k. 3; rep. from * to end.

3rd row.—* P. 3, k. 2; rep. from * to last st., p. 1.

4th row—As 2nd row.

5th row.—* P. 3, m. 1, k. 2 tog.; rep. from * to last st., p. 1.

6th row.—As 2nd row.

7th row.—As 3rd row.

8th row.—As 2nd row.

Rep. these 8 rows.

"Rabbit" Stitch

Number of stitches divisible by 8

1st row.—* K. 5, p. 3; rep. from * to end.

2nd row.—* K. 1, m. 1, k. 2 tog., p. 5; rep. from * to end.

3rd row.—Same as the 1st row.

4th row.—P.

5th row.—K. 1, * p. 3, k 5; rep. from * ending with k. 4.

6th row.—P. 4, * k. 1, m. 1, k. 2 tog., p. 5; rep. from * ending with p. 4.

7th row.—Same as 5th row.

8th row.—P.

Rep. these 8 rows.

"Cat" Stitch

Number of stitches divisible by 10, plus 1 stitch.

1st row.—K. 1, * k. 1, k. 2 tog., m. 1, k. 1, p. 1, k. 1, m. 1, sl. 1, k. 1, p.s.s.o. k. 1, p. 1; rep. from * to end.

2nd row.—P.

3rd row.—K. 1, * k. 1, m. 1, sl. 1, k. 1, p.s.s.o., k. 1, p. 1, k. 1, k. 2 tog. m. 1, k. 1, p. 1; rep. from * to end.

4th row.—P.

Rep. these 4 rows.

"Sandcastle" Stitch

Number of stitches divisible by 6, plus 4 stitches.

1st row.—K. 4, * k. into the back of the 2nd st. on the left needle, k. the 1st st., then slip both sts. off the needle (referred to as twist 2 back), k. 4; rep. from * to end.

2nd and alternate rows.—P.

3rd row.—K. 3, * k. into the front of the 2nd st., k. the 1st st., then slip both sts. off the needle (referred to as twist 2 front), twist 2 front once more, k. 2; rep. from * finishing k. 3 instead of k. 2.

5th row.—Like the 1st row.

7th row.—K. 1, * twist 2 back, k. 4; rep. from *, finishing k. 1 instead of k. 4.

9th row.—* Twist 2 front twice, k. 2; rep. from *, finishing twist 2 front twice.

11th row.—Like the 7th row.

12th ow.—P. Rep. these 12 rows.

"Hopscotch" Stitch

Number of stitches divisible by 2.

1st row.—Sl. 1 p.w., * p. 1, k. into back of next st.; rep. from * to last st., p. 1.

2nd row.—Sl. 1 p.w., * p. into back of next st., k. 1; rep. from * to last st., p. into back of last st. Rep. these 2 rows.

"Snowman" Stitch

Number of stitches divisible by 4, plus 2 stitches.

1st row.—K. to end.

2nd row.—P. to end.

3rd row.—K. 1, * sl. 2, k. 2; rep. from * to last st., k. 1.

4th row.—K. 1, * p. 2, sl. 2; rep. from * to last st., k. 1.

5th row.—K. to end.

6th row.—P. to end.

7th row.—K. 1, * k. 2, sl. 2; rep. from * to last st., k. 1.

8th row.—K. 1, * sl. 2, p. 2; rep. from * to last st., k. 1.

Rep. these 8 rows.

"Double Life" Methods

FOR KNITTED GARMENTS

CHILDREN wear their knitted clothes through at the toes, heels, elbows and knees long before the garments are worn out, or even before they are outgrown. It is well worth the extra trouble, therefore, to reinforce the garments when they are new.

Heels and toes and knees and elbows can be either knitted with double wool, which produces a rather bulky fabric but a very hard-wearing one, or a matching mercerized cotton thread can be knitted in with the wool. For elbows and knees weave the thread behind, holding the cotton yarn in the left hand and taking it over and under the needle in turn so that it is looped from stitch to stitch behind and does not interfere with the pattern.

Preventive darns can be made on the back of the work, taking the loops at the back of the knitting, so that very little is seen from the front. The best way is to darn diagonally across the fabric.

The tips of glove fingers should be reinforced as they wear out first and are very "fiddling" to re-knit.

The cast-on and -off rows of welts often break in wear, and these should be knitted with double wool, using the thumb method, to make a strong elastic edge.

for Sun Suit—

—Sleeveless Pullover

—Cardigan

Stitch Suggestions for hard-wearing
Woollies.

Three More Stitches

WHICH MAKE A SECOND CHOICE FOR DESIGNS ON PAGES 160 TO 180

"Smocking" Stitch

Number of stitches divisible by 8, plus 6.

1st row (right side of work).—K. 1, * sl. 1, k. 2, sl. 1, k. 4; rep. from *, ending k. 1 instead of k. 4.

2nd row.—P. 1, * sl. 1, p. 2, sl. 1, p. 4; rep. from *, ending p. 1 instead of p. 4.

3rd row.—K. 1, * sl. next 3 sts. on to spare needle, leave at back of work, k. next st., then sl. 2nd and 3rd sts. on spare needle back on to left-hand needle, leaving spare needle with first st. at the front of work; k. 2, then k. st. from spare needle. (This will be referred to as "twist 4 sts.") K. 4; rep. from *, ending k. 1 instead of k. 4.

4th row.—P.

5th row.—K. 1, * k. 4, sl. 1, k. 2, sl. 1; rep. from * until 5 sts. remain, k. 5.

6th row.—P. 1, * p. 4, sl. 1, p. 2, sl. 1; rep. from * until 5 sts. remain, p. 5.

7th row.—K. 1, * k. 4, twist 4 sts.; rep. from * until 5 sts. remain, k. 5.

8th row.—P.

These 8 rows form the patt.

Detail of "Smocking" Stitch.

"Cross-stitch Rib" Stitch

Number of stitches divisible by 3, plus 1 stitch.

1st row (wrong side of work facing).—K. 1, * p. 2, k. 1; rep. from * to end.

2nd row.—P. 1, * keeping wool to front sl. 1, p. 1, wool over and round needle, p.s.s.o. these 2 sts., p. 1; rep. from * to end.

Rep. these 2 rows.

Detail of the "Cross-stitch rib" Stitch.

"Outfit" Stitch (See opposite page)

Number of stitches divisible by 11, plus 1 stitch.

1st row.—K. 3, * p. 2, k. 2, p. 2, k. 5; rep. from * until 9 sts. remain, p. 2, k. 2, p. 2, k. 3.

2nd row.—K. 1, p. 2, * k. 2, p. 2, k. 2, p. 5; rep. from * until 9 sts. remain. k. 2, p. 2, k. 2, p. 2, k. 1.

3rd row.—Same as 2nd row.

4th row.—Same as 1st row.

Rep. these 4 rows.

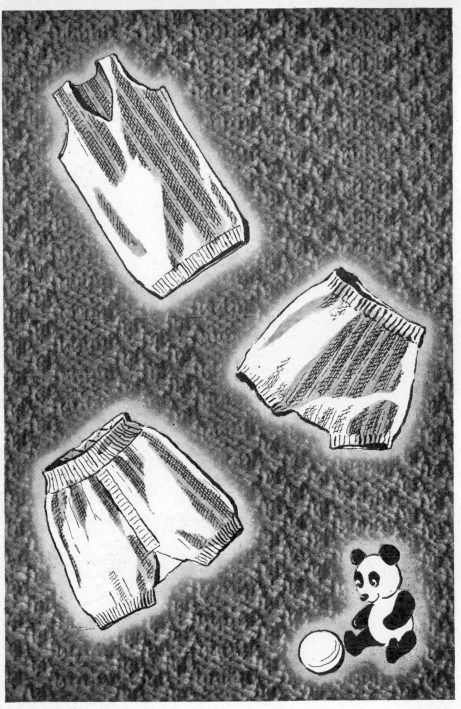

A simple but effective stitch for underwear.

Twin Set

FOR THE SCHOOLGIRL IN HER 'TEENS

MATERIALS

11 oz. of 3-ply wool for set (5 oz. for jersey, 6 oz. for cardigan).
2 No. 9 and 2 No. 12 knitting needles.
4 No. 9 and 4 No. 12 needles with points at both ends for jersey collar.
11 buttons for cardigan.

MEASUREMENTS

Jersey.—Length, 16½ ins.
Chest, 30 ins.
Sleeve seam, 3½ ins.
Cardigan.—Length, 17 ins.
Chest, 32 ins.
Sleeve seam, 15½ ins.

TENSION

7½ sts. to 1 in.

THE JERSEY

The Front.—With No. 12 needles cast on 93 sts. and work in following patt:—

1st row.—* K. 2, p. 1, k. 1, p. 1, k. 1, p. 1; rep. from * to last 2 sts., k. 2.

2nd row.—* P. 3, k. 1, p. 1, k. 1, p. 1; rep. from * to last 2 sts., p. 2.

Rep. these 2 rows until work measures 3 ins., ending with row on wrong side (with a 2nd row of patt.). Change to No. 9 needles and work 4 rows in patt. Continue in patt., inc. for side shaping thus:—

1st row.—K. twice into 1st st., (k. into st. and before slipping it off, k. again into back of loop), k. 1, * (p. 1, k. 1) twice, p. 1, k. 2; rep. from * to last 7 sts., (p. 1, k. 1) twice, p. 1, k. twice into next st., p. 1

2nd row.—P. 4, * (k. 1, p. 1) twice, p. 3; rep. from * to end.

3rd row.—P. 1, * k. 2, (p. 1, k. 1) twice, p. 1; rep. from * to last 3 sts., k. 2, p. 1.

4th row.—As 2nd row.

5th and 6th rows.—Rep. 3rd and 4th rows once.

7th row.—K. twice into 1st st., * k. 2, (p. 1, k. 1) twice, p. 1; rep. from * to last 3 sts., k. 1, k. twice into next st., k. 1.

8th row.—K. 1, * p. 4, k. 1, p. 1, k. 1; rep. from * to last 5 sts., p. 4, k. 1.

9th row.—K. 1, p. 1, * k. 2, (p. 1, k. 1) twice, p. 1; rep. from * to last 4 sts., k. 2, p. 1, k. 1.

10th row.—As 8th row.

11th and 12th rows.—Rep. 9th and 10th rows once.

13th row.—K. twice into 1st st., p. 1, * k. 2, (p. 1, k. 1) twice, p. 1; rep. from * to last 4 sts., k. 2, k. twice into next st., p. 1.

14th row.—P. 1, k. 1, * p. 4, k. 1, p. 1, k. 1; rep. from * to last 6 sts., p. 4, k. 1, p. 1.

15th row.—P. 1, k. 1, p. 1, * k. 2, (p. 1, k. 1) twice, p. 1; rep. from * to last 5 sts., k. 2, p. 1, k. 1, p. 1.

16th row.—As 14th row.

17th and 18th rows.—Rep. 15th and 16th rows.

19th row.—K. twice into 1st st., k. 1, p. 1, * k. 2, (p. 1, k. 1) twice, p. 1; rep. from * to last 5 sts., k. 2, p. 1, k. twice into next st., k. 1.

20th row.—K. 1, p. 1, k. 1, * p. 4, k. 1, p. 1, k. 1; rep. from * to end.

21st row.—(K. 1, p. 1) twice, * k. 2, (p. 1, k. 1) twice, p. 1; rep. from * to last 6 sts., k. 2, (p. 1, k. 1) twice.

22nd row.—As 20th row.

23rd and 24th rows.—Rep. 21st and 22nd rows.

25th row.—K. twice into 1st st., p. 1, k. 1, p. 1, * k. 2, (p. 1, k. 1) twice, p. 1;

Every schoolgirl will appreciate a matching cardigan and jersey. This set is simple to make and youthful in style, with the cardigan buttoning up to a square throat line. The jersey has a tiny collar.

The jersey is in moss stitch rib and close-up of stitch is shown below.

rep. from * to last 6 sts., k. 2, p. 1, k. 1, k. twice into next st., p. 1.

26th row.—(P. 1, k. 1) twice, * p. 4, k. 1, p. 1, k. 1; rep. from * to last st., p. 1.

27th row.—* (P. 1, k. 1) twice, p. 1, k. 2; rep. from * to last 5 sts., (p. 1, k. 1) twice, p. 1.

28th row.—As 26th row.

29th and 30th rows.—Rep. 27th and 28th rows.

31st row.—K. twice into 1st st., (k. 1, p. 1) twice, * k. 2, (p. 1, k. 1) twice, p. 1; rep. from * to last 7 sts., k. 2, p. 1, k. 1, p. 1, k. twice into next st., k. 1.

32nd row.—P. 2, k. 1, p. 1, k. 1, * p. 4, k. 1, p. 1, k. 1; rep. from * to last 2 sts., p. 2.

33rd row.—K. 1; * (p. 1, k. 1) twice, p. 1, k. 2; rep. from * to last 6 sts., (p. 1, k. 1) twice, p. 1, k. 1.

34th row.—As 32nd row.

35th and 36th rows.—Rep. 33rd and 34th rows.

37th row.—K. twice into 1st st., * (p. 1, k. 1) twice, p. 1, k. 2; rep. from * to last 6 sts., (p. 1, k. 1) twice, k. twice into next st., k. 1.

38th row.—P. 2, * (p. 1, k. 1) twice, p. 3; rep. from * to end.

39th row.—K. 2, * (p. 1, k. 1) twice, p. 1, k. 2; rep. from * to end.

This completes side shaping (107 sts. on needle).

Continue in pattern without shaping until work measures 11 ins., ending with row on wrong side.

Shape for Armholes thus:—

1st row.—Cast off 5 sts., work in patt. to end.

2nd row.—As 1st row.

3rd row.—K. 2 tog., work in patt. to last 2 sts., k. 2 tog.

Rep. 3rd row 7 times.

This completes armhole shaping and 81 sts. remain on needle.

Continue in patt., allowing for decreased sts. at each side, until work measures 15 ins., ending with row on wrong side.

Shape for Neck thus:—

Next row.—Work in patt. across 33 sts., turn.

Work on this set of sts. only for one side of neck thus:—

Next row.—K. 2 tog., work in patt. to end.

Next row.—Work in patt. to last 2 sts., k. 2 tog.

Rep. last 2 rows twice.

Next row.—K. 2 tog., work in patt. to end.

This completes neck shaping and 26 sts. remain.

Continue in patt. without shaping until work measures 16½ ins. from lower edge, ending at armhole edge.

Shape for Shoulder thus:—

Next row.—Cast off 9 sts., work in patt. to end.

Next row.—Work in patt. to end.

Rep. last 2 rows once.

Cast off remaining 8 sts.

Return to remaining 48 sts., slip centre 15 sts. on to a spare needle and leave for collar. Now rejoin wool at neck edge to 33 sts. for second side of neck and work decreasings and shoulder shapings exactly as given for first side of neck.

The Back.—Work exactly as given for front until armhole shapings are completed and 81 sts. remain.

Continue in patt., allowing for decreased sts., until work measures 16½ ins. ending with row on wrong side.

Shape for Neck and Shoulders thus:—

Next row.—Cast off 9 sts., there now being 1 st. on right-hand needle, work in patt. across 18 sts., k. 2 tog., turn.

Continue on these 20 sts. for one shoulder thus:—

1st row.—K. 2 tog., work in patt. to end.

2nd row.—Cast off 9 sts., work in patt. to last 2 sts., k. 2 tog.

3rd row.—As 1st row.

Cast off remaining 8 sts.

Return to remaining 51 sts., slip centre 21 sts. on to a spare needle and leave for collar, now rejoin wool at neck edge to 30 sts. for second shoulder and work in patt. to end of row.

Next row.—Cast off 9 sts., work in patt. to last 2 sts., k. 2 tog.

Next row.—K. 2 tog., work in patt. to end.

Rep. last 2 rows once.

Cast off remaining 8 sts.

The Sleeves.—With No. 12 needles cast on 82 sts. and work in moss st. thus:—

1st row.—* P. 1, k. 1; rep. from * to end.

2nd row.—* K. 1, p. 1; rep. from * to end.

Rep. these 2 rows for 1 in.

Change to No. 9 needles and continue in patt. as follows:—

1st row.—* P. 1, k. 1, p. 1, k. 1, p. 1, k. 2; rep. from * to last 5 sts., p. 1, k. 1, p. 1, k. 1, p. 1.

2nd row.—P. 1, k. 1, p. 1, k. 1, * p. 4, k. 1, p. 1, k. 1; rep. from * to last st., p. 1.

Rep. these 2 rows until work measures 3½ ins., from lower edge.

Shape for Top thus:—

1st row.—K. 2 tog., work in patt. to last 2 sts., k. 2 tog.

2nd row.—Work in patt. to end.

Rep. last 2 rows 5 times.

13th row.—K. 2 tog., work in patt. to last 2 sts., k. 2 tog.

Rep. last row until 30 sts. remain on needle.

Cast off these 30 sts. in patt.

The Collar.—Join shoulder seams neatly.

Work with right side of work facing and use 4 No. 12 needles.

Slip the 15 sts. at centre front on to 2 needles, 7 sts. on one needle, 8 sts. on other needle.

Now take another needle (this will be

The cardigan is knitted in stocking stitch, with moss stitch borders at the neck, front, sleeves and waist. With the jersey, it makes a gay and smart outfit for the girl who is just becoming " clothes conscious."

the first needle), join wool to centre front and work across the 8 sts. thus: (p. 1, k. 1) 4 times; now on to this same needle, k. up 16 sts. neatly along neck edge to shoulder seam.

Take a second needle, k. up 5 sts. neatly along neck edge to back of neck sts. on spare needle, then work across these 21 sts. thus: (k. 1, p. 1) 10 times, k. 1; now on to this same needle, k. up 5 sts. neatly along neck edge to shoulder seam.

Take a third needle and k. up 16 sts. neatly along neck edge to remaining 7 sts. at centre front, then work across these 7 sts. thus: (k. 1, p. 1) 3 times, k. 1 (78 sts.).

Work in rounds of moss st. thus:—

1st round.—* K. 1, p. 1; rep. from * to end.

2nd round.—* P. 1, k. 1; rep. from * to end.

Rep. these 2 rounds once.

Change to No. 9 needles.

The work is now divided at centre front

and worked in rows instead of rounds for the collar.

1st row.—* K. 1, p. 1; rep. from * to centre front (end of third needle), turn.

2nd row.—* P. 1, k. 1; rep. from * to centre front (end of 1st needle), turn.

Rep. these 2 rows for 2 ins.

Cast off loosely in moss st.

Make-up.—Press work lightly with hot iron and damp cloth.

Join side and sleeve seams.

Sew sleeves into armholes, placing seams to side seams and arranging any extra fullness at top of sleeve. Press seams.

THE CARDIGAN

The Back.—With No. 12 needles cast on 97 sts. and work in moss st. thus:—

1st row.—* K. 1, p. 1; rep. from * to last st., k. 1.

Rep. this row for 1 in., then continue in st.st. thus:—

1st row.—K. to end.

2nd row.—P. to end.

Rep. these 2 rows until work measures 3 ins. ending with a p. row.

Change to No. 9 needles and continue in st.st., inc. 1 st. at both ends of next row (by working twice into 1st st. and last st. but one thus: k. into st., then before slipping it off, k. again into back of loop), then on every following 6th row until there are 113 sts. on the needle.

Continue without shaping until work measures 11 ins. from lower edge, ending with a p. row.

Shape for Armholes thus:—

1st row.—Cast off 7 sts., k. to end.

2nd row.—Cast off 7 sts., p. to end.

3rd row.—K. 2 tog., k. to last 2 sts. k. 2 tog.

4th row.—P. 2 tog., p. to last 2 sts., p. 2 tog.

Rep. last 2 rows 3 times (83 sts. remain). Continue without shaping until work measures 16½ ins. from lower edge, ending with a p. row.

Begin Neck Border thus:—

Next row.—K. 21, * p. 1, k. 1; rep. from * to last 22 sts., p. 1, k. 21.

Next row.—P. 21, * p. 1, k. 1; rep. from * to last 22 sts., p. 22.

Rep. last 2 rows until work measures 17 ins. from lower edge, ending with row on wrong side.

Shape Shoulders thus:—Work in st.st. with moss st. neck border and cast off 9 sts. at beg. of the next 4 rows, then cast off 10 sts. at beg. of next 2 rows.

Now cast off remaining 27 sts. in moss st.

The Right Front.—With No. 12 needles cast on 45 sts. and work 1 in. in moss st. as given for back.

Continue in st.st. until work measures 3 ins., ending with a p. row.

Now leave these sts. and work the front border thus:—

Using No. 9 needles cast on 7 sts.

Work 3 rows in moss st., then make a buttonhole in next 2 rows thus:—

Next row.—Moss st. 2, cast off 3 sts., moss st. to end.

Next row.—Moss st. 2, cast on 3 sts., moss st. 2.

Continue in moss st. until work measures 1½ ins. from commencement of the previous buttonhole, then make another buttonhole in next 2 rows.

Continue in moss st. until work measures 3 ins. from lower edge.

Now join moss st. border to main part of front thus:—

Using No. 9 needles, moss st. 7 sts. for front border, then with right side of work facing, k. across 45 sts. for main part, inc. at side edge by working twice into last st. but one in the row.

Now continue to work in st.st. with moss st. front border of 7 sts. making further buttonholes in border at regular intervals of 1½ ins. measured from commencement of each previous buttonhole. (*N.B.*—To ensure regularity of buttonholes it is helpful to count number of rows worked between first and second buttonholes, then always to work this same number of rows between successive buttonholes.)

At the same time continue to inc. at side edge on every following 6th row until there are 60 sts. on needle.

Still making buttonholes in front border, continue without shaping at side edge until work measures 11 ins. from lower edge, ending at side edge.

Shape for Armhole thus:—

1st row.—Cast off 7 sts., p. to last 7 sts., moss st. 7.

2nd row.—Moss st. 7, k. to last 2 sts., k. 2 tog.

3rd row.—P. 2 tog., p. to last 7 sts., moss st. 7.

Rep. last 2 rows 3 times (45 sts. remain).

Continue in st.st. with moss st. front border and buttonholes until work measures 14½ ins. from lower edge, ending at front edge.

Begin Neck Border thus:—

Next row.—(K. 1, p. 1) 12 times, k. to end.

The jersey is knitted in a different stitch from the cardigan, and gives to the set a smart "grown-up" effect. The set can be knitted in contrasting colours if that is preferred to a matching set.

Next row.—P. 21, (p. 1, k. 1) 12 times.

Rep. last 2 rows until work measures 15½ ins. from lower edge, making an eleventh buttonhole in front edge as before and finishing at front edge.

Next row.—Cast off 17 sts., work in moss st. to last 21 sts., k. 21.

Next row.—P. 21, moss st. 7.

Next row.—Moss st. 7, k. 21.

Rep. last 2 rows until work measures 17 ins. from lower edge, ending at armhole edge.

Shape Shoulder thus:—

Next row.—Cast off 9 sts., p. to last 7 sts., moss st. 7.

Next row.—Moss st. 7, k. to end.

Rep. last 2 rows once.

Cast off remaining 10 sts.

The Left Front.—With No. 12 needles cast on 45 sts. and work as given for right front until work measures 3 ins., ending with a p. row.

Now leave these sts. and work the front border thus:—

Using No. 9 needles cast on 7 sts. and work 3 ins. in moss st., then join moss st. border to main part of front thus:—

Using No. 9 needles work across 45 sts. for main part thus: K. twice into 1st st., k. to end, then work in moss st. across 7 sts. for front border.

Now continue to work in st.st. with moss st. front border of 7 sts. and inc. 1 st. at side edge on every following 6th row until there are 60 sts. on needle.

Continue without shaping until work measures 11 ins. from lower edge, ending at side edge.

Shape for Armhole thus:—

1st row.—Cast off 7 sts., k. to last 7 sts., moss st. 7.

2nd row.—Moss st. 7, p. to last 2 sts., p. 2 tog.

3rd row.—K. 2 tog., k. to last 7 sts., moss st. 7.

Rep. last 2 rows 3 times (45 sts. remain).

Continue in st.st. with moss st. front border until work measures 14¼ ins. from

lower edge, ending at front edge.

Begin Neck border thus:—

Next row.—(K. 1, p. 1) 12 times, p. to end.

Next row.—K. 21, (p. 1, k. 1) 12 times.

Rep. last 2 rows until work measures 15½ ins. from lower edge, ending at front edge.

Next row.—Cast off 17 sts., work in moss st. to last 21 sts., p. 21.

Next row.—K. 21, moss st. 7.

Next row.—Moss st. 7, p. 21.

Rep. last 2 rows until work measures 17 ins., ending at armhole edge.

Shape Shoulder thus:—

Next row.—Cast off 9 sts., k. to last 7 sts., moss st. 7.

Next row.—Moss st. 7, p. to end.

Rep. last 2 rows once.

Cast off remaining 10 sts.

The Sleeves.—With No. 12 needles cast on 51 sts. and work 1 in. in moss st. as given for back.

Continue in st.st. until work measures 3 ins., ending with a p. row.

Change to No. 9 needles and continue in st.st., inc. at both ends of next row (by working twice into first and last st. but one in row), and on every following 6th row until there are 89 sts. on needle.

Continue without shaping until work measures 15½ ins., ending with a p. row.

Shape Top thus: Dec 1 st. at both ends of every row until 27 sts. remain.

Cast off remaining sts.

Make-up.—Press each piece of work lightly on wrong side with hot iron over a damp cloth.

Join shoulder seams, matching up moss st. neck borders on front shoulders to corresponding stitches on back shoulders.

Join side and sleeve seams. Sew sleeves into armholes, placing sleeve seams to side seams.

Sew buttons on to centre of left front border to match up with buttonholes in right front border.

Press seams.

Vest and Knickers

AN ESSENTIAL OUTFIT FOR THE WINTER

MATERIALS

4 oz. of 3-ply wool for the vest.
3 oz. for the knickers.
1 pair each Nos. 12, 10 and 8 needles.
A medium-size crochet hook.
Elastic for waist.

MEASUREMENTS

Vest: Length, 28 ins.
Bust, to fit 32 ins.
Knickers: Waist to crutch, 14 ins.

TENSION

Using No. 8 needles, 13 sts. to measure 2 ins. for vest.
Using No. 10 needles, 15 sts. to measure 2 ins. over ribbing for knickers.

THE VEST

The Back.—Using No. 8 needles cast on 97 sts. and work in rib as follows:—

1st row.—K. 3, * p. 1, k. 5; rep. from * to last 4 sts., p. 1, k. 3.

2nd row.—P. 3, * k. 1, p. 5; rep. from * to last 4 sts., k. 1, p. 3.

Continue in rib until work measures $14\frac{1}{2}$ ins.

Change to No. 12 needles and work in k. 1, p. 1 rib for 3 ins.

Change to No. 8 needles and continue in lace patt. as follows:—

1st row.—* K. 5, m. 1, sl. 1, k. 2 tog., p.s.s.o., m. 1, k. 4; rep. from * to the last st., k. 1.

2nd and alternate rows.—P. to end.

3rd row.—* K. 3, k. 2 tog., m. 1, k. 3, m. 1, sl. 1, k. 1, p.s.s.o., k. 2; rep. from * to last st., k. 1.

5th row.—As 1st row.

7th row.—K. to end.

9th row.—K. 2 tog., * m. 1, k. 9, m. 1, sl. 1, k. 2 tog., p.s.s.o.; rep. from * to end, ending the last rep. with m. 1, sl. 1, k. 1, p.s.s.o. instead of m. 1, sl. 1, k. 2 tog., p.s.s.o.

11th row.—* K. 2, m. 1, sl. 1, k. 1,

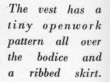

The vest has a tiny openwork pattern all over the bodice and a ribbed skirt.

The girl in her 'teens who longs for pretty undies, will find this design for her vest and knickers just what she wants. This vest was in pale blue, but the knickers in dark blue, to wear underneath her school frock.

p.s.s.o., k. 5, k. 2 tog., m. 1, k. 1; rep. from * to the last st., k. 1.

13th row.—Rep. 9th row.

15th row.—K. to end.

16th row.—P. to end.

These 16 rows form the patt. Continue in patt. until work measures 21 ins.

Shape Armholes thus: Cast off 4 sts. at beg. of the next 2 rows, then dec. 1 st. at both ends of every row until there are 73 sts. on needle.

Continue without further dec. until work measures 26 ins., ending with row on wrong side of work.

Shape Neck thus: Work in patt. on 24 sts., cast off the next 25 sts., work in patt. to end.

Now continue on the last set of 24 sts., dec. 1 st. every row at neck edge until 13 sts. remain.

Continue without further dec. until work measures 28 ins., ending with row on right side of work.

Shape Shoulders thus: Cast off 4 sts. at beg. of the next 2 rows from armhole edge.

Cast off remaining 5 sts.

Rejoin wool to the other 24 sts. at neck edge and work to match first side.

The Front.—Work exactly as given for back until work measures 23 ins., ending with row on wrong side.

Shape Neck thus:—

Next row.—Work in patt. on 30 sts., cast off the next 13 sts., work to end.

Now work on the last 30 sts., dec. 1 st. every row at neck edge until 13 sts. remain. Continue without further dec. until work measures 28 ins., ending with row on right side of work.

Shape Shoulder as for Back.—Rejoin wool at neck edge to the last 30 sts. and work to match first side.

The Neck Border.—Using No. 12 needles cast on 6 sts. and work in moss st. for about 20 ins. Cast off.

The Armhole Borders.—Using No. 12 needles cast on 6 sts. and work in moss st. for about 16 ins. Cast off.

Make a second piece the same way.

Make-up.—Press work lightly.

Join side and shoulder seams with a narrow backstitch.

Stitch moss st. borders round neck and armholes. Press all seams.

THE KNICKERS

Before commencing front make a pocket lining.

Using No. 10 needles cast on 25 sts. and work in rib as for lower part of vest until work measures 3½ ins. Leave sts. on a spare needle.

The Front. The Right Leg.—Using No. 12 needles cast on 64 sts. and work in k. 1, p. 1 rib for 1 in. Leave these sts. on a spare needle.

The Left Leg.—Work exactly as given for right leg.

Now join legs and work gusset thus:—

Change to No. 10 needles and work on sts. of left leg as follows:—

1st row.—K. 3, (p. 1, k. 5) 10 times, p. 1, cast on 26 sts. for gusset, then work on right leg sts., p. 1, (k. 5, p. 1) 10 times, k. 3.

2nd row.—P. 3, (k. 1, p. 5) 10 times, k. 1, p. 26, k. 1, (p. 5, k. 1) twice, turn.

The knickers are ribbed for close, snug fitting; they have a pocket in one leg.

3rd row.—P. 1, (k. 5, p. 1) twice, sl. 1, k. 1, p.s.s.o., k. 22, k. 2 tog., p. 1, (k. 5, p. 1) twice, turn.

4th row.—K. 1, (p. 5, k. 1) twice, p. 24, k. 1, (p. 5, k. 1) 4 times, turn.

5th row.—P. 1, (k. 5, p. 1) 4 times, sl. 1, k. 1, p.s.s.o., k. 20, k. 2 tog., p. 1, (k. 5, p. 1) 4 times, turn.

6th row.—K. 1, (p. 5, k. 1) 4 times, p. 22, k. 1, (p. 5, k. 1) 6 times, turn.

7th row.—P. 1, (k. 5, p. 1) 6 times, sl. 1, k. 1, p.s.s.o., k. 18, k. 2 tog., p. 1, (k. 5, p. 1) 6 times, turn.

8th row.—K. 1, (p. 5, k. 1) 6 times, p. 20, k. 1, (p. 5, k. 1) 8 times, turn.

9th row.—P. 1, (k. 5, p. 1) 8 times, sl. 1, k. 1, p.s.s.o., k. 16, k. 2 tog., p. 1, (k. 5, p. 1) 8 times, turn.

10th row.—K. 1, (p. 5, k. 1) 8 times, p. 18, k. 1, (p. 5, k. 1) 9 times, turn.

11th row.—P. 1, (k. 5, p. 1) 9 times, sl. 1, k. 1, p.s.s.o., k. 14, k. 2 tog., p. 1, (k. 5, p. 1) 9 times, turn.

12th row.—K. 1, (p. 5, k. 1) 9 times, p. 16, k. 1, (p. 5, k. 1) 10 times, p. 3, turn.

13th row.—K. 3, p. 1, (k. 5, p. 1) 10 times, sl. 1, k. 1, p.s.s.o., k. 12, k. 2 tog., p. 1, (k. 5, p. 1) 10 times, k. 3.

14th row.—Work in rib on 64 sts., p. 14, rib 64.

15th row.—Rib 64 sts., sl. 1, k. 1, p.s.s.o., k. until 66 sts. remain, k. 2 tog., rib to end.

16th row.—Rib 64 sts., p. the gusset sts., rib to end.

Rep. the last 2 rows until 2 gusset sts. remain.

Next row.—Rib 63 sts., p. 2 tog. twice, rib 63 sts.

Next row.—Rib 63 sts., k. 2, rib 63.

Next row.—Rib 63, p. 2 tog., rib. 63.

Continue in rib on all sts. for 5 rows.

Now commence shaping up centre front at each side of the centre p. st.

Next row.—Rib 61, k. 2 tog., p. 1, k. 2 tog., rib to end. Work 5 rows on these sts.

Next row.—Work in rib, dec. on either side of centre p. st. as before.

Rep. the last 6 rows 4 times more (115 sts. remain).

At the same time, when work measures 8 ins., ending with a row on wrong side insert pocket thus:—

Next row.—Rib 19 sts., work in moss st. on the next 25 sts., rib to end.

Continue in this way for 6 rows, keeping the 25 sts. in moss st.

Next row.—Rib 19 sts., cast off the 25 moss sts., rib to end.

Next row.—Insert the pocket lining in place of sts. cast off in the previous row.

Continue in rib on 115 sts., until work measures 12 ins., ending with row on wrong side.

Change to No. 12 needles and work in k. 1, p. 1 rib for 2 ins.

Cast off loosely in rib.

The Back.—Work exactly as given for front but omitting pocket, until work measures 12 ins. Now shape back thus:—

1st and 2nd rows.—Work in wide rib until 12 sts. remain, turn.

3rd and 4th rows.—Work in rib until 24 sts. remain, turn.

5th and 6th rows.—Work in rib until 36 sts. remain, turn.

7th and 8th rows.—Work in rib until 48 sts. remain, turn.

9th and 10th rows.—Work in rib on all sts.

Change to No. 12 needles and work in k. 1, p. 1 rib for 2 ins.

Cast off loosely in rib.

Make-up.—Press work lightly.

Join side seams with a narrow backstitch. Sew the short ribbed leg seams together.

Using a medium-size crochet hook, work casing for elastic at waist thus:—

Join wool at side seam to top edge, with wrong side of work facing, * 4 ch., take hook down and sl.st. into ribbing ½ in. from edge and ½ in. to the left, 4 ch., sl.st. into top edge ½ in. further to left; rep. from * all round.

Press seams. Thread elastic through casing.

Here is a close-up of the jerkin the brother and sister are wearing in the frontispiece picture on page 2. Both jerkins are made from the same set of instructions; the girl's in pattern, the boy's in stocking stitch.

Sleeveless Jerkin

FOR BOY OR GIRL

MATERIALS

4 oz. 3-ply wool.
2 No. 10 and 2 No. 12 knitting needles.

MEASUREMENTS

Length, 19 ins.
Chest, 34 ins.

TENSION

7½ sts. to 1 in.

THE BOY'S JERKIN

The Front.—With No. 12 needles cast on 104 sts.

Work 3 ins. in k. 1, p. 1 rib.

Change to No. 10 needles.

Continue in st.st. inc. 1 st. both ends of next row and every following 6th row until 128 sts. are on needle.

Detail of stitch for girl's jerkin.

Continue straight until work measures 11½ ins., finishing p. row.

Shape Armholes thus: Cast off 7 sts. beg. of next 2 rows, dec. 1 st. both ends of next 6 rows, then dec. 1 st. both ends of every alternate row until 94 sts. remain. Continue without shaping until work measures 17 ins., finishing p. row.

Shape Neck and Shoulders thus:—

Next row.—K. 34, cast off 26 sts., k. to end.

Continue on last set of 34 sts., dec. 1 st. at neck edge on every row until 30 sts. remain, then at same edge on every alternate row until 28 sts. remain.

Continue straight until work measures 19 ins., finishing armhole edge.

Next row.—Cast off 9 sts., work to end.

Next row.—Work to end.

Rep. last 2 rows once.

Cast off.

Rejoin wool at needle point and work on other 34 sts. to match first side.

The Neck Border.—With No. 12 needles and right side facing, pick up and k. 80 sts. round neck.

Work 8 rows in k. 1, p. 1 rib. Cast off loosely in rib.

The Back.—Continue as for front to end of armhole shapings.

Continue without shaping on 94 sts. until work measures 19 ins., finishing p. row.

Next row.—K. 32 sts., cast off 30 sts., k. to end.

Work on the last 32 sts., casting off 9 sts. at the armhole edge twice and at the same time dec. 1 st. at the neck edge on every row until 10 sts. remain.

Cast off.

The left-hand jerkin, made originally in bright yellow, has a small all-over design similar to double moss stitch. The other jerkin, originally made in russet, is in stocking stitch, with ribbed welt and arm bands.

Rejoin wool at needle point and work the other 32 sts. to correspond to the shoulder you have just knitted.

The Neck Border.—Work as for front border but pick up only 50 sts.

The Armhole Borders.—Join shoulder seams.

With right side of work facing and using No. 12 needles, k. up 160 sts.

Work 8 rows in k. 1, p. 1 rib, dec. 1 st. at both ends of each row.

Cast off.

Make-up.—Press work lightly on wrong side with hot iron over damp cloth, omitting the ribbing.

Join side seams.

THE GIRL'S JERKIN

This is made in exactly the same way as the boy's jerkin except that a small block patt. is substituted for the st.st.

The patt. is worked as follows:—

1st and 2nd rows.—* K. 2, p. 2; rep. from * to end.

3rd and 4th rows.—* P. 2, k. 2; rep. from * to end.

Rep. these 4 rows.

The shape of the jerkin is simple enough to be an excellent basis for variation.

Many of the sts. to be found in various stitch sections in this book could be successfully used instead of the st.st.

Bathing Suit

IN A FIRM WAVY STITCH

MATERIALS

5 oz. 3-ply wool.

2 No. 12 and 2 No. 14 knitting needles.

MEASUREMENTS

Shoulder to crutch, 22 ins.

All round above gusset, 30 ins.

Chest, 26 ins.

TENSION

About 10½ sts. to 1 in. measured over patt. (2 complete patts. 16 sts., measure about 1½ ins.)

The Front.

The Right Leg Border.—With No. 12 needles cast on 68 sts.

Change to No. 14 needles, work ½ in. in g.st.

Next row.—K. to end, cast off 8 sts. Break off wool.

The Left Leg Border.—With No. 12 needles cast on 68 sts.

Change to No. 14 needles, work ½ in. in g.st.

Next row.—Cast off 8 sts., k. to end. Break off wool.

The Gusset.—With No. 12 needles cast on 25 sts.

Work 8 rows in st.st., finishing p. row. Break off wool.

Using No. 12 needles assemble all sts. on to one needle thus:—

Begin at straight edge of left leg border, k. across all sts., inc. in every 3rd st. to make 80 sts. for leg.

K. 25 sts. for gusset, then work across sts. for right leg border, beg. at edge where sts. were cast off, and inc. in every 3rd st. as for left leg (185 sts. on needle).

P. 1 row, then shape legs and gusset thus:—

Break off wool and, with right side of work facing, sl. 76 sts. of left leg on to right-hand needle, rejoin wool and work thus:—

1st row.—K. last 4 sts. of left leg, sl. 1 k. 1, p.s.s.o., k. 21, k. 2 tog., k. 4, turn.

2nd row.—P. 35, turn.

3rd row.—K. 1, sl. next 2 sts. on to spare needle, leave at front of work, k. next 2 sts., k. 2 sts. from spare needle (this will be called " 1st twist "), k. 3, sl. 1, k. 1, p.s.s.o., k. 19, k. 2 tog., k. 1, 1st twist next 4 sts., k. 3, turn.

4th row.—P. 41, turn.

5th row.—K. 7, 1st twist next 4 sts., k. 1, sl. 1, k. 1, p.s.s.o., k. 17, k. 2 tog., k. 3, 1st twist next 4 sts., k. 5, turn.

Detail of swim-suit stitch.

For swimming or sun bathing! This beautifully fitting costume is knitted in an attractive " wavy " design, which makes a firm fabric that will not stretch in the water. Detail of the stitch is shown on page 205.

6th row.—P. 47, turn.

7th row.—K. 3, sl. next 2 sts. on to spare needle, leave at back of work, k. next 2 sts., k. 2 sts. from spare needle (this will be called " 2nd twist "), k. 4, 2nd twist next 4 sts., k. 1, sl. 1, k. 1, p.s.s.o., k. 15, k. 2 tog., k. 3, 2nd twist next 4 sts., k. 4, 2nd twist next 4 sts., k. 1, turn.

8th row.—P. 53, turn.

9th row.—K. 4, (k. 1, 2nd twist next 4 sts., k. 3) twice, sl. 1, k. 1, p.s.s.o., k. 13, k. 2 tog., (k. 1, 2nd twist next 4 sts., k. 3) twice, k. 4.

10th row.—P. 59, turn.

11th row.—(K. 1, 1st twist next 4 sts., k. 3) 3 times, sl. 1, k. 1, p.s.s.o., k. 11, k. 2 tog., (k. 1, 1st twist next 4 sts., k. 3) 3 times, turn.

12th row.—P. 65, turn.

13th row.—K. 4, (k. 3, 1st twist next 4 sts., k. 1) 3 times, sl. 1, k. 1, p.s.s.o., k. 9, k. 2 tog., (k. 3, 1st twist next 4 sts., k. 1) 3 times, k. 4, turn.

14th row.—P. 71, turn.

15th row.—(K. 3, 2nd twist next 4 sts., k. 1) 4 times, sl. 1, k. 1, p.s.s.o., k. 7, k. 2 tog., (k. 3, 2nd twist next 4 sts., k. 1) 4 times, turn.

16th row.—P. 77, turn.

17th row.—K. 4, (k. 1, 2nd twist next 4 sts., k. 3) 4 times, sl. 1, k. 1, p.s.s.o., k. 5, k. 2 tog., (k. 1, 2nd twist next 4 sts., k. 3) 4 times, k. 4, turn.

18th row.—P. 83, turn.

19th row.—(K. 1, 1st twist next 4 sts., k. 3) 5 times, sl. 1, k. 1, p.s.s.o., k. 3, k. 2 tog., (k. 1, 1st twist next 4 sts., k. 3) 5 times.

20th row.—P. 89, turn.

21st row.—K. 4, (k. 3, 1st twist next 4 sts. k. 1) 5 times, sl. 1, k. 1, p.s.s.o., k. 1, k. 2 tog., (k. 3, 1st twist next 4 sts., k. 1) 5 times, k. 4, turn.

22nd row.—P. 95, turn.

23rd row.—(K. 3, 2nd twist next 4 sts., k. 1) 6 times, sl. 1, k. 2 tog., p.s.s.o. (k. 3, 2nd twist next 4 sts., k. 1) 6 times.

24th row.—P. 101 sts., turn.

25th row.—K. 4, (k. 1, 2nd twist next 4 sts., k. 3) 6 times, k. 2 tog., (2nd twist next 4 sts., k. 4) 6 times, k. 3, turn.

26th row.—P. 108 sts., turn.

27th row.—(K. 1, 1st twist next 4 sts., k. 3) 14 times, turn.

28th row.—P. 116, turn.

29th row.—K. 4, (k. 3, 1st twist next 4 sts., k. 1) 14 times, k. 4, turn.

30th row.—P. 124 sts., turn.

31st row.—(K. 3, 2nd twist next 4 sts., k. 1) 16 times, turn.

32nd row.—P. 132, turn.

33rd row.—K. 4, (k. 1, 2nd twist next 4 sts., k. 3) 16 times, k. 4, turn.

34th row.—P. 140, turn.

35th row.—(K. 1, 1st twist next 4 sts., k. 3) 18 times, turn.

36th row.—P. 148, turn.

37th row.—K. 4, (k. 3, 1st twist next 4 sts., k. 1) 18 times, k. 4, turn.

38th row.—P. to end.

39th row.—(K. 3, 2nd twist next 4 sts., k. 1) 20 times.

40th row.—P. to end.

Continue in the 8-row patt., dec. 1 st. at both ends of 5th row and every following 4th row until 128 sts. remain, keeping patt. correct throughout.

Continue straight in patt. until work measures 11 ins. from cast-on gusset sts., finishing p. row.

Change to No. 14 needles and work 2 ins. in patt.

Change to No. 12 needles and continue in patt. until work measures 16 ins. from cast-on gusset sts., finishing row on right side.

Begin Armhole Borders and Shape Armholes thus:—

1st row.—K. 8, p. to last 8 sts., k. 8.

2nd row.—K. 8, patt. to last 8 sts., k. 8.

Rep. last 2 rows once, then 1st row again.

6th row.—Cast off 5 sts., k. 3 including st. already on right-hand needle, patt. to last 8 sts., k. 3, cast off 5.

Rejoin wool at needle point.

7th row.—K. 3, p. 2 tog., p. to last 5 sts., p. 2 tog., k. 3.

8th row.—K. 3, sl. 1, k. 1, p.s.s.o., patt. to last 5 sts., k. 2 tog., k. 3.

Rep. last 2 rows 4 times.

17th row.—K. 3, p. 22, k. 48, p. 22, k. 3.

18th row.—K. 3, sl. 1, k. 1, p.s.s.o., patt. 20,.k. 48. patt. 20, k. 2 tog., k. 3.

19th row.—K. 3, p. 21, k. 48, p. 21, k. 3.

20th row.—K. 3, sl. 1, k. 1, p.s.s.o., patt. 19, k. 48, patt. 19, k. 2 tog., k. 3.

21st row.—K. 3, p. 20, k. 48, p. 20, k. 3.

22nd row.—K. 3, sl. 1, k. 1, p.s.s.o., patt. 18, k. 3, cast off 42, k. 3, including st. already on right-hand needle after casting off, patt. 18, k. 2 tog., k. 3.

Work on last set of 25 sts. thus:—

23rd row.—K. 3, p. to last 3 sts., k. 3.

24th row.—K. 3, patt. to last 5 sts., k. 2 tog., k. 3. Rep. last 2 rows twice.

Continue in patt. with g.st. borders on 22 sts. until work measures 22 ins. from cast-on gusset sts., finishing p. row.

Cast off.

Rejoin wool at needle point and work on other 25 sts. thus:—

1st row.—K. 3, p. to last 3 sts., k. 3.

2nd row.—K. 3, sl. 1, k. 1, p.s.s.o., patt. to last 3 sts., k. 3.

Rep. last 2 rows twice.

Continue on 22 sts. to match first side.

The Back.—Continue as for front until work measures 11 ins. from cast-on gusset sts., finishing p. row.

Shape for Back thus:—

1st and 2nd rows.—Patt. to last 8 sts., turn.

3rd and 4th rows.—Patt. to last 16 sts., turn.

5th and 6th rows.—Patt. to last 24 sts., turn.

7th and 8th rows.—Patt. to last 32 sts., turn.

9th and 10th rows.—Patt. to end.

Change to No. 14 needles and work 2 ins. in patt.

Change to No. 12 needles and complete as for front.

Make-up.—Press work lightly on wrong side with hot iron over damp cloth.

Join side and shoulder seams.

Join gusset seams, then sew cast-off leg borders along side edges of gusset, then sew up borders.

Press seams.

'Teen-age girls will love this smart little bathing costume. The original was made in canary yellow.

School Sweater

IN A CABLE RIB

MATERIALS

9 oz. 4-ply wool in main shade.
1 oz. 4-ply wool in contrasting shade.
2 No. 8 and 2 No. 10 knitting needles.
Spare needle for cable.

MEASUREMENTS

Length, 20½ ins.
Chest, 32 ins.
Sleeve seam, 17½ ins.

TENSION

About 7 sts. to 1 in. measured over slightly stretched patt.

The Back.—With No. 10 needles and main shade cast on 118 sts. Work in rib.

1st row.—K. 1, * p. 2, k. 1; rep. from * to end.

2nd row.—P. 1, * k. 2, p. 1; rep. from * to end.

Rep. these 2 rows for 3 ins., finishing 2nd row.

Change to No. 8 needles and patt:—

1st row.—* K. 1, p. 2, k. 4, p. 2; rep. from * to last st., k. 1.

2nd row.—* P. 1, k. 2, p. 4, k. 2; rep. from * to last st., p. 1.

3rd and 4th rows.—As 1st and 2nd rows.

5th row.—* K. 1, p. 2, sl. next 2 sts. on to spare needle, leave at front of work, k. next 2 sts., k. 2 sts. from spare needle, p. 2; rep. from * to last st., k. 1.

6th row.—As 2nd row.

These 6 rows form patt.

Continue in patt. until work measures 13¾ ins., finishing row on wrong side.

Shape Armholes thus: Keeping continuity of patt., cast off 6 sts. beg. of next 2 rows, dec. 1 st. both ends of every row until 86 sts. remain.

Continue straight until work measures 19½ ins., finishing row on wrong side.

Shape Shoulders thus: Keeping continuity of patt., cast off 10 sts. beg. of next 6 rows.

Cast off remaining sts.

The Front.—Continue as for back, working in patt. until work measures 13 ins., finishing row on wrong side.

Divide for Neck Opening thus:—

Next row.—Patt. 47, turn, leave remaining sts. on spare needle.

Continue in patt. on these 47 sts. until work measures 13¾ ins., finishing side edge.

Shape Armholes thus: Keeping continuity of patt., cast off 6 sts. beg. of next

Knit this practical cable rib sweater in his school colours. Any schoolboy would be as proud to wear it as you will be to knit it.

row, then dec. 1 st. at armhole edge on next 10 rows, at the same time dec. 1 st. at edge on next row and every following 4th row.

Now continue with armhole edge straight, dec. on every 4th row at neck edge until 19 sts. remain.

Continue straight on 19 sts. until work measures 20½ ins., finishing armhole edge.

Shape Shoulders thus:—

Next row.—Cast off 10 sts., patt. to end.

Next row.—Patt. to end.

Cast off 9 sts.

Return to main sts., sl. centre 24 sts. on spare needle, rejoin wool and work on remaining 47 sts. to match first side.

With right side of work facing and using No. 10 needles and contrasting wool, k. first 6 sts. of remaining 24 sts.

Work in st.st. on these 6 sts. until band measures same as shaped neck edge to centre back.

Cast off.

Leave the centre 12 sts. on spare needle and work on last 6 sts. to match band just worked.

Cast off.

Rejoin main shade of wool to remaining 12 sts. with right side of work facing, and, using No. 10 needles, work 8 rows in g.st.

Next row.—K. 6, turn.

Continue in g.st. on these 6 sts. until band is same length as st.st. band. Cast off.

Rejoin wool to remaining 6 sts. and work in g.st. until this band is same length as st.st. band.

Cast off.

The Sleeves.—With No. 10 needles and main shade of wool cast on 55 sts.

Work 2½ ins. in k. 1, p. 2 rib as given for back welt, finishing 2nd row.

Change to contrasting wool and work 1 in. in st.st., finishing p. row.

Change to No. 8 needles and main shade and continue in patt. as given for back, inc. 1 st. both ends of 7th row and every following 6th row until 91 sts. are on needle, working extra sts. into patt.

Continue straight until work measures 17½ ins., finishing row on wrong side.

Shape Top thus: Keeping continuity of patt., dec. 1 st. both ends of every row until 30 sts. remain.

Cast off 6 sts. beg. of next 2 rows. Cast off remaining sts.

Make-up.—Press work lightly on wrong side with hot iron over damp cloth.

Join side, shoulder and sleeve seams.

Sew sleeves into armholes.

Sew st.st. borders neatly round neck edge, then sew g.st. borders to the st.st. border, joining at back of neck.

Press seams.

Cotton Gloves

FOR RIDING OR CYCLING

MATERIALS

2 oz. knitting cotton.

2 No. 12 and 2 No. 14 knitting needles.

To fit average size.

TENSION

7 sts. to 1 in. with No. 12 needles.

The Right-hand Glove.—With No. 12 needles cast on 50 sts.

Change to No. 14 needles, work 2 ins. in k. 1, p. 1 rib.

Change to No. 12 needles and patt.:—

1st row.—* P. 1, k. 1; rep. from * to end.

Every schoolboy hankers after a sweater with his school colours knitted into it. Here is a good design, with colour introduced at the neck and cuffs. Knit it in white for summer wear, or grey for winter.

2nd row.—As 1st row.

3rd row.—* K. 1, p. 1; rep. from * to end.

4th row.—As 3rd row.

These 4 rows form patt.

Begin Thumb Gusset thus:—

5th row.—(P. 1, k. 1) 13 times, p. 1, m. 1 by picking up thread between st. just worked and next st. and k. 1 st. into back of loop (work all m. 1 in this way), k. 1, m. 1, (p. 1, k. 1) 11 times.

6th row.—(P. 1, k. 1) 11 times, k. 1, p. 1, k. 1, (k. 1, p. 1) 13 times, k. 1.

7th row.—(K. 1 p. 1) 13 times, k. 2, p. 1, k. 1, (k. 1, p. 1) 11 times.

8th row.—(K. 1, p. 1) 11 times, p. 1, k. 1, p. 1, (p. 1, k. 1) 13 times, p. 1.

9th row.—(P. 1, k. 1) 13 times, p. 1, m. 1, p. 1, k. 1, p. 1, m. 1, (p. 1, k. 1) 11 times.

Work 3 rows in patt.

13th row.—(P. 1, k. 1) 13 times, p. 1, m. 1, (k. 1, p. 1) twice, k. 1, m. 1, (p. 1, k. 1) 11 times.

Work 3 rows in patt., allowing for inc. sts.

Continue in this way, inc. 2 sts. in gusset on next and every 4th row, keeping continuity of patt. throughout until there are 62 sts. on needle.

Work 3 rows after last inc. row.

Next row.—Patt. 40, turn, cast on 2 sts.

Next row.—Patt. 15, turn, cast on 2 sts.

Continue in patt. on 17 sts. for 2¼ ins. or length required, finishing row on wrong side.

Shape Top thus:—

Next row.—(Patt. 1, work 2 tog.) 5 times, work 2 tog.

Next row.—Patt. to end.

Next row. — (Work 2 tog.) 5 times, patt. 1.

Break off thread and thread end through remaining sts. Draw up and fasten off, then sew down side edges.

With right side of work facing, rejoin wool and k. up 3 sts. at base of thumb. Continue in patt. on 52 sts. for 1¼

ins., finishing row on wrong side.

Next row.—Patt. 6, sl. these sts. on to a safety-pin for fourth finger, cast on 1 st., patt. to last 6 sts., sl. these sts. on to a second safety-pin, cast on 1 st.

Work 3 rows in patt. on 42 sts., thus finishing row on wrong side.

Work for Fingers thus:—

The First Finger:—

Next row.—Patt. 28, turn, cast on 1 st.

Next row.—Patt. 15, turn, cast on 1 st.

Continue in patt. on 16 sts. for 2¾ ins. or length required, finishing row on wrong side.

Shape Top thus:—

Next row.—(Patt. 1, work 2 tog.) 5 times, patt. 1.

Next row.—Patt. 11.

Next row.—(Work 2 tog.) 5 times, patt. 1.

Break off thread and complete to match thumb.

The Second Finger.—With right side of work facing, rejoin thread and k. up 2 sts. at base of first finger, patt. next 7 sts., turn, cast on 1 st.

Next row.—Patt. 17, turn, cast on 1 st.

Continue in patt. on 18 sts. for 3¼ ins. or length required, finishing row on wrong side.

Shape Top thus:—

Next row.—(Patt. 1, work 2 tog.) 6 times.

Next row.—Patt.

Next row.—(Work 2 tog.) 6 times.

Break off thread and complete to match thumb.

The Third Finger.—With right side of work facing, rejoin thread and k. up 2 sts. at base of second finger, patt. to end.

Continue in patt. on 16 sts. for 2¾ ins. or length required, finishing row on wrong side.

Shape Top and complete to match thumb.

The Fourth Finger:—Slip the two sets of

The gloves are knitted in bright-coloured knitting cotton in double moss stitch. They are very "tough" and most suitable for hard wear.

sts. from safety-pins on to needles and, with right side of work facing, rejoin wool and k. up 2 sts. at base of third finger, patt. to end.

Continue in patt. on 14 sts. for 2¼ ins., finishing on wrong side.

Shape Top thus:—

Next row.—(Work 2 tog., patt. 1) 4 times, work 2 tog.

Next row.—Patt.

Next row.—(Work 2 tog.) 4 times, patt. 1.

Break off thread and complete to match thumb, sewing down side edges to wrist edge.

The Left-hand Glove.—Work wrist ribbing as for right-hand glove. Change to No. 12 needles and patt.:—

1st row.—* K. 1, p. 1; rep. from * to end.

2nd row.—As 1st row.

3rd row.—* P. 1, k. 1; rep. from * to end.

4th row.—As 3rd row.

Begin Thumb Gusset thus:—

5th row.—(K. 1, p. 1) 11 times, m. 1, k. 1, m. 1, (p. 1, k. 1) 13 times, p. 1.

6th row.—K. 1, (p. 1, k. 1) 13 times, k. 1, p. 1, k. 1, (k. 1, p. 1) 11 times.

7th row.—(P. 1, k. 1) 11 times, k. 1, p. 1, k. 1, (k. 1, p. 1) 13 times, k. 1.

8th row.—P. 1, (k. 1, p. 1) 13 times, p. 1, k. 1, p. 1, (p. 1, k. 1) 11 times.

9th row.—(K. 1, p. 1) 11 times, m. 1, p. 1, k. 1, p. 1, m. 1, (p. 1, k. 1) 13 times, p. 1.

Work 3 rows in patt.

13th row.—(K. 1, p. 1) 11 times, m. 1, k. 1, (p. 1, k. 1) twice, m. 1, (p. 1, k. 1) 13 times, p. 1.

Work 3 rows in patt. allowing for inc. sts.

Continue inc. in this way until 62 sts. are on needle.

Work 3 rows after last inc. row.

Next row.—Patt. 35, turn, cast on 2 sts.

Next row.—Patt. 15, turn, cast on 2 sts.

Complete the thumb, rest of hand and fingers as given for the right-hand glove.

Press lightly with hot iron over damp cloth.

Cap and Scarf

IN COLOURED KNITTING

THE CAP

MATERIALS

1 oz. 4-ply wool, dark or neutral colour (original grey).

A small ball 4-ply wool, medium colour (original red).

A small ball 4-ply wool, light colour (original green).

2 No. 13 knitting needles.

A crochet hook.

MEASUREMENTS

Round head, about 22 to 23 ins. slightly stretched.

Depth, about 7½ ins.

TENSION

8½ sts. to 1 in. over st.st.

Detail of coloured knitting stitch.

ADDITIONAL ABBREVIATIONS

Dk. = dark; md. = medium; lt. = light.

With No. 12 needles and dk. wool cast on 180 sts.

Work ½ in. in k. 1, p. 1 rib. Continue in patt., taking wools very loosely across back of work.

1st row.—* K. 1 dk., k. 1 lt., k. 3 dk., (k. 1 md., k. 1 dk.) 3 times, k. 1 dk.; rep. from * to end.

2nd row.—* P. 3 dk., p. 1 md., p. 1 dk., p. 1 md., p. 3 dk., p. 3 lt.; rep. from * to end.

3rd row.—As 1st row.

4th row.—* P. 1 dk., (p. 1 md., p. 1 dk.) 4 times, p. 3 dk.; rep. from * to end.

5th row.—* K. 3 dk., k. 1 md., k. 1 dk., k. 1 md.; rep. from * to end.

6th row.—* P. 1 dk., p. 1 md., p. 5 dk., p. 1 md., (p. 1 dk., p 1 md.) twice; rep. from * to end.

7th row.—* (K. 1 dk., k. 1 md.) twice, k. 3 dk., k. 1 lt., k. 3 dk., k. 1 md.; rep. from * to end.

8th row.—* P. 3 dk., p. 3 lt., p. 3 dk., p. 1 md., p. 1 dk., p. 1 md.; rep. from * to end.

9th row.—As 7th row.

10th row.—As 6th row.

11th row.—As 5th row.

12th row.—As 4th row.

13th-24th rows.—Rep. rows 1 to 12 inclusive once.

25th-27th rows.—Rep. rows 1 to 3 inclusive.

28th row.—With dk. p. to end.

Break off dk. and md. wools. Continue

The cap can be worn at several jaunty angles, and no doubt there will be a good deal of peering into mirrors to get just the right set. Choose three good contrasting colours for the patterned bands on the scarf and the cap.

A cap and scarf for out of school hours. The original was in grey with red and green used in the patterned bands of the set.

k. 21; rep. from * to end.

57th row.— * (Work 2 tog.) 3 times, k. 18; rep. from * to end.

59th row. — * (Work 2 tog.) 3 times, k. 15; rep. from * to end.

61st row.— * (Work 2 tog.) 3 times, k. 12; rep. from * to end.

63rd row.— * (Work 2 tog.) 3 times, k. 9; rep. from * to end.

65th row.— * (Work 2 tog.) 3 times, k. 6; rep. from * to end.

67th row.— * (Work 2 tog.) 3 times, k. 3; rep. from * to end.

69th row.— * (Work 2 tog.); rep. from * to end.

Break off wool, thread through remaining sts., draw up and fasten off.

Press work lightly on wrong side with hot iron over damp cloth, taking care not to stretch the ribbed band.

Join back seam very neatly with a narrow backstitch. Press seam. Make a crochet cord of the 3 colours and attach a tassel to one end. Sew other end to centre top of cap.

with lt. wool only. Work 4 rows in st.st.

33rd row.— * (Work 2 tog.) 3 times, k. 39; rep. from * to end.

Work 3 rows in st.st.

37th row.— * (Work 2 tog.) 3 times, k. 36; rep. from * to end.

Work 3 rows in st.st.

41st row.— * (Work 2 tog.) 3 times, k. 33; rep. from * to end.

Work 3 rows in st.st.

45th row.— * (Work 2 tog.) 3 times, k. 30; rep from * to end.

Work 3 rows in st.st.

49th row.— * (Work 2 tog.) 3 times, k. 27; rep. from * to end.

Work 3 rows in st.st.

53rd row.— * (Work 2 tog.) 3 times, k. 24; rep. from * to end.

Work 1 p. row after each dec. row.

55th row.— * (Work 2 tog.) 3 times,

SCARF

MATERIALS

3 oz. 4-ply wool, dark or neutral colour (original grey).

A small ball 4-ply wool, medium colour (original red).

3 oz. 4-ply wool, light colour (original green).

2 No. 9 knitting needles.

MEASUREMENTS

Length, 40 ins.

Width, 8 ins.

TENSION

7 sts. to 1 in.

ADDITIONAL ABBREVIATIONS

Dk. = dark; md. = medium; lt. = light.

With No. 9 needles and dk. wool cast on 55 sts. Work ½ in. in g.st.

Continue in patt. taking wools loosely across back of work when working with 3 shades.

1st row.—K. 2 dk., * k. 1 dk., k. 1 lt., k. 3 dk., (k. 1 md., k. 1 dk.) 3 times, k. 1 dk.; rep. from * to last 5 sts., k. 1 dk., k. 1 lt., k. 3 dk.

2nd row.—K. 2 dk., * p. 3 lt., p. 3 dk., p. 1 md., p. 1 dk., p. 1 md., p. 3 dk.; rep. from * to last 5 sts., p. 3 lt., k. 2 dk.

3rd row.—As 1st row.

4th row.—K. 2 dk., * p. 4 dk., (p. 1 md., p. 1 dk.) 4 times; rep. from * to last 5 sts., p. 3 dk., k. 2 dk.

5th row.—K. 2 dk., * k. 3 dk., k. 1 md., k. 1 dk., k. 1 md.; rep. from * to last 5 sts., k. 5 dk.

6th row.—K. 2 dk., * (p. 1 md., p. 1 dk.) 3 times, p. 4 dk., p. 1 md., p. 1 dk.; rep. from * to last 5 sts., p. 1 md., p. 1 dk., p. 1 md., k. 2 dk.

7th row.—K. 2 dk., * (k. 1 dk., k. 1 md.) twice, k. 3 dk., k. 1 lt., k. 3 dk., k. 1 md.; rep. from * to last 5 sts., k. 1 dk., k. 1 md., k. 3 dk.

8th row.—K. 2 dk., * p. 1 md., p. 1 dk., p. 1 md., p. 3 dk., p. 3 lt., p. 3 dk.; rep. from * to last 5 sts., p. 1 md., p. 1 dk., p. 1 md., k. 2 dk.

9th row.—As 7th row.

10th row.—As 6th row.

11th row.—As 5th row.

12th row.—As 4th row.

13th-24th rows.—Rep. rows 1 to 12 inclusive once.

25th-27th rows.—Rep. rows 1 to 3 inclusive once.

With dk. wool p. 1 row, then work ½ in. in g.st., finishing row on wrong side.

With dk. wool work in rib thus:—

1st row.—K. 2, * k. 7, p. 2; rep. from * to last 8 sts., k. 4, k. twice into next st., k. 3.

2nd row.—K. 2, * p. 7, k. 2; rep. from * to end.

3rd row.—K. 2, * k. 7, p. 2; rep. from * to last 9 sts., k. 9.

Rep. last 2 rows until work measures 36 ins., finishing row on right side.

Next row.—K. 2, p. 2 tog., p. 5, * k. 2, p. 7; rep. from * to last 2 sts., k. 2.

Work ½ in. in g.st., finishing row on wrong side.

Now rep. patt. rows 1 to 27 inclusive once.

Using dk. wool, work ½ in. in g.st. Cast off.

The Lining.—With No. 9 needles and lt. wool, cast on 55 sts. and work ½ in. in g.st.

Continue in st.st. keeping 2 sts. at each edge in g.st. until lining is the same length as scarf except for the final g.st. border.

Work ½ in. in g.st.

Cast off.

To Make-up.—Press both pieces of the scarf lightly on the wrong side under a damp cloth, pressing out the rib and Fair Isle patt. to match the lining in width.

Stitch the two sides lightly together on the wrong side leaving the ends open, turn inside out, press again, and finish off the ends with a fringe, in any of the colours, knotted through both edges.

Three-quarter Socks

IN THREE SIZES FOR BOY OR GIRL

MATERIALS

3 oz. 3-ply wool for size 1.
4 oz. for size 2, 4 oz. for size 3.
4 No. 12 knitting needles.

MEASUREMENTS

Length of Foot: Size 1, 7½ ins. to 8 ins.; size 2, 8½ ins. to 9 ins.; size 3, 9½ ins. to 10 ins.

Length of Leg (from top to bottom of heel): Size 1, 18 ins.; size 2, 19½ ins.; size 3, 21 ins.

This allows for 3 ins. to 3½ ins. to be turned over at the top and the turn-over can be less as the child grows.

N.B.—For size 1 work as given; for size 2 work as given but follow first number of stitches, rows or inches in brackets for original number; for size 3 work as given but follow second number of stitches, rows or inches in brackets for original number.

TENSION

8½ sts. to 1 in.

Cast on 72 (80, 88) sts. (24 on each of 3 needles for size 1; 24, 32, 24 for size 2; 32, 24, 32 for size 3) and work in rounds of rib thus:—

1st round.—* K. 2, p. 1, k. 4, p. 1; rep. from * to end.

Rep. this round until work measures 8 (9½, 10½) ins., finishing at end of third needle.

Shape for Leg thus:—

1st round.—K. 2 tog., p. 1, work in rib to end.

2nd round.—K. 1, p. 1, work in rib to end.

Rep. 2nd round 4 times.

7th round.—K. 1, p. 1, k. 2 tog., k. 2, p. 1, work in rib to last 5 sts., k. 2, sl. 1, k. 1, p.s.s.o., p. 1.

8th round.—K. 1, p. 1, k. 3, p. 1, work in rib to last 4 sts., k. 3, p. 1.

Rep. 8th round 4 times.

13th round.—K. 1, p. 1, k. 3, p. 1, k. 2 tog., p. 1, work in rib to last 7 sts., sl. 1, k. 1, p.s.s.o., p. 1, k. 3, p. 1.

14th round.—K. 1, p. 1, k. 3, p. 1, k. 1, p. 1, work in rib to last 6 sts., k. 1, p. 1, k. 3, p. 1.

Rep. 14th round 4 times.

19th round.—K. 1, p. 1, k. 3, p. 1, k. 1, p. 1, k. 2 tog., k. 2, p. 1, work in rib to last 11 sts., k. 2, sl. 1, k. 1, p.s.s.o., p. 1, k. 1, p. 1, k. 3, p. 1.

20th round.—(K. 1, p. 1, k. 3, p. 1) twice, work in rib to last 10 sts., k. 3, p. 1, k. 1, p. 1, k. 3, p. 1.

Rep. 20th round 4 times.

25th round.—(K. 1, p. 1, k. 3, p. 1) twice, k. 2 tog., p. 1, work in rib to last 13 sts., sl. 1, k. 1, p.s.s.o., p. 1, k. 3, p. 1, k. 1, p. 1, k. 3, p. 1.

26th round.—(K. 1, p. 1, k. 3, p. 1) twice, k. 1, p. 1, work in rib to last 12 sts., (k. 1, p. 1, k. 3, p. 1) twice.

Rep. 26th round 4 times.

31st round.—(K. 1, p. 1, k. 3, p. 1) twice, k. 1, p. 1, k. 2 tog., k. 2, p. 1, work in rib to last 17 sts., k. 2, sl. 1, k. 1, p.s.s.o., p. 1, (k. 1, p. 1, k. 3, p. 1) twice.

Continue thus, dec. 2 sts. on every 6th round until 54 (60, 66) sts. remain. Now continue in rib of k. 1, p. 1, k. 3, p. 1 until work measures 16½ (18, 19½) ins., finishing at end of third needle.

Work for Heel thus: With wrong side of work facing sl. 13 (14, 16) sts. from end of third needle on to first needle, then sl. 4 (3, 7) sts. from end of first needle on to second needle, thus leaving 27 (29, 33) sts. on first needle for the heel and 27 sts. to be arranged, evenly on two needles and left for the instep.

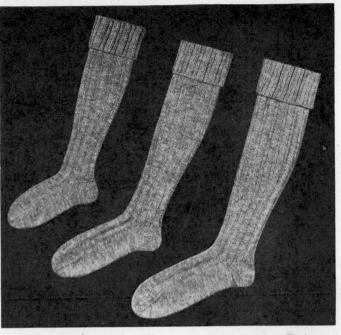

Schoolboys and schoolgirls alike will approve of these warm, ribbed socks. Instructions are given for three sizes.

Break off wool, rejoin at beg. of heel sts. and work thus:—

1st row.—K. all but last st. of previous row, turn.

2nd row.—P. all but last st. of previous row, turn.

Rep. last 2 rows 8 (9, 10) times.

Next row.—K. sts. of previous row, then lift up loop before next st. and k. tog. with next st., turn.

Next row.—P. sts. of previous row, then lift up loop before next st. and p. tog. with next st., turn.

Continue thus, taking up 1 st. extra on every row until all sts. are worked on to one needle (27 (29, 33) sts.).

Work foot thus: K. 13 (14, 16) sts. on to one needle for first needle, sl. 27 (31, 33) sts. for instep on to one needle, k. remaining 14 (15, 17) sts. of heel on to second needle, with third needle work in rib across instep sts.

Next round. 1st needle.—K. to end. **2nd needle.**—K. to end. **3rd needle.**—Rib to end.

Rep. this last round until work measures 5¾ ins. for a 7½-in. foot, 6¼ ins. for 8-in., 6¾ ins. for 8½-in., 7¼ ins. for 9-in., 7¾ ins. for 9½-in., 8¼ ins. for 10-in.), finishing at end of 3rd needle.

Shape for Toe thus:—

1st round. 1st needle.—K. **2nd needle.**—K. **3rd needle.** K.

2nd round. 1st needle.—K. 1, sl. 1, k. 1, p.s.s.o., k. to end.

2nd needle.—K. to last 2 sts., k. 2 tog.

3rd needle.—K. 1, sl. 1, k. 1, p.s.s.o., k. to last 3 sts., k. 2 tog., k. 1.

Rep. last 2 rounds until 18 (20, 22) sts. remain.

Slip sts. from 2nd needle on to 1st needle and graft two sets of sts. tog.

Press lightly with warm iron and damp cloth.

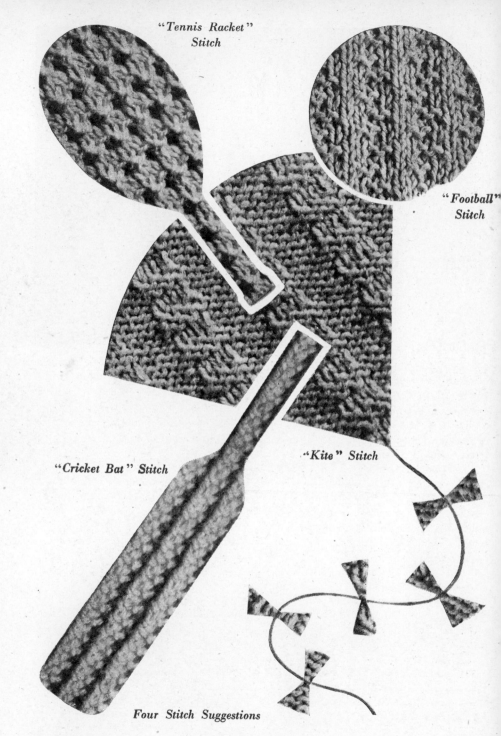

"Tennis Racket" Stitch

"Football" Stitch

"Cricket Bat" Stitch

"Kite" Stitch

Four Stitch Suggestions

Alternative Stitches

FOR USE FOR CHILDREN'S GARMENTS AND ACCESSORIES SHOWN ON PAGES 190 TO 219

IF you would like to make a plain garment into a patterned one or to substitute a simple stitch for an elaborate one, make your choice from the opposite page. "Tennis Racket" stitch and "Cricket Bat" stitch both have an attractive bumpy surface and a slightly open texture which make them specially suitable for girls' garments. Try either of these for the top of the girl's vest on page 198, or for the plain twin set on page 190, keeping the moss stitch borders as before. Either of these stitches could be used, too, for the patterned jerkin on page 204.

"Football" stitch and "Kite" stitch are two broken rib patterns, very easy to knit, and good for both boys' and girls' garments. The stocking stitch jerkin on page 203 would look well knitted in either of these ribs. Remember them, too, for variations on the plain twin set on page 190, keeping the moss stitch borders in the case of "Football" stitch and substituting garter stitch borders in the case of "Kite" stitch to match the garter stitch effect of the rib. Either of these stitches could be used for the turnover tops of the three-quarter socks on page 218.

"Tennis Racket" Stitch

An odd number of stitches.
1st row.—K.
2nd row.—P.
3rd row.—K. 1, * k. 2 tog.; rep. from * to end.
4th row.—K. 1, * pick up and knit the thread between the sts., k. 1; rep. from * to end.
Rep. these 4 rows.

"Football" Stitch

Number of stitches divisible by 4, plus 2 stitches.
1st row.—P. 2, * k. 2, p. 2; rep. from * to end.
2nd row.—P.
3rd row.—K. 1, * p. 2, k. 2; rep. from * ending p. 1.
4th row.—P.
Rep. these 4 rows.

"Kite" Stitch

Number of stitches divisible by 6, plus 7 stitches.
1st row.—K.
2nd row.—P.
3rd row.—K. 2, * p. 3, k. 3; rep. from * ending p. 3, k. 2.
4th row.—P. 2, * k. 3, p. 3; rep. from * ending k. 3, p. 2.
Rep. these 4 rows.

"Cricket Bat" Stitch

Number of stitches divisible by 2.
1st row.—* K. 1, p. 1; rep. from * to end.
2nd row.—K. 1, * p. into previous row of next st. leaving the st. on left-hand needle, k. 2 tog. through the backs of the loops.
Rep. from * to last st., k. 1.
Rep. these 2 rows.

"Artist" Stitch

Number of stitches divisible by 4, plus 2 stitches.

1st row.—K. 2, * k. 2nd st. on left-hand needle, then k. 1st st. and sl. both sts. off needle tog. (this will be called "twist"), k. 2; rep. from * to end.

2nd row.—P. 2, * k. 2, p. 2; rep. from * to end.

3rd row.—K.

4th row.—P.

5th row.—Twist first 2 sts., * k. 2, twist next 2 sts.; rep. from * to end.

6th row.—K. 2, * p. 2, k. 2; rep. from * to end.

7th row.—K.

8th row.—P.

Rep. these 8 rows.

"Singing" Stitch

Number of stitches divisible by 6, plus 1 for edge stitch.

1st row.—Sl. 1, k. 2 tog., * m. 1, k. 1, m. 1, k. 1, sl. 1, k. 2 tog., p.s.s.o., k. 1; rep. from * to last 4 sts., m. 1, k. 1, m. 1, k. 2 tog., k. 1.

2nd row.—P.

Rep. these 2 rows.

"'Cello" Stitch

Number of stitches divisible by 4, plus 2 stitches.

1st row.—K. 2, * w.fd., sl. 2 p.w. (always taking wool very loosely across front of these sl.sts.), w.bk., k. 2; rep. from * to end.

2nd and alternate rows.—P.

3rd row.—K. 3, * w.fd., sl. 2 p.w., w.bk., k. 2; rep. from * to last 3 sts., w.fd., sl. 2 p.w., w.bk., k. 1.

5th row.—Keeping wool to front sl. 2 p.w., w.bk., * k. 2, w.fd., sl. 2 p.w., w.bk.; rep. from * to end.

7th row.—K. 1, * w.fd., sl. 2 p.w., w.bk., k. 2; rep. from * to last st., k. 1.

8th row.—P.

Rep. these 8 rows.

MAKING UP HINTS

BEAUTIFULLY knitted garments are often ruined by careless making up. So take the trouble to sew them up properly.

After pinning out the pieces of the garment to measurement on an ironing blanket, press them before seaming.

If you have taken care to knit your first and last stitches firmly, you will have a neat edge to sew up, and any of the following seams can be used.

For children's garments generally the edge-to-edge method is the best. Hold the two pieces of work flat with the edges meeting and the right side facing you, and join with a "lacing" stitch, taking one loop from each side.

The backstitch method will produce a ridge, but if done close to the edge, can be quite neat. Place the right sides of the work together and backstitch them firmly as near to the edge as possible, taking quite small stitches.

For cardigans and any garment which has not to be pulled over the head, machine stitching is very satisfactory, but use a fairly loose tension as the fabric is springy and will pull up if the stitches are too tight.

Front bands should be stretched well when sewn on. Pin them into position, stretching all the way round, then over-sew them neatly into place. The bands sewn on to necks should be particularly stretched.

When sewing in sleeves, unless otherwise stated, the centre of the sleeve top should be sewn to the shoulder seam. Pin in this way before sewing up, and use the backstitch method.

*for Sleeved
Sweater—*

*—Youthful
Jumper*

Three Artistic Stitches

Telephone No. 888.
PRIVATE BRANCH EXCH.

GREENWOOD'S,

WOOLS & HANDICRAFTS

13-15, VICTORIA STREET and 12, QUEEN STREET,

:: HUDDERSFIELD. ::

194

Miss V. A. Jaques,
40 Rectory Road, Barnes,
London, S.W. 13.

Youthful Ingenuity

STITCHES PLANNED FOR 'TEEN AGE ACCESSORIES AND ENSEMBLES

Detail of the "Feather Rib" Stitch.

"Feather Rib" Stitch

Number of stitches divisible by 11, plus 5 stitches.

P. 1 row before beginning patt.

1st row.—* P. 5, sl. next st. on spare pin, leave in front of work, k. 2, then k. sts. from spare pin, sl. next 2 sts. on spare pin, leave at back of work, k. 3rd st., then k. 2 from spare pin; rep. from * to last 5 sts., p. 5.

2nd row.—P.

Rep. these 2 rows.

Two-colour Check Stitch

An even number of stitches.

l. = light colour; d. = dark colour.

1st row.—K. with l.

2nd row.—As 1st row.

3rd row.—K. with d.

4th row.—As 3rd row. Change to l.

5th row.—K. 1, * k. 2 tog., pick up and

k. l. st. in 2nd row; rep. from * to last st., k. 1.

6th row.—K.

7th row.—As 3rd row.

8th row.—As 4th row. Change to l.

9th row.—K. 1, * pick up and k. l. st. in 6th row, k. 2 tog.; rep. from * to last st., k. 1.

10th row.—K.

Rows 3 to 10 form patt.

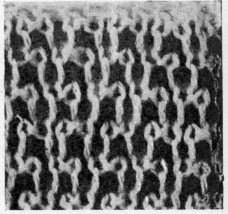

Detail of Two-colour Check Stitch.

"Outfit" Stitch (opposite page)

Number of stitches divisible by 4.

1st row.—* K. 1, p. 1; rep. from * to last 2 sts., k. 2.

2nd row.—* K. 1, p. into the previous row of following st., leaving it on left-hand needle. K. tog. through the backs of the loops this st. with the next (plain) st., k. 1; rep. from * to end.

Rep. these 2 rows.

A neat rib stitch designed for the 'teen age outfit illustrated here.

Household Section

Mats and Runner

FOR THE SMART HOUSEWIFE'S TABLE

MATERIALS

4 4-oz. hanks of fine string (for 4 mats and 1 runner).

1 pair No. 12 knitting needles.

A fine crochet hook.

MEASUREMENTS

Mats: 9½ ins. by 13 ins.

Runner: 9½ ins. by 31 ins.

TENSION

About 8 sts. to 1 in.

THE MATS

Cast on 77 sts. and work in m.st.:—

1st row.—K. 1, * p. 1, k. 1; rep. from * to end. Rep. this row for 1 in. Continue in patt.:—

1st and alternate rows.—M.st. 8. p. to last 8 sts., m.st. 8.

2nd row.—M.st. 8, * k. 9, m. 1, sl. 1, k. 2 tog., p.s.s.o., m. 1, k. 8. Rep. from * twice, k. 1, m.st. 8.

4th row.—M.st. 8, * k. 7, k. 2 tog., m. 1, k. 3, m. 1, sl. 1, k. 1, p.s.s.o., k. 6; rep. from * twice, k. 1, m.st. 8.

6th row.—M.st. 8, * k. 6, k. 2 tog., m. 1, k. 5, m. 1, sl. 1, k. 1, p.s.s.o., k. 5; rep. from * twice, k. 1, m.st. 8.

8th row.—M.st. 8 * k. 5, k. 2 tog., m. 1, k. 7, m. 1, sl. 1, k. 1, p.s.s.o., k. 4; rep. from * twice, k. 1, m.st. 8.

10th row.—M.st. 8, * k. 4, k. 2 tog., m. 1, k. 9, m. 1, sl. 1, k. 1, p.s.s.o., k. 3; rep.

from * twice, k. 1, m.st. 8.

12th row.—M.st. 8, * k. 3, k. 2 tog., m. 1, k. 11, m. 1, sl. 1, k. 1, p.s.s.o., k. 2; rep. from * twice, k. 1, m.st. 8.

14th row.—M.st. 8, * k. 2, k. 2 tog., m. 1, k. 13, m. 1, sl. 1, k. 1, p.s.s.o., k. 1; rep. from * twice, k. 1, m.st. 8.

16th row.—M.st. 8, * k. 1, k. 2 tog., m. 1, k. 5, k. 2 tog., m. 1, k. 1, m. 1, sl. 1, k. 1, p.s.s.o., k. 5, m. 1, sl. 1, k. 1, p.s.s.o.; rep. from * twice, k. 1, m.st. 8.

18th row.—M.st. 8, k. 2 tog., * m. 1, k. 5, k. 2 tog., m. 1, k. 3, m. 1, sl. 1, k. 1, p.s.s.o., k. 5, m. 1, sl. 1, k. 2 tog., p.s.s.o.; rep. from * twice, ending 2nd rep. with sl. 1, k. 1, p.s.s.o., m.st. 8.

20th row.—M.st. 8, * k. 2, m. 1, sl. 1, k. 1, p.s.s.o., k. 5, m. 1, sl. 1, k. 2 tog., p.s.s.o., m. 1, k. 5, k. 2 tog., m. 1, k. 1; rep. from * twice, k. 1, m.st. 8.

22nd row.—M.st. 8, * k. 3, m. 1, sl. 1, k. 1, p.s.s.o., k. 11, k. 2 tog., m. 1, k. 2; rep. from * twice, k. 1, m.st. 8.

24th row.—M.st. 8, * k. 4, m. 1, sl. 1, k. 1; p.s.s.o., k. 9, k. 2 tog., m. 1, k. 3; rep. from * twice, k. 1, m.st. 8.

26th row.—M.st. 8, * k. 5, m. 1, sl. 1, k. 1, p.s.s.o., k. 7, k. 2 tog., m. 1, k. 4; rep. from * twice, k. 1, m.st. 8.

28th row.—M.st. 8, * k. 6, m. 1, sl. 1, k. 1, p.s.s.o., k. 5, k. 2 tog., m. 1, k. 5; rep. from * twice, k. 1, m.st. 8.

30th row.—M.st. 8, * k. 7, m. 1, sl. 1, k. 1, p.s.s.o., k. 3, k. 2 tog., m. 1, k. 6;

rep. from * twice, k. 1, m.st. 8.

32nd row.—M.st. 8, * k. 8, m. 1, sl. 1, k. 1, p.s.s.o., k. 1, k. 2 tog., m. 1, k. 7; rep. from * twice, k. 1, m.st. 8.

33rd to 47th rows.—Rep. 1st to 15th rows inclusive.

48th row.—M.st. 8, * k. 1, k. 2 tog.. m. 1, k. 5, k. 2 tog., m. 1, k. 1, m. 1, sl. 1, k. 1, p.s.s.o., k. 5, m. 1, sl. 1, k. 1, p.s.s.o., * k. 1, k. 2 tog., m. 1, k. 15, m. 1, sl. 1, k. 1, p.s.s.o., rep. from * to * once, k. 1, m.st. 8.

50th row.—M.st. 8, k. 2 tog., * m. 1, k. 5, k. 2 tog., m. 1, k. 3, m. 1, sl. 1, k. 1, p.s.s.o., k. 5, m. 1, * sl. 1, k. 2 tog., p.s.s.o., m. 1, k. 17, m. 1, sl. 1, k. 2 tog., p.s.s.o.; rep. from * to * once, sl. 1, k. 1, p.s.s.o., m.st. 8.

52nd row.—M.st. 8, * k. 2, m. 1, sl. 1, k. 1, p.s.s.o., k. 5, m. 1, sl. 1, k. 2 tog., p.s.s.o., m. 1, k. 5, k. 2 tog., m. 1, * k. 3, m. 1, sl. 1, k. 1, p.s.s.o., k. 13, k. 2 tog., m. 1, k. 1; rep. from * to * once, k. 2, m.st. 8.

53rd to 64th rows.—Rep. 21st to 32nd rows inclusive.

Now rep. patt. rows 33 to 64 inclusive once, then patt. rows 1 to 32 inclusive once, then 1st, 2nd and 3rd patt. rows again. Work 1 in. in m.st. across all sts.

Cast off in m.st.

Work 3 more mats in same way.

THE RUNNER

Continue as given for the mats to end of the 64th row. Now rep. patt. rows 33 to 64 inclusive 6 times.

Rep. patt. rows 1 to 32 inclusive once, then 1st, 2nd and 3rd patt. rows again.

Work 1 in. in m.st. across all sts.

Cast off in m.st.

Work a row of d.c. all round each mat and runner, working 1 d.c., 1 ch., 1 d.c. into each corner to keep work flat.

Press carefully on wrong side with a hot iron over a damp cloth, pinning out to shape if necessary.

The knitted mats and runner look very dainty on a polished table. Instructions for crocheting the napkin edges are given on page 228.

Simple Crochet Edgings

CROCHET edgings can be used to trim such articles as handkerchiefs, table napkins, tray cloths, etc., according to the thickness of cotton used, and the linen. For instance, cotton from 40 to 60 should be used for handkerchiefs and 20, 10 or 5 for napkins and tray cloths, according to the weight of linen. The tray cloth edging shown on page 229 was worked in a very coarse thread as a heavy linen was used.

A narrow hem should be turned and tacked in place but the corners should be sewn in place carefully.

The first row of crochet is worked over the hem into the linen, and if possible a special number of loops (as given) worked. If this cannot be arranged, discretion must be used in working the appropriate rows to make the pattern fit at each corner. For instance, in edging No. 1 for handkerchiefs an extra 2 ch. may be worked just before corner to make the 7 trs. come at the corner loop, or the 2 ch. may be omitted. When any variation is made, it should be worked both sides of that particular corner.

The Table Napkin Edgings (*illustrated on page 227*).—Use No. 20 crochet cotton and a steel hook, size 4.

Turn a narrow hem and work 1st row over this.

Edging No. 1 (*in forefront of photograph on page 227*). **1st row.**—* 1 d.c. into linen, 2 ch.; rep. from * all round, working 3 d.c. with 2 ch. between at each corner.

2nd row.—1 d.c. into first 2 ch., * 5 ch., miss next 2 ch., 1 d.c. into next 2 ch.; rep. from * all round, working an extra 5 ch. loop at each corner.

3rd row.—3 d.c., 4 ch., 3 d.c. into each 5 ch. loop. Break off.

Edging No. 2 (*in background of photograph on page 227*). **1st row.**—As 1st row of Edging No. 1, working an odd number of 2 ch. to each side before turning corner with 5 ch. Join with sl.st.

2nd row.—6 ch., * miss 2 ch., 3 tr. into next 2 ch.,

Crochet edges add loveliness to handkerchiefs and runners,

3 ch.; rep. from * all round working 3 tr., 3 ch., 3 tr. into each corner loop, and ending round with 2 tr. and sl.st. into third of first 6 ch.

3rd row.—* 6 tr. into each 3 ch. loop, 1 d.c. into centre of each group of 3 tr.; rep. from * all round. Break off.

The Handkerchief Edgings.—Use No. 40 crochet cotton and a fine steel hook.

Edging No. 1 (*top of picture on page 228*).—Commence at corner and work 1 d.c. into linen, * 3 ch., miss a small space, 1 d.c. into linen; rep. from * all round, working 5 ch. at each corner.

2nd row.—1 d.c. into first 3 ch., * (1 tr., 2 ch.) 4 times, 1 tr. into next 3 ch., 1 d.c. into next 3 ch., 2 ch., 1 d.c. into next 3 ch.; rep. from * all round, working 7 tr. with 2 ch. between at each corner.

3rd row.—3 ch., 1 d.c. into each 2 ch. of last round. Break off.

Edging No. 2 (*centre of picture on page 228*).—Commence at one corner and work 1 d.c. into linen, * 5 ch., miss a small space of hem (about equal to 3 ch.), 1 d.c. into linen; rep. from * all round, making an odd number of d.c. to each side and turning corners with 5 ch.

2nd row.—* 1 d.c. into 5 ch., 4 ch.; rep. from * all round, working 1 d.c., 4 ch., 1 d.c. into each corner, 5 ch.

3rd row.—* 1 d.c. into first 4 ch., 3 tr., 3 ch., 3 tr. into next 4 ch.; rep. from * all round, working 3 tr., 3 ch., 3 tr. into each corner loop. Break off.

The Runner Border.—The runner photographed beneath the handkerchiefs on opposite page, was made from an odd piece of linen with a simple crochet border. The edge is turned down, 1 d.c.; 2 ch. worked over it and the chart on page 230 followed for the rest of the work. More or fewer holes may be worked before and after corners according to the length of the linen.

The corners are turned by working 4 tr., 5 ch., 4 tr. The border is the same as for the pillow-case edging on page 230.

The Tray Cloth Edging.—This was worked with coarse cotton (No. 3) and a No. 1 hook as a heavy linen was used.

Each pattern takes about 2 ins. in width, so that it is necessary to measure the linen and mark where each will come in order to keep the corners even.

1st row.—1 d.c. into corner, 1 ch., 1 d.c. into linen, 1 ch., 1 d.c., * 8 ch., miss small space of linen, (1 d.c., 1 ch.) 10 times; rep. from *, working only 3 d.c. with 1 ch. between before corners and 5 ch. at corner.

2nd row.—* Into each 8 ch. loop work (4 double tr., 3 ch., 1 d.c. into top of last tr. forming picot) 3 times, 4 double tr., 3 ch., 1 d.c. between 5th and 6th d.c. of last row, 3 ch.; rep. from * all round.

This pretty tray cloth edging is very quick to work.

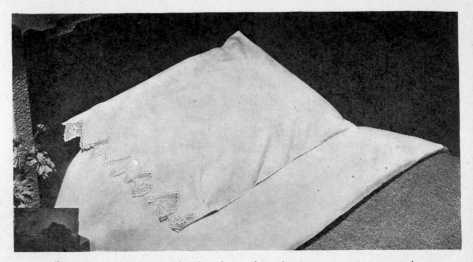

The lovely pillow case border shown here is easy to crochet from the chart below, yet it will give an air of distinction to your bed linen.

PILLOW CASE BORDER

The illustration shows an unusual way of trimming linen with crochet. The material was machine hem-stitched in a series of right-angled points and a row of d.c. worked into these holes. The little pattern can be followed from the chart, working into the d.c. for 1st row and slip-stitching to the other slope of d.c. at ends of rows when turning. The open squares indicate a square mesh of 1 tr., 2 ch. and the solid squares, blocks of 3 tr.

The picot edging is worked last as follows:—

* 2 d.c. into first 2 ch., 2 d.c. into next, 3 ch.; rep. from *.

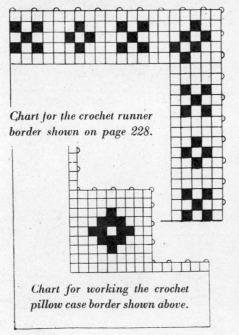

Chart for the crochet runner border shown on page 228.

Chart for working the crochet pillow case border shown above.

KNITTED BLANKET

A knitted blanket worked on large needles with bouclé or looped yarn will give maximum warmth with minimum weight. A single-bed size blanket takes about 3 lb. of "loop" yarn and, to avoid the inconvenience of a large number of stitches, should be made in three strips, 20 ins. wide and 80 ins. long, knitted on No. 6 needles in stocking stitch with 1-in. garter-stitch borders. Join these strips by overlapping the borders and working two rows of machine stitching through both thicknesses, finishing with two rows of machine stitching round all outside edges to prevent them curling.

Bath Mat

MATERIALS

8 oz. dishcloth cotton.
1 pair No. 6 needles.

MEASUREMENTS

28 ins. by 34 ins.

TENSION

About 3½ sts. to 1 in.

Cast on 101 sts.
1st row.—K.
2nd row.—K. 1, * insert right-hand needle k.w. in next st., wind cotton k.w. round this needle and first two fingers of left hand twice, then k. st., k. 1; rep. from * to end.

3rd row.—P.

K. next 6 rows in g.st.

Rep. from 2nd row until mat measures 34 ins., ending with a 3rd row. Cast off.

To strengthen the mat and make it more absorbent, it is a good idea to back it with a piece of old towelling, stitching the two thicknesses together right across in several places.

Make your bath mats in different colours to match your towels.

Knitted Counterpane

DISTINCTIVE, MADE IN COTTON OR WOOL

English knitted quilts have been famous for a hundred and fifty years, and great ingenuity of pattern is shown in those which have survived. The pattern given here is called Apricot Leaf with Feather Pattern border. In pastel-coloured wool, it would make a wonderful quilt and blanket combined, but almost any yarn, provided it is not too thick, could be used. The original was made of cotton yarn on size 16 needles.

The counterpane is composed of squares each made up of four smaller squares knitted cornerways and sewn together. The size of the counterpane will depend on the number of squares.

Begin by casting on 2 sts.

1st row.—K. 1, m. 1, k. 1.

2nd and alternate rows.—P.

3rd row.—(K. 1, m. 1) twice, k. 1.

5th row.—(K. 1, m. 1) 4 times, k. 1.

7th row.—K. 1, m. 1, p. 1, k. 2, m. 1 k. 1, m. 1, k. 2, p. 1, m. 1, k. 1.

Four of these squares form a pattern.

8th row.—P. 2, k. 1, p. 7, k. 1, p. 2.

9th row.—K. 1, m. 1, p. 2, k. 3, m. 1, k. 1, m. 1, k. 3, p. 2, m. 1, k. 1.

10th row.—P. 2, k. 2, p. 9, k. 2, p. 2.

11th row.—K. 1, m. 1, p. 3, k. 4, m. 1, k. 1, m. 1, k. 4, p. 3, m. 1, k. 1.

12th row.—P. 2, k. 3, p. 11, k. 3, p. 2.

13th row.—K. 1, m. 1, p. 4, k. 5, m. 1, k. 1, m. 1, k. 5, p. 4, m. 1, k. 1.

14th row.—P. 2, k. 4, p. 13, k. 4, p. 2.

15th row.—K. 1, m. 1, p. 5, k. 6, m. 1, k. 1, m. 1, k. 6, p. 5, m. 1, k. 1.

16th row.—P. 2, k. 5, p. 15, k. 5, p. 2.

17th row.—K. 1, m. 1, p. 6, sl. 1, k. 1, p.s.s.o., k. 11, k. 2 tog., p. 6, m. 1, k. 1.

18th row.—P. 2, k. 6, p. 13, k. 6, p. 2.

19th row.—K. 1, m. 1, p. to centre panel, sl. 1, k. 1, p.s.s.o., k. to last 2 sts. of centre panel, k. 2 tog., p. to last st., m. 1, k. 1.

20th row.—P., k. and m. sts. and k. p. sts. of previous row.

Rep. last 2 rows 4 times.

29th row.—K. 1, m. 1, p. 12, sl. 1, k. 2 tog., p.s.s.o., p. 12, m. 1, k. 1.

30th row.—P.

31st row.—K. to end, inc. 1 st. each end of row (31 sts.).

32nd and 33rd rows.—As 30th row.

34th row.—K. 2 tog., * m. 1, k. 2 tog.; rep. from * to last 3 sts., m. 1, k. 3 tog.

35th row.—P.

36th row.—P., dec. 1 st. each end of row.

37th row.—K.

38th row.—As 36th row

39th row.—P.

Rep. rows 34 to 39 inclusive 3 times, then rows 34 to 37 inclusive once more. P. 3 tog. and fasten off.

COUNTERPANE BORDER

The border is made separately and then added to the counterpane. It is knitted "shortways" and can be of any desired width. The fringe, which is worked afterwards, consists of 12-in. lengths of yarn, knotted twice.

There are 17 sts. plus 1 st. to each patt.
1st row.—P. **2nd row.**—K.

3rd and 4th rows.—As 1st and 2nd rows.

5th row.—K. 1, * m. 1, k. 6, k. 2 tog., sl. 1, k. 1, p.s.s.o., k. 6, m. 1, k. 1; rep. from * to end.

6th row.—P.

7th to 16th rows.—Rep. 5th and 6th rows 5 times. These 16 rows form patt. Rep. as required.

This beautiful counterpane has retained its loveliness after a century of use. Instructions for the Apricot Leaf motif and Feather border are given here.

Principles of Knitting and Crochet

KNITTING and crochet, amongst the earliest handicrafts, are based on a few simple movements of the hands. From the clear photographs and step-by-step instructions on the following pages, the beginner will master these movements without difficulty and can then proceed from simple stitches to the more intricate patterns.

ABBREVIATIONS. — The following abbreviations are those in general use. If, in any pattern, an abbreviation occurs which is applicable to that pattern only, details are given at the beginning of the instructions.

* = asterisk. In knitting instructions this is used as a sign of repetition, and indicates that the instructions written after a * or between two *s have to be repeated to the end of the row, or the number of times stated. For example: * k. 1, p. 1; rep. from * 3 times, means that you have to repeat the k. 1, p. 1, 3 times after having done it once; that is, 4 times in all.

beg. = beginning.

k. = knit (see page 245).

p. = purl (see page 246).

st. = stitch.

sts. = stitches.

sl. = slip. Instead of knitting or purling the next stitch on the left-hand needle, simply transfer it to the right-hand needle without putting the wool over to knit it.

g.st. = garter stitch (see page 243).

st.st. = stocking stitch (see page 247).

inc. = increase or increasing.

dec. = decrease or decreasing.

p.w. = purlwise, that is, by inserting the point of the right-hand needle into the front of the stitch, as if to purl.

k.w. = knitwise; inserting the point of the right-hand needle into the front of the stitch and out at the back as if to knit.

p.s.s.o. = pass slip stitch over. Slip one stitch on to the right-hand needle without knitting it. Knit the next stitch and then lift the slipped stitch over the knitted stitch with the point of the left-hand needle. Where more than one stitch has to be slipped, the instructions will read: "p.s.sts.o."

m. = make. Various methods of making stitches are shown on page 244.

w.fd. = wool forward (see page 243).

w.r.n. = wool round needle (see page 243).

w.o.n. = wool over needle (see page 244).

w.b. = wool back.

t.b.l. = through back of loop or loops.

rep. = repeat.

tog. = together.

ins. = inches.

patt. = pattern.

ch. = chain. Used in crochet (see page 239).

s.c. = single crochet (see page 239).

d.c. = double crochet (see page 239).

tr. = treble. Used in crochet (see page 240).

l.tr. = long treble (see page 240).

BUTTONS. Four crochet buttons are shown in **Fig. 1.** For the square button make 7 ch. Work 1 d.c. into 6 ch., 1 ch., turn and work 7 rows more, taking hook through both loops of stitches of previous row. Fold over to form a square and work 1 row of d.c. through both edges thus joining together for three sides. Fill with wool and complete fourth side.

For the round button, make 4 ch. with double wool and medium crochet hook, and join in a ring. Into the ring work 16 tr. Break off wool, leaving fairly long end, and thread into darning needle. Take a stitch into the top of each treble, pull threads tightly together and sew across.

The larger round button consists of a wooden mould covered with a square of moss stitch.

The lozenge button is worked with a medium hook and single yarn. Make 11 ch., turn and work 1 d.c. into each of 10 ch., turn with 1 ch., and work 5 rows more, taking hook through back loop only. Sew up one end, fill with wool, sew bottom and other end.

BUTTONHOLES. By working 3 or more d.c., then 3 ch., leaving a space and then repeating, a very simple buttonhole for the edge of a fabric can be made (**Fig. 2**).

For horizontal buttonholes cast off a number of stitches in one row and cast on the same number on the return row (**Fig. 3**). For vertical buttonholes divide work at required place and knit both sides separately to the required depth (**Fig. 4**).

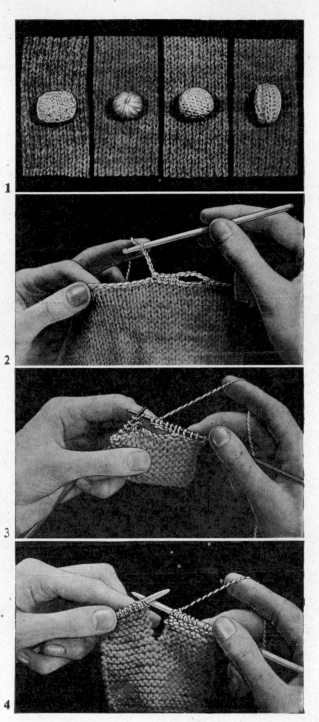

1

2

3

4

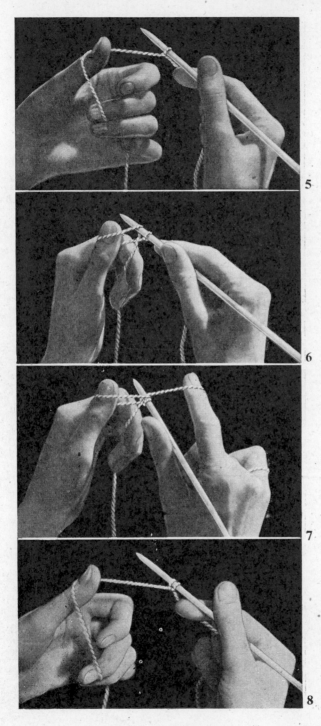

CASTING ON (*Thumb Method*).

Casting on in knitting means making the first row of loops on a needle, and is the basis on which the rest of the knitting is worked. There are several ways of casting on, but for all general purposes the thumb method is the most satisfactory, as it forms a firm but elastic edge which is almost indistinguishable from the rest of the knitted fabric. It is worked with the thumb of the left hand and one needle, held in the right hand.

Fig. 5 shows the first step in the thumb method of casting on. Leaving an end of wool—about a yard for an average garment—make a slip loop and put it on a needle held in the right hand. Now pass the end of wool over and round the thumb of the left hand, keeping the wool from the ball on the right-hand side.

Put the needle into the loop of wool round left-hand thumb, keeping the end of wool firmly between the fingers of the left hand, as shown in Fig. 6.

Using the wool from the ball, wind it round the point of the needle still holding the end of wool firmly in the left hand (Fig. 7).

Draw the loop of wool round the needle through the thumb loop, letting the wool then drop off the thumb (Fig. 8).

Repeat for as many stitches as given in the knitting instructions and then continue knitting with 2 needles, in the usual way.

CASTING ON (*Two-needle Method*). Instead of the thumb and one needle method, two needles can be used for casting on, but this results in an untidy, loopy edge which can only be avoided if the first row is knitted into the back of the cast-on stitches—a slow laborious process which produces an inelastc edge. It is not advisable, for instance, to use it for children's garments which have to be pulled on over the head.

The first step in the two-needle method of casting on is to make a loop in the wool, without leaving a long end, and put both needles into the loop, the left-hand needle over the right (**Fig. 9**).

Now pass the wool, from the ball, between the points of the needles as shown in **Fig. 10**.

Using the right - hand needle, draw this loop of wool through the loop around the 2 needles so that you now have a loop on each needle (**Fig. 11**).

Slip the loop of wool at present on the right-hand needle on to the left-hand needle as shown in **Fig. 12**, and repeat for as many stitches as are required, then continue knitting.

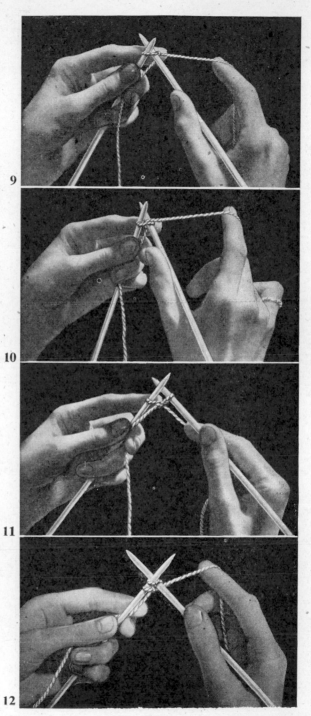

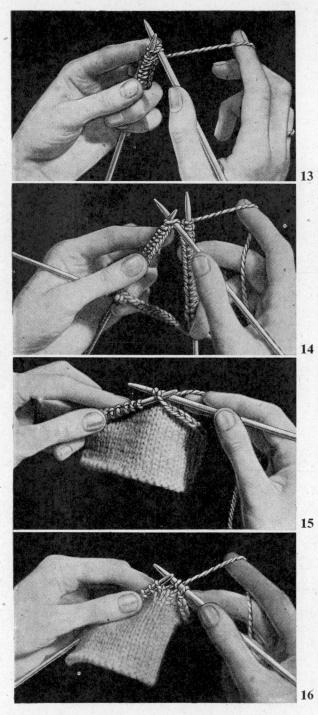

CASTING ON (*Corded Method*). This makes a suitably strong edge for garments subjected to hard wear. Work exactly as for casting on with 2 needles and when there are 2 stitches on the left-hand needle, insert the right-hand needle between them and knit the loops as before (**Fig. 13**).

13   For knitting in rounds for socks, stockings, etc., cast on with the thumb method the total number of stitches required, and then divide them between 3 needles as given in the knitting instructions.

Fig. 14 shows the fourth needle in position to begin the first round of knitting.

CASTING OFF means securing the last row of
14 stitches to prevent them running. The casting-off row is usually worked at the same tension as the rest of the garment, but where an elastic edge is required, a needle two sizes larger than those used for the rest of the garment should be used.

For *simple casting off* knit the first 2 stitches, and, with the left-hand needle, slip the first stitch over the
15 second (**Fig. 15**). Continue until the last stitch, break off the wool and pull it through the last loop.

Double casting off is re-commended for extra elasticity. Knit the first stitch, then pick up the thread which lies between that stitch and the next on the left-hand needle and knit into it. Slip the first stitch over this one and continue
16 in this way (**F.g. 16**).

CROCHET. The correct position of the hands for crochet is shown in **Fig. 17**. The hook is held firmly n the right hand, the work rests between the thumb and first finger of the left hand while the thread is kept taut by the second and third fingers and looped under the little finger.

The *chain* is the basis on which crochet is worked. Make a slip knot and put it on the hook, pass the hook under the thread and draw a loop through the slip-knot (**Fig. 17**). Continue in this way until chain is required length, then work back along this chain with single, double or treble crochet, according to the instructions.

For *single crochet* or *slip-stitch*, insert the hook through the chain or the previous row of crochet, draw a loop through on to the hook and through the loop originally on hook (**Fig. 18**).

Fig. 19 shows the *double crochet* stitch. Insert the hook through the chain or previous row of crochet and draw a loop through. Pass the hook under the thread and draw this through the two loops on the hook (**Fig. 20**) so that there is only 1 loop remaining on hook.

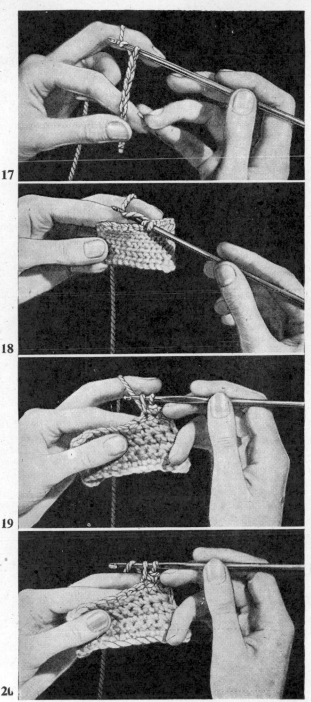

17

18

19

20

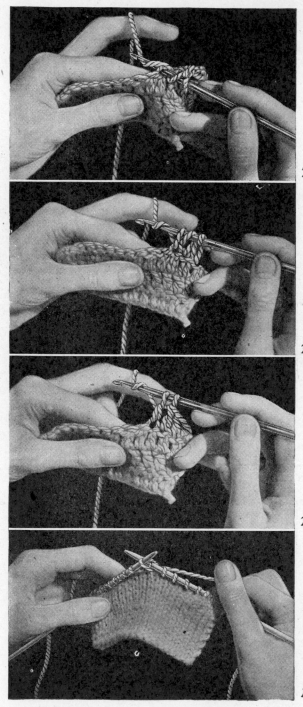

CROCHET (*Treble crochet*). The third basic stitch in crochet is treble crochet. Pass the hook under the thread, insert the hook into the chain or previous row of crochet and draw a loop of thread through (**Fig. 21**).

21 There are now 3 loops on the hook. Pass the hook under the thread again and draw the thread through the first 2 loops on the hook (**Fig. 22**) thus reducing the number of stitches on the hook by two.

22 Finally, as shown in **Fig. 23**, pass the hook under the thread again and draw this through the 2 remaining loops on the hook. Double treble, triple treble and quadruple treble stitches are worked in the same way, passing the hook under the thread two, three or four times before inserting in the chain. The hook is then passed under the thread and drawn through 2 loops at a time until only 1 loop remains on the hook.

23

DECREASING (*p.s.s.o.*). There are various methods of decreasing in knitting, and the *pass slip stitch over* method is widely used. Slip a stitch off the left-hand needle on to the right-hand needle without knitting it. Knit the next stitch and then with the point of the left-hand needle, lift the slipped stitch over the **24** last knitted stitch (**Fig. 24**).

DECREASING (*Knitting 2 together*). All knitted garments require a certain amount of shaping; for example, most jumpers need shaping at the sides above the waist, at the armholes and also at the neck. The positions of decreasings and increasings are given in the knitting instructions, but there are various methods of reducing the number of stitches. The most usual way of doing this is by knitting or purling 2 stitches together.

To knit 2 stitches together, put the right-hand needle through the first 2 stitches on the left-hand needle, loop the wool round and draw it through both stitches, thus reducing the number of stitches by one (**Fig. 25**).

The same method is used to decrease on a purl row, but the right-hand needle is inserted purlwise into the first 2 stitches of the left-hand needle (**Fig. 26**).

In order to keep the continuity of a fancy pattern it is sometimes necessary to knit or purl into the back of the 2 stitches when decreasing. **Fig. 27** shows the decreasing being worked in this way on a knitted row.

Fig. 28 illustrates a decreasing by purling into the back of 2 stitches on a purl row. The right-hand needle is passed round the back of the work and into the second stitch of the left-hand needle first.

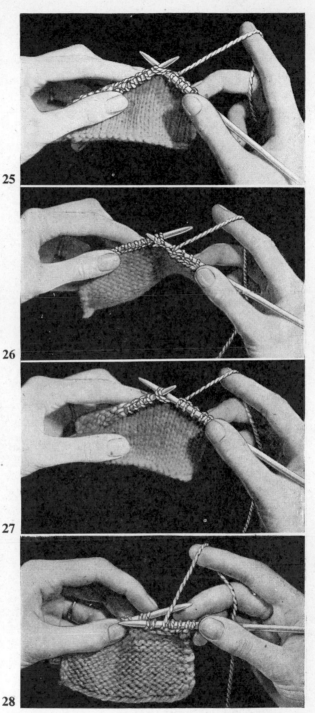

25

26

27

28

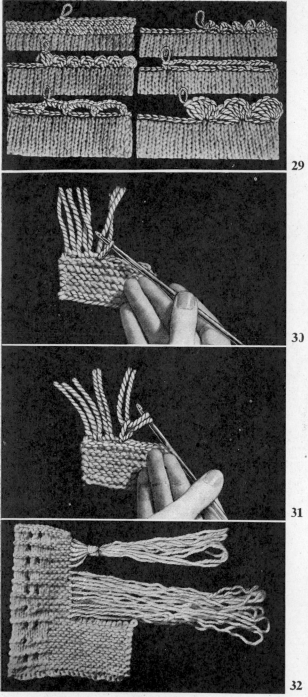

EDGINGS. For baby garments and underwear crochet edgings make a dainty finish and six are shown in **Fig. 29.** From left to right they are:—

Double Crochet. One or more rows of double crochet.

Picot. 1 s.c. into first st., * 3 ch. 1 d.c. into the first of these chain sts. miss 1 st., 1 s.c. into the next; rep. from * to end.

Small Shell. * 1 s.c. and 2 tr. into same st., leave a small space; rep. from *.

Small Loop. * 1 d.c. into edge, 3, 4, 5 or more ch. (according to length of loop required); rep. from *.

Large Loop. Work first row as given for loop edging. Second row.—* d.c. into d.c., then 1 d.c. into each ch.; rep. from *.

Large Shell. * 1 s.c., 6 long tr. into same st., leave a space; rep. from *.

FRINGE. Cut a strip of cardboard slightly wider than the depth of the fringe required. Wind the wool round this and then cut along one edge to form strands. Take a single strand of this cut wool, fold in half and draw the loop end through the edge of the garment, with a crochet hook (**Fig. 30**). Now draw the two ends through the loop and pull tight (**Fig. 31**).

Alternatively add extra stitches to the work, according to the depth of fringe required (**Fig. 32**), and when knitting is completed, cast off all stitches except on this additional border. When these are unravelled they form a fringe which can be left in loops or knotted.

GARTER STITCH or "plain" knitting is produced by knitting every row in a knit stitch (**Fig. 33**).

GRAFTING is a method of joining two sets of stitches in a flat join. Divide the stitches equally on to two needles with the wrong sides facing. Thread a needle with a length of wool, pass this needle purlwise through the first stitch on the front needle, leaving the stitch on the knitting needle, then pass the wool needle knitwise through the first stitch on the back knitting needle, again leaving the stitch on the knitting needle. *Pass the wool needle knitwise through the first stitch on the front needle and slip it off, pass the wool needle purlwise through the second stitch on the front needle and leave it on. Now pass the wool needle purlwise through the first stitch on the back needle and slip it off. Pass the wool needle through the second stitch on the back needle, leaving it on. Repeat from * until all the stitches are joined.

Fig. 34 shows grafting when the work has been taken off the knitting needles and pressed to prevent stitches running. The method is the same.

HOLES for threading ribbon, decoration or small buttonholes, are made in three ways. Between knit stitches the wool is passed forward between the needle points (w.fd.) and the next stitch knitted in the ordinary way (**Fig. 35**). Between purl stitches the wool is passed from the front of the work over the right-hand needle and between the needle points (w.r.n.) (**Fig. 36**).

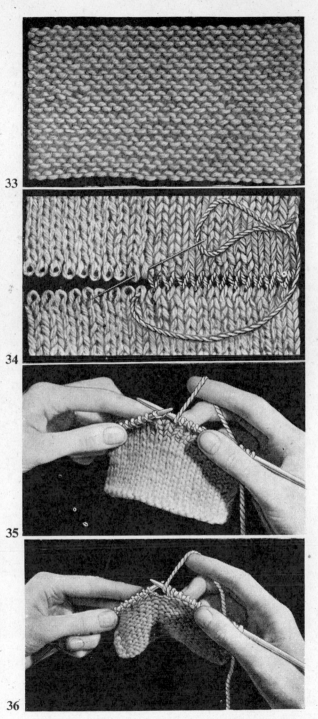

33

34

35

36

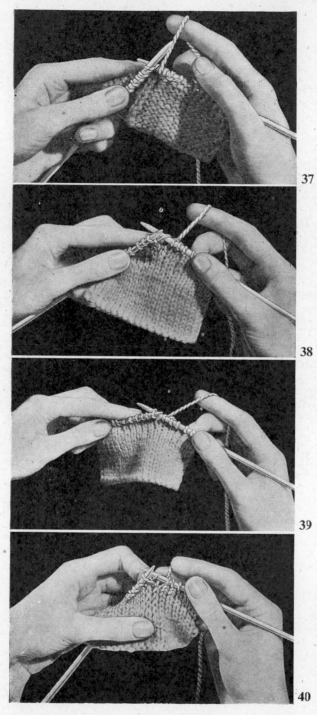

HOLES (*Third Method*). When the hole has to be made between a purl and a knit stitch, the wool, which is at the front, in the purl position, is passed over the right-hand needle (w.o.n.), thus making an extra stitch and bringing the wool into the correct position for knitting the next knit stitch (**Fig. 37**). With all three methods of making holes, the next two stitches are knitted or purled together to compensate for the "made" stitch.

INCREASING. One method of increasing the number of stitches in a garment to produce the necessary shaping is shown in **Fig. 38**. With the right-hand needle, pick up the loop between the stitches and, bringing the wool round the point of the needle, knit in the usual way to make an extra stitch.

This method makes a small hole unless the loop is twisted.

Another method of increasing is to knit first into the front and then into the back of the same stitch. **Fig. 39** shows the position of the needle ready for knitting into the back of the stitch.

Where it is important that the increasing be almost invisible as in the centre of a garment, the most satisfactory method is to knit or purl into the stitch in the previous row, as well as into the stitch itself (**Fig. 40**). This gives a neat and scarcely visible increasing.

KNIT or PLAIN STITCH. This stitch is the basis of all knitting. Having cast on the number of stitches required, hold the needle containing the stitches in the left hand, with the point about ½ in. above the thumb and first finger. Hold the other needle in the right hand, and insert the point in the first stitch, putting it in the front of the stitch and through to the back (Fig. 41).

In plain knitting the wool is kept at the back of the work. With the first finger of the right hand, pass the wool between the points of the two needles as shown in Fig. 42.

Keeping the wool held firmly between the first and second fingers of the right hand, draw the loop of wool through the first stitch on the left-hand needle with the point of the right-hand needle (Fig. 43).

Allow the first stitch on the left-hand needle to slip off, leaving the new stitch thus formed on the right-hand needle (Fig. 44). Continue in this way, transferring the stitches from the left-hand needle to the right. The knitting illustrated on this page is "stocking" stitch which is achieved by knitting one row and purling the next. The purl side is illustrated on page 246.

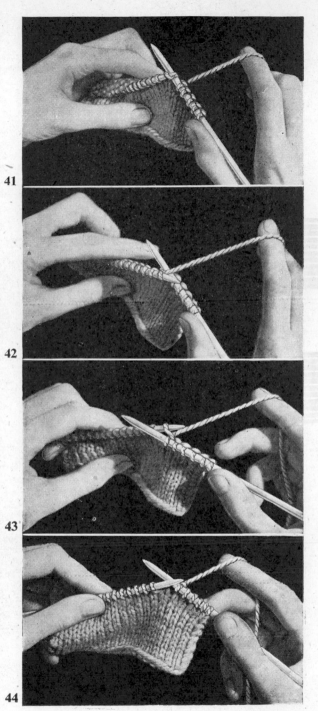

41

42

43

44

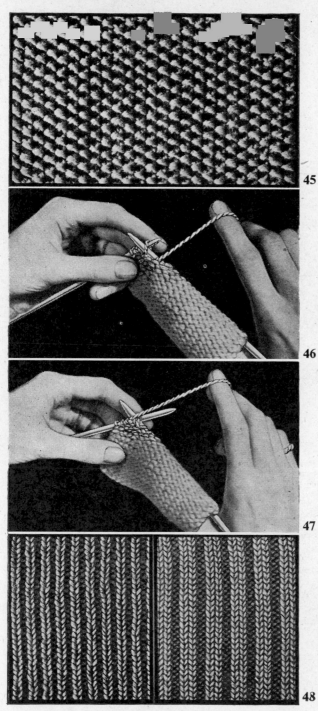

MOSS STITCH. This produces a reversible fabric showing plain and purl stitches alternately, both horizontally and vertically. An odd number of stitches is cast on and each row is worked in k. 1, p. 1. If, in any particular pattern, an even number of stitches is necessary, the moss-stitch effect can still be achieved by commencing each row **45** with the same stitch as the last one of the previous row. An example of moss stitch is shown in **Fig. 45.**

PURL. This is the other basic stitch in knitting. Hold the work in the left hand as for the knit stitch. Pass the point of the right-hand needle through the front of the first stitch on the left-hand needle, keeping the right-hand needle to **46** the front. The wool is also kept at the front of the work in purling (**Fig. 46**).

With the first finger of the right hand, bring wool between the two needles and round the point of the right-hand needle (**Fig. 47**). Draw the loop through with the point of the needle, **47** allowing the first stitch to slip off the left-hand needle.

RIBBING. This is produced by a combination of plain and purl stitches, forming vertical ridges. The ribbing on the left of **Fig. 48** is in k. 1, p. 1, while the one on the right is k. 2, p. 2. Ribbing is used for welts, neck bands, etc., to contract **48** the fabric and make it fit.

STOCKING STITCH.

This consists of alternate rows of knit stitch and purl stitch, giving a smooth surface on one side and a ridged one on the other. The smooth surface is generally considered the right side of the work, but the purl surface can be used very effectively as the right side. In **Fig. 49**, the purl side is shown at the top and the plain side below.

TENSION and Needles.

Fig. 50 shows how the size of needles affects the finished fabric. With the smaller needle (No. 12) there are more stitches to the inch than when the larger needle (No. 8) is used, although the wool is the same in both cases. A garment will not result in the correct measurements unless the size of needle and thickness of wool are those specified in the instructions.

The "tension" at which knitting is worked will also affect the size of the finished garment and it is well worth while knitting a small piece, with the wool and needles specified, and checking the tension of this with the aid of pins and an inch tape (**Figs. 51** and **52**) before commencing the garment.

Average tensions in stocking stitch are as follows:—

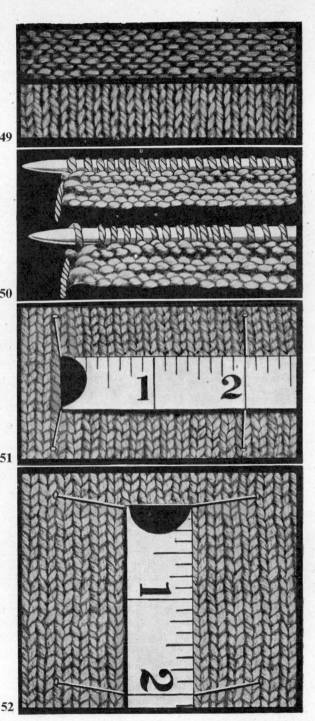

Wool	Needles	Stitches to 1 inch
2-ply	9	$7\frac{1}{2}$
,,	10	8
,,	11	$8\frac{1}{2}$
,,	12	9
3-ply	8	$6\frac{1}{2}$
,,	9	7
,,	10	$7\frac{1}{2}$
,,	11	8
4-ply	7	$5\frac{1}{2}$
,,	8	6
,,	9	$6\frac{1}{2}$
,,	10	7

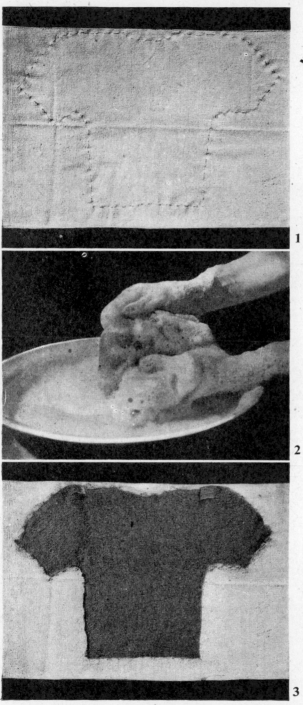

PRACTICAL TIP
AND REPAIRIN

WASHING. Knitted garments which have taken a long time to make are often ruined by careless washing before they are worn out. Iı the following few simple rules are observed, the garments will keep their shape and fresh looks. Even a garment which has been laundered carelessly can be put right.

First mark out with pins on an ironıng blanket or towel, the outline of the garment's original shape as a guide to re-blocking (**Fig. 1**).

Squeeze the garment—not rub—in fairly hot soapy water (**Fig. 2**). Knitted fabrics should never be rubbed, for this " felts " them quicker than anything.

Rinse in two clear waters of the washing water temperature and squeeze as dry as possible. (Never wring a knitted garment by hand.) Lay the garment on the towel and push it gently into shape, pınning or tacking it to the outline, as shown in **Fig. 3**. Where there is ribbing, such as welts, cuffs oı neck band, push the ribs close together to contract the fabric.

Hints

ON RENOVATING KNITTED GARMENTS

DRYING. Cover the garment with a second towel, as shown in **Fig. 4**, then put garment and towels through a slack wringer to remove surplus moisture. Spread out flat and leave to dry.

By this method a garment made of good wool will regain its shape and elasticity and even mixture yarns and rayons that are not easily reconditioned, can be greatly improved.

In winter and wet weather, when woollies cannot be dried out of doors, the following method can be used: spread at least two thicknesses of newspaper on a table and lay the garment out to its shape on these. Place two more thicknesses of paper on top, folding the sleeves over the top of these (**Fig. 5**).

Finish off with two more thicknesses of paper and then roll paper and garment tightly together as shown in **Fig. 6**. Leave this roll overnight until most of the moisture has been absorbed into the paper. The garment can then be hung — not pegged—over a line. Finish off by pressing under a damp cloth.

4

5

6

UNRAVELLING WOOL. Even when a knitted garment is torn and worn, there is generally enough good yarn left in it for re-knitting into something smaller, or for combining with other woo to make another garment.

Unpick all seams carefully, avoiding cutting the loops of wool so that there will not be too many joins. Commence unravelling the garment from the cast-off edge, pulling gently to disengage the loops. As the wool is freed, wind it round a large book, pastry board, or other suitable article. **Fig. 7** shows the unravelled wool wound round a book.

· When a good amount of wool has been wound in this way, take it carefully off the book and tie it in three or four places to make a skein (*see* **Fig. 8**).

After unpicking the whole garment in this way, wash the skeins gently in soapy water, or if necessary, dye them. It is not always necessary to re-dye patchy wool as the uneven colour can be quite attractive when re-knitted, provided the contrast is not too violent. Now thread or tie the wet skeins on a line to dry, fastening a weight on to the bottom of them, to take out the crinkles. **Fig. 9** shows the weighted skein drying on a line.

PATCHING and MENDING. Elbows and knees and other parts of knitted garments that wear out quickly can be patched by knitting in a new piece of fabric. With a sharp pair of scissors cut away the worn and thin parts in a neat square or oblong shape (**Fig. 10**).

Carefully pull out the short ends of wool until there is a clear row of loops top and bottom of the space.

Slip the top row of stitches on to a needle so that they will not "run," and the bottom row on to the same size needles with which the garment was knitted (**Fig. 11**). Now knit a new piece of fabric the size of the hole and graft the last row of stitches to the top row of loops. (Grafting instructions are on page 243.) Finally, sew the sides of the new piece of knitting to the sides of the hole in the garment.

RE-KNITTING WELTS. It frequently happens that welts "run"—that is, the cast-on stitches break and the knitting becomes unravelled, usually because of a too-tight casting-on in a garment subjected to stretching. The best method of repairing this damage is to re-knit the whole of the welt. The first step is to pull a thread where the welt joins the main part of the garment, as shown in **Fig. 12.**

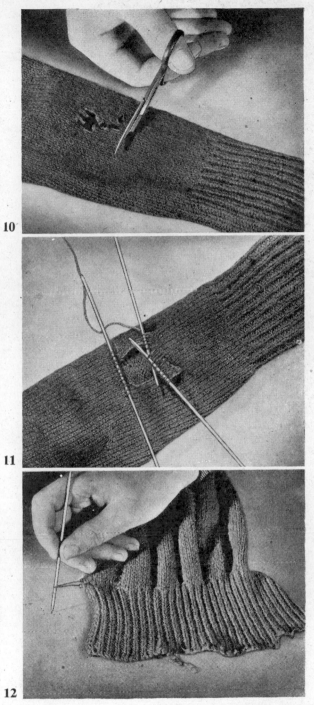

10

11

12

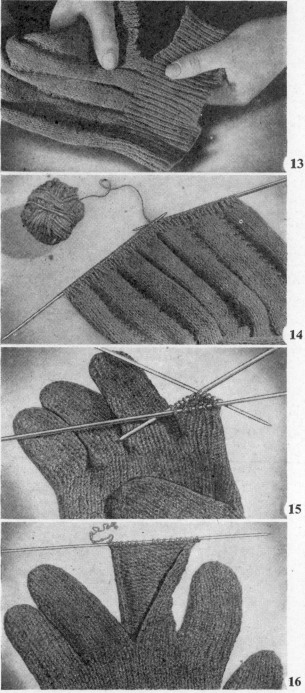

RE-KNITTING WELTS
—*continued*. Pull this thread up as tightly as possible and then cut it at the beginning of the row. Now pull the stitches apart gently at each side of the thread, as illustrated in **Fig. 13**, and the worn part will come away neatly.

13 Pick up the stitches on the main part of the garment, as in **Fig. 14**, and knit on a new welt. Contrasting wool could be used quite effectively, if none of the original wool is available.

14 ## NEW FINGERS in gloves.
Almost invariably, the finger-tips of knitted gloves wear out first, but they are well worth re-knitting if the rest of the glove is in good condition.

For gloves that are knitted on four needles the following method should be used. Cut away the worn part, pull out any short ends of wool remaining, until there is a clear row of loops. Pick up these stitches and re-knit the finger, following the original instructions (**Fig. 15**).

15

Fig. 16 shows the renovation being worked on a glove which was knitted on two needles. In this case, unp.ck the finger seam, cut off the worn part of the knitted fabric, pick up the stitches and re-knit as before, finally rejoining the seams. Glove welts can be re-knitted as shown in **Figs. 12, 13** and **14** and finger-tips and welts would look very effective if knitted in a **16** contrasting colour.

RE-FOOTING Socks and Stockings. Socks and stockings usually wear into holes at the heels and toes first, and when time and trouble have been expended on hand-knitting them, it is well worth while re-knitting the heels and toes instead of merely darning the holes.

If both the heels and the toes have worn thin the best plan is to unravel the entire foot as far as the commencement of the heel flap and re-knit the foot from the original instructions. If there is not sufficient wool available odd wool can be used for the toe as this will not be seen.

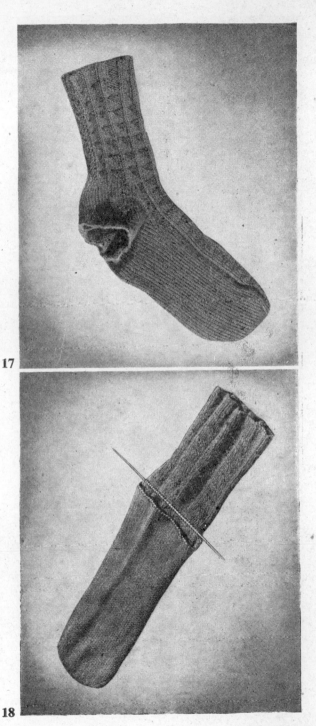

17

Fig. 17 shows a sock which has worn out at the heel only and which can be re-heeled as follows: cut away the worn part of the heel flap and pull out all the short ends of wool until there is a complete row of loops across the heel flap and the stitches which were originally picked up along the sides of the flap are free.

With 2 needles the same size as used for knitting the sock, pick up the same number of heel flap stitches as mentioned in the original instructions. Fig. 18 shows the heel flap stitches on a needle ready for re-knitting. **18**

19

20

21

RE-FOOTING Socks and Stockings—*continued*. With the heel flap stitches on one needle, pick up the side and sole stitches on two other needles, as shown in **Fig. 19**. Knit the heel flap, joining it to the side stitches as follows: * knit to the end of the row, slipping the first stitch from the side needle and knitting it with the last stitch of the heel flap (**Fig. 20**). Turn and purl back, transferring a stitch as before and knitting it with the last stitch on the centre needle. Repeat from * until the heel flap is complete.

The stitches which are left on the other two needles are the sole stitches. Count these and put them on to one needle. Now turn the heel as in the original instructions, leaving the same number of stitches as on the spare needle. Graft these two sets of stitches together. (Grafting instructions are on page 243.)

RE - KNITTING TOES. When the toes of socks are worn, cut away the thin part, and unravel the knitting until there is a clear round of loops. Set these stitches on to three needles and re-knit the toe according to the original instructions (**Fig. 21**).

For socks that have been knitted on two needles, unpick the foot seams, unravel the worn parts until a clear row of loops is left. Pick up these stitches and re-knit. Top and bottom of the toe can be re-knitted in this way and seamed as before.

USING WOOL ODD-MENTS. Short lengths of wool should never be thrown away, but should be tied together and wound into multi-coloured balls and kept on one side for making knitted blankets. These are excellent for children's cots and beds and, indeed, for adults' beds as well, although a too large expanse of wool tends to sag in wear unless it is very tightly knitted and the yarn is well spun.

One method of making these sectional blankets is to knit a quantity of 4-in. squares in garter stitch and sew them together to the required size. Another and perhaps more attractive way is to knit small "shells," such as those in **Fig. 22**.

Using No. 12 needles, cast on 41 stitches and knit about 8 rows. Still working in garter stitch, knit 2 together each side of the centre stitch on alternate rows until 3 sts. remain (**Fig. 23**). Knit these 3 sts. together and fasten off.

When a good number of these "shells" have been made, sew them carefully together, beginning from the middle of the blanket so that the colours can be arranged in a pleasing pattern of light and dark shades. The blanket will be most effective with a border of "shells" in the same colour. **Fig. 24** shows some of the finished "shells" sewn together.

22

23

24

INDEX

S. 1/45 T.   *Made and Printed by C. Tinling & Co., Ltd., Liverpool, London and Prescot.*